Queer and Deleuzian Temporalities

Queer and Deleuzian Temporalities

Toward a Living Present

Rachel Loewen Walker

BLOOMSBURY ACADEMIC
LONDON • NEW YORK • OXFORD • NEW DELHI • SYDNEY

BLOOMSBURY ACADEMIC
Bloomsbury Publishing Plc
50 Bedford Square, London, WC1B 3DP, UK
1385 Broadway, New York, NY 10018, USA
29 Earlsfort Terrace, Dublin 2, Ireland

BLOOMSBURY, BLOOMSBURY ACADEMIC and the Diana logo are
trademarks of Bloomsbury Publishing Plc

First published in Great Britain 2022
This paperback edition published 2023

Copyright © Rachel Loewen Walker, 2022

Rachel Loewen Walker has asserted her right under the Copyright, Designs and
Patents Act, 1988, to be identified as Author of this work.

For legal purposes the Acknowledgments on pp. ix–xii constitute an
extension of this copyright page.

Cover image: Abstract background (© traffic_analyzer / Getty Images)

All rights reserved. No part of this publication may be reproduced or transmitted in
any form or by any means, electronic or mechanical, including photocopying,
recording, or any information storage or retrieval system, without prior permission
in writing from the publishers.

Bloomsbury Publishing Plc does not have any control over, or responsibility for, any
third-party websites referred to or in this book. All internet addresses given in this
book were correct at the time of going to press. The author and publisher regret any
inconvenience caused if addresses have changed or sites have ceased to exist, but
can accept no responsibility for any such changes.

A catalogue record for this book is available from the British Library.

Library of Congress Cataloging-in-Publication Data
Names: Loewen Walker, Rachel., author.
Title: Queer and Deleuzian Temporalities : Toward a Living Present / Rachel Loewen Walker.
Description: London, UK ; New York : Bloomsbury Academic, 2021. |
Includes bibliographical references and index.
Identifiers: LCCN 2021026057 (print) | LCCN 2021026058 (ebook) |
ISBN 9781350184343 (hb) | ISBN 9781350184350 (epdf) | ISBN 9781350184367 (ebook)
Subjects: LCSH: Deleuze, Gilles, 1925–1995. | Time. | Queer Theory. | Feminist Criticism.
Classification: LCC B2430.D454 W354 2021 (print) | LCC B2430.D454 (ebook) |
DDC 306.7601–dc23
LC record available at https://lccn.loc.gov/2021026057
LC ebook record available at https://lccn.loc.gov/2021026058

ISBN: HB: 978-1-3501-8434-3
PB: 978-1-3501-8549-4
ePDF: 978-1-3501-8435-0
eBook: 978-1-3501-8436-7

Typeset by Newgen KnowledgeWorks Pvt. Ltd., Chennai, India

To find out more about our authors and books visit www.bloomsbury.com
and sign up for our newsletters.

Lies 1: There is only the present and nothing to remember.
Lies 2: Time is a straight line.
Lies 3: The difference between the past and the future is that one has happened while the other has not.
Lies 4: We can only be in one place at a time.
Lies 5: Any proposition that contains the word "finite" (the world, the universe, experience, ourselves …)
Lies 6: Reality as something which can be agreed upon.
Lies 7: Reality is truth.

—Jeanette Winterson, *Sexing the Cherry*

The future is literally right here and now and consequently there is no time to waste.

—Rosi Braidotti, *Posthuman Knowledge*

Contents

List of Figures	viii
Acknowledgments	ix
Preface: The Monomyth	xiii
Introduction	1
1 Telling Time: From Deleuze to Heraclitus and from Queer Theory to Indigenous Ways of Knowing	17
2 The Living Present: A Co-Creative Conversation between Deleuze and Winterson	37
3 Quantum Materialism: Bringing Time and Matter Together in a Feminist Future	65
4 "An Erratic and Uneasy Becoming": Queering Time, Reworking the Past	89
5 Thick Time: Echoes of the Anthropocene	117
6 An Ethics of Entanglement	139
Notes	155
References	177
Index	191

Figures

I.1	Thick time	3
2.1	Pebble diffraction	40
3.1	1927 Solvay Conference on Quantum Mechanics	66
4.1	The thick time of coming out	106
5.1	Human evolution	118
5.2	Tentative phylogenetic schemes for hominid evolution	119

Acknowledgments

In a journey that is about the entanglement of bodies and theories in the making of time, I find myself wanting to thank hundreds of coconspirators who have intervened along the way. I have had many divergent communities of practice around me as I completed this manuscript during the last four years, including colleagues from the University of Saskatchewan, the University of Alberta, the nonprofit sector of Saskatoon, Saskatchewan, and a national community of 2SLGBTQ leaders and service providers in Canada.

I am especially grateful to the members of the Deleuze and feminist reading groups who always brought text to life, life to text—Danielle Peers and Lindsay Eales, our collaborative queer imaginings forever changed the conversation, and Yasmin Sari, you have always brought a breath of fresh air, in spirit and ideas. To my women's and gender studies mentors, colleagues, and friends, especially Joan Borsa and Marie Lovrod, thank you for decades of support backward and forward. And thank you to the distinct and international group of new feminist materialist scholars that rippled through my life with impeccable timing, especially Astrida Neimanis for contributing to my thinking and writing around climate and accountability, Peta Hinton for limitless brainstorming that inspires me to this day, and the many others who shaped this important time in my intellectual growth, which helped to shape many of the chapters ahead.

Thank you to the community of support at OUTSaskatoon during my time as the executive director (2013–20) and while I precariously balanced leadership responsibilities and writing deadlines. Being entrusted as a community leader in this way is the greatest honor of my life thus far. It taught me as much about the temporality of social justice as it did about the timing of letting go.

To those who lent their expertise directly to the manuscript: Elena del Rio, Cressida Heyes, and Jan Jagodzinski, thank you all for incisive feedback paired with enthusiastic support. Claire Colebrook, thank you for questions and critique that always stretch me well beyond the text. It has been a gift to read your work for the duration of my academic career and I am honored that you took the time to read mine. And to my graduate supervisor, turned dear friend, Marie-Eve Morin: thank you for your sharp and ingenious mind, for regularly understanding my work better than I did, and for sharing meals and laughter alongside deep dives into duration, intensity, and immanence. A special thank you to Jade Grogan and the editorial team at Bloomsbury—it has been an absolute pleasure from start to finish. Thank you to Isabelle MacLean for meticulous indexing expertise, and to three anonymous reviewers for comprehensive and challenging feedback that resulted in expansive revisions and a book that I am truly proud of.

My final thank yous are to all of those who hold pieces of my heart and so are as much a part of this work as I. To my parents: my mom, Amy Walker, our memories are woven into this work and our conversations have become its content; my dad, Harold Loewen, you are always the steady ground from which I venture; and to Lynn Loewen, your exuberant support has been unwavering. Thank you to all of my siblings (Shauna Weiss, Kris Loewen, and Trevor Weiss) and their families for endless encouragement. And to dear friends new and old, some of whom fill my heart, others my mind, and all of whom make time stand still. Thank you to my favourite nonprofit warriors Sheryl Harrow-Yurach, Chantelle Johnson, and Heather Hale; to Jan Braun and Marjorie Beaucage, who are both kindred writers and soulful friends; to Amanda Mitchell and Andrew Hartman, for both reading early chapters of your own free will; to Laura Harms, Brad Harms, Kelly Woodley, and Robin Koutecky for more years of encouragement than I could ever count; to Lee Pirot, for always being in my corner; and to Troy Boyenko, for support without measure and for continually reminding me that when the chips are down, it is laughter that gets us through.

Most importantly, thank you to my love, my heart, Estefan Cortes-Vargas. You make all memories vibrant, all pages dance, and all futures open-ended. In all the worlds of space and time, I need only a moment with you.

* * *

I am grateful to both the Social Sciences and Humanities Research Council of Canada and the Ariel F. Sallows Endowment in Human Rights from the College of Law, at the University of Saskatchewan. Both of these have given me the gift of time so needed to do justice to complex and careful research.

This is an original work, though portions include adaptations of previously published material. Both the introduction and Chapter 2 include material that was previously published in Rachel Loewen Walker, "The Living Present as a Materialist Feminist Temporality," *Woman: A Cultural Review* 25, no. 1 (2014): 46–61. Reprinted with permission of Taylor & Francis Ltd. Chapter 5 includes material that was previously published in Rachel Loewen Walker, "Environment Imagining Otherwise," *Journal of Curriculum and Pedagogy* 10, no. 1 (2013): 34–7. Reprinted with permission of Taylor & Francis Ltd.

The author and publisher gratefully acknowledge the permission granted to reproduce copyright material in this book, and in particular the following for permission to reprint excerpt(s) from the sources indicated:

Sexing the Cherry by Jeanette Winterson, copyright © 1989 Jeanette Winterson. Reprinted by permission of Vintage Canada/Alfred A. Knopf Canada, a division of Penguin Random House Canada Limited. All rights reserved.

The Posthuman by Rosi Braidotti, copyright © 2013 Rosi Braidotti. Reprinted by permission of Polity Books.

Gilles Deleuze's Philosophy of Time: A Critical Introduction and Guide by James Williams, copyright © 2011 James Williams. Reprinted by permission of the Licensor through PLSclear.

The Order of Time by Carlo Rovelli, copyright © 2017 by Adelphi Edizioni SPA, Milano. Translation copyright © 2018 by Simon Carnell and Erica Segre. Used by permission of Riverhead, an imprint of Penguin Publishing Group, a division of Penguin Random House LLC. All rights reserved.

How It Is: The Native American Philosophy of V.F. Cordova by Kathleen Dean Moore (ed.) and V. F. Cordova, copyright © 2007. Used by permission of University of Arizona Press.

The Stone Gods by Jeanette Winterson, copyright © 2007 Jeanette Winterson. Reprinted by permission of Vintage Canada/Alfred A. Knopf Canada, a division of Penguin Random House Canada Limited. All rights reserved.

Beyond Weird: Why Everything You Thought You Knew about Quantum Physics Is Different by Phillip Ball, copyright © 2018 by Phillip Ball. Used by permission of Zed Books, Bloomsbury Publishing Plc.

Cosmodolphins: Feminist Cultural Studies of Technology, Animals, and the Sacred by Mette Bryld and Nina Lykke, copyright © 2000 Mette Bryld and Ninna Lykke. Reprinted by permission of Zed Books, Bloomsbury Publishing Plc.

The Untimeliness of Feminist Theory by Elizabeth Grosz in NORA-Nordic Journal of Feminist and Gender Research, "The Untimeliness of Feminist Theory," NORA-Nordic Journal of Feminist and Gender Research, copyright © 2010 Elizabeth Grosz. Reprinted by permission of Taylor & Francis Ltd.

The Pace of Queer Time by Lila in Autostraddle March 16, 2016: https://www.autostraddle.com/the-pace-of-queer-time-329459/.

Theorizing Queer Temporalities by Carolyn Dinshaw et al. in GLQ: A Journal of Lesbian and Gay Studies, copyright © 2007. Used by permission of Duke University Press.

Resisting Medicine, Re/Modeling Gender by Dean Spade, copyright © 2003 by the Regents of the University of California. Reprinted from the Berkeley's Women's Law Journal 18 Berkeley Women's L.J. 15 (2003), by permission of the Regents of the University of California.

The Anthropocene and the Archive by Claire Colebrook accessed through The Memory Network (http://thememorynetwork.net/the-anthropocene-and-the-archive/) copyright © 2014 Claire Colebrook. Reprinted by permission of the author. Holocene by Bon Iver, track 3 on Bon Iver, April Base Publishing, 2011, compact disc.

McKenzie Wark, as quoted on the back cover of Twilight of the Anthropocene Idols by Tom Cohen et al., copyright © 2016. Reprinted with permission of the author.

Feeling Backward: Loss and the Politics of Queer History by Heather Love, Cambridge, MA: Harvard University Press, copyright © 2007 by the President and Fellows of Harvard College.

Every effort has been made to trace copyright holders and to obtain their permission for the use of copyright material. The publisher apologizes for any errors or omissions in the above list and would be grateful if notified of any corrections that should be incorporated in future reprints or editions of this book.

Preface: The Monomyth

As the storyteller, I have the privilege of being able to pick and choose from thousands of different stories that have been told over time—stories about the "waves" of feminist theory, about the timelines of ancient Greece, about queer theory and new feminist materialisms, and about Indigenous temporalities. I also get to tell stories about climate change, how I learned to ride a bike, the love lives of homo sapiens and robo sapiens, the living present, and many other tales. With every story told, I know that each one is only and ever the product of my own entangled experiences as a complex body in an even more complex world. I am a white settler, a cisgender, queer woman. I knew I was a feminist in elementary school, but was never brave enough to think my crushes on girls meant anything more than curiosity. I learned how to bake bread from runaway Hutterites in my teens, I worked with nationally renowned Indigenous scholars at a community-based research center in my twenties, and I was the executive director of a queer community center for most of my thirties before returning to academia. At the same time, I have changed paths hundreds of times within this tale. I have loved and been broken; I dropped out of university twice. I tried to drop out of high school. I experienced great trauma as a girl, and I was failed by a court system that is forever too cowardly to hold men accountable for their crimes. Each of these experiences has co-created the chapters and conversations that lie ahead. Every choice that I have ever made has ruptured a linear tale, linearities that are only ever retroactive attempts to make "reality" into truth and to turn ruptures into finitudes.

Just as I tell the stories of my life, I make cuts and slices, comparisons and critiques, in the work that lies ahead. This is the power of the storyteller and, as the storyteller, I have attempted to make the power dynamics of these cuts transparent, but it is impossible to attend to every cut and such a quest toward transparency betrays the fact that there is no other way to speak, write, act, or *be in the world*, outside of our *tellings* of self, time, being, desiring. As such, my method is less a quest toward transparency as it is an honesty about the closeness between author and text. In the work that follows you will hear the *I*, you will hear my opinions, memories, stories, and thoughts as you traverse the pages, as you read story after story about philosophers, political crises, community narratives, and theoretical arguments. Does this mean that the work is autobiographical? *Of course it is autobiographical. Has there ever been anything else?* Whether it is a *Treatise on Human Nature*, an exploration of the *Logic of Sense*, or a novel about *Sexing the Cherry*, the author is always entangled with their text. The story is always a product of what matters to its teller at any given time. Our storied pasts are always the first acts of present behavior, just as a collection of texts forms the evidence for an argument. And so, the closeness to the "I" that characterizes this book both makes visible the closeness that is always already there in our storytelling as much as in our history-making and philosophizing. This transparency serves as a methodological tactic as it enacts the entanglement between the bodies, ideas, memories, and skin that makes the timescape of a living present possible.

I also try to resist the monomyth, or the hero's journey, in the work that follows. Whether narrative or not, we write our theoretical and philosophical texts with the allure of a happy ending. I'll try instead to work toward unraveling our familiar methods of storytelling, questioning temporal singularities, and thickening our lone heroes. These stories may not be packed with the action that we are used to, but they illustrate the ways that every *new* story is a line of flight: a creative burst from the original tale that connects with possibilities outside itself.[1] And so, I invite you to imagine time otherwise, to embody a living present where time is multiple and the future has already passed. *I invite you to "close your eyes and dream. This is one story. There will be another."*[2]

Introduction

We live as time makers—anything exists as a maker of time.
—James Williams, *Gilles Deleuze's Philosophy of Time*

Travel back to your seven-year-old self. Do you remember playing outside in the yard for three hours without stopping, waiting for your parents to get home from work, counting down the days until Christmas holidays? There was a sense in which the months dragged on forever; waiting an hour for something was excruciating, a year felt like a lifetime. Often my young self couldn't even think back far enough to the previous year, much less comprehend any continuity between that six-year-old starting first grade and the seven-year-old heading in to second. William James believed that children and youth "felt" time much slower because of the fact that so many upcoming experiences were brand new[1]—do you remember the first time you rode a bike? *Yes, of course*. Do you remember the second? The tenth? Scientists have taken up a similar cause, looking at subjective experiences of time relative to the age of the subject, and studies have shown that there is a correlation between age and the perception of time's speed.[2] As we age, we experience time as moving faster—which seems to align with my inability to determine whether an (otherwise memorable) event happened last year or the year before, compared to my precise, and still agonizing, memory of cheating on a spelling test in November of my eighth year.

Scientists aren't as concerned with the relationship between our subjective experience of time and its role in memory production as philosophers might be, but if we think about our growing seven-year-old, experiencing many things for the first time—whether riding a bike, taking a math test, going on a family vacation, having a fight with her best friend—by the time she reaches fifteen years, she's traveled through each of these experiences many times, some thousands of times, and each repeated experience adds another layer of understanding. The uniqueness fades, the body habitually moves through the movements of pedals and breaks, and the fights with friends layer a thicker skin upon a previously open heart. It is not only the case that the memories no longer take up as much space in our great mental stores, but also that the reflexive movement between past, present, and future becomes our modus operandi as we build our unique multilayered pasts.

It is this contraction of time that lies at the heart of this text—whether ordinary and mundane contractions of time and understanding such as the hand reaching for a boiling kettle, just moments before it squeals, or the profound contractions of memory such as adult fingers that unconsciously type out a phone number from childhood. I borrow the concept of "contraction" from Gilles Deleuze, who uses it alongside his description of the living present to refer to the present's envelopment of the past in all present experiences or understandings.[3] To contract is to expand a single experience into every smell, touch, or sound that came before it. For me, contraction is thirty-nine years of habit and memory housed on the head of a pin. Contraction is both an expansion and a narrowing (or even an abridging) of the past in order that one's present understanding and comportment be composed of a whole lifetime of experience and memories. Such instantaneous access is not granted through consciousness but through an embodied entanglement with bodies, streets, smells, and other experiences. Think about the compression of an accordion or the stretching of a child's Slinky™ toy, as both of these movements express the work of temporal contraction. To contract the past is to experience the growth and the shrinking of each of these objects as they are pushed and pulled and, in so doing, to witness the constitution of time itself.

Take this example: I can think back to the morning I was walking along a quiet street and recognized a childhood friend from behind. I had not seen this friend in twenty years, in which time we had both aged from adolescence to adulthood, and yet, I knew them immediately—an unconscious memory of movement, rhythm, and gait that I had somehow stored away. I contracted a long past in an instant and in that moment my timeline both narrowed and stretched. This instinctive knowledge speaks to all range of things including how we communicate with a stranger, or why we prefer one grocery store to another. Each of these moments is born out of the instantaneous contractions of past, present, and future that we conduct unconsciously and which demonstrate the imperceptible ways that we travel through time in any given moment. Here it bears mentioning that the book at hand is not about time's minutes, days, months, or hours, nor is it about whether time is real, abstract, relational, or substantive (although I will explore each of these stories about time). This book is about time's architecture, its materiality, thickness, productivity, and action. Time is less an abstract, intangible concept, than it is the deep well of experience and understanding that frames and produces all matters of encounter in very grounded and embodied ways. If I think back to riding a bike at age seven, I cannot extract the memory from my parent's divorce for it is the only time I remember them together. The memories tumble together and bring with them feelings of sorrow and nostalgia, while at the same time stretching around thirty-five years of life lived with parents apart, stepsiblings, new bikes, different houses. This act of contraction participates in what could be called a *thick time*, or a "transcorporeal stretching between present, future, and past."[4] Rather than thinking of time as the unspooling of a horizontal chronology, with the familiar tick marks tracking significant events, a thick time takes a vertical slice from within the middle of a horizontal timeline.

Figure I.1 shows thick time as a deep dive into a particular moment; it brings into relief all significant pasts that have contributed to such a moment, and rather than narrating a causal chronology (this happened, and then this happened, and therefore and so on) the pasts, presents, and futures are stacked. They bleed in and through one another as they are brought to bear on a thickened present experience or what we may call the *living present*.

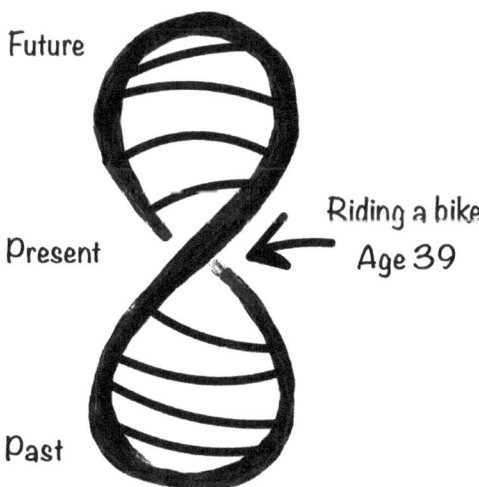

Figure I.1 Thick time
Source: Author.

The "living present" used in this way was coined by Deleuze in *Difference and Repetition* (1994) and *The Logic of Sense* (1969). It describes the present moment as a passive contraction of the past and an anticipation of the future in its creation of meaning and understanding; or the way in which the seven-year-old learning to ride a bike draws upon the previous day's lesson as she pushes one foot down on the pedal and struggles to make the other follow suit. Our bike rider has learned this rhythm already, and so it is familiar; it starts to become a habit. At the same time she knows that she cannot stop mid-pedal because she stretches toward a future where she moves along the path smoothly, continuously. Or likewise, there is a future where she jolts along and then crashes to the sidewalk following a forgotten movement (a habit not yet formed). Note, however, that the living present is not merely a "drawing on the past" and "anticipation of the future" so that the present action has meaning, but rather it actually *changes* the past and future of self and other through continuous, reverberating waves.

Within this frame, *selfhood* or *subjectivity* is also a contraction of habit and memory, comprising thousands of conscious and unconscious moments/expressions/experiences that make up our changing present.[5] There would be no self without such habitual processes and, further, the self-making-past-making-future is ever-changing: "The self does not undergo modifications, it is itself a modification."[6] We can understand this through an example of a drumstick hitting a drum, covered with deposits of colored sand: "One side is the past and another the future, each shaking and forming different shapes as the drumsticks hit towards the centre."[7] The drumstick is a time traveler as it stretches and contracts through multiple temporalities and, more importantly, it is itself changed through every beat just as our young bike rider changes with every successful or failed attempt.

Most significant, then, is that the living present extends well beyond mere "human" activity. In the sense that human beings live as time-makers, continually contracting and remaking past and present, so too does the tree outside my window. In a Canadian climate, a poplar tree has a concentric ring of growth for each year gone by. We can read these rings like a map of the tree's past: How much water did the tree get? How cold was that winter four years ago? On the other hand, a tree in Costa Rica, where the seasons don't change on an annual clock, may develop a range of rings in the course of a year, depending on the changing climate. Both trees are material manifestations of thick time, and yet they are unique and incompatible maps. Further, their maps are dynamic: they are unpredictable and created in relation to the water, air, sunlight, or earth. This interconnectedness reminds us that we are fundamentally relational beings.

There is nothing that we experience, understand, or know, that is not the product of our engagement with another, *an other*. Whether it is another human being, our pets, a red banana-seat bicycle, or an old, cracked, pink bar of soap, our memories are fiercely collaborative as they are shaped and cemented, changed, or forgotten in relation to all entities with which we are entangled (people, objects, cities, trees).

Take another example: the other day my partner was telling me a story about being in a helicopter as a child. They were only two years old, but talked about how they remembered the intensity and the sounds of the experience. They noted that every time they saw a helicopter on television, it brought them back to this childhood experience. The curious element of this memory is that according to psychologists, the vast majority of people cannot recall experiences from earlier than three years old.[8] And as my partner told the story, they joked that they weren't sure if they actually remembered the experience or if their father had told them about it so many times that it had lodged itself in the body as a virtual experience. Many of us can relate to the confluence of memory and story. Do I really remember blowing out the candles on my fourth birthday, or have I simply paged through the photo album documenting the event so many times that the photographed experience has become four-dimensional? Psychologists Akhtar and colleagues call these implanted stories "fictional first memories" and indicate that a variety of factors outside of actual experience such as photographs or familial retellings lend toward their recollection. More interesting, however, is that the researchers found that these early "fictional" memories were largely connected to the individual's overall autobiographical narrative, such that they were shaped in an effort to add coherence to one's present. Thus, despite the fact that "all memories contain some degree of fiction" they operate to give sense, context, and shape to our *selves*, alongside our relationships to *others*, whether that *other* is a home, a person, or an object.[9]

This is the reach of the living present; it is a dynamic stretching back and reaching forward in order to make sense of our present selves. If we take a deep breath and really feel the impacts of such a limitless process of change and innovation, we can release long histories of reliance on fixed, linear timelines, recognizing that the significance of the examples described above is not that my partner nor I remembered *incorrectly*, nor that memory itself is suspect, as many have claimed throughout history. Instead, it is that memory is inextricable from the stories that we tell, past, present, and future. We might want to tell multiple stories, as though they sit alongside one another in alternative temporal universes. And we need not be after the truth of what is remembered in the body and what is crafted in the mind and instead be interested in the impact of "what happened" and how it produced many offshoots of experience and understanding. A two-year-old's experience of the intensity of a helicopter ride may be the embodied frame within which their father's storytelling memorializes the experience at the same time that it propels an adult forward in experiencing moments and activities that recreate that intensity in other forms.

When we reframe our timelines, we enact the Deleuzian attempt to imagine time that is "out of joint" or out of step.[10] Rather than subordinating time to its historic points or the movements that it is accustomed to measuring (hours, years, growth), time is "liberated from its overly circular figure, freed from the events which made up its content."[11] This challenges us to rethink the safety and security of being able to tell causal stories about the present. As I will discuss at length in later chapters, causal stories are often hinged on progress narratives; they reach toward a supposed "improvement" or a normalized pattern of development. Though there is great value in a quest toward improvement (i.e., improving one's math skills so as to attain a job as a bookkeeper), our memories have experiential force in our present. They produce retroactive causality embodying something of the "erotic effect of memory itself" as Deleuze describes it, dancing and weaving through our self-making-past-making-future, and turning it into weighted stories about our younger selves.[12] As I will show in the pages to come, whether "fictional first memories" or not, we learn much more about ourselves and those around us by looking at memories through the frame of the living present, than we do from relying on an "accurate" timeline.

The Pull of (Linear) Time: Resisting the Monomyth

In any discussion of narrative, we must recognize that we are hardwired to tell linear tales—tales where we follow a familiar plot that starts with character/subject development and then moves to an inciting action that rises to the climax. Once the climax is resolved, we tie up our loose ends, make sense of all conflict, and carry on with a swelling sense of completion. As this plays out within our storytelling tropes, the pattern is a common story arc called the monomyth, or the hero's journey. Setting out on their own, our swashbuckling hero lets go of the world that they know—Harry Potter's cupboard bedroom on Privet Drive; Katniss Everdeen's home in District 12; Bilbo Baggins' comfortable existence in the Shire—crosses a threshold of crisis, great challenge, or adversity—Harry faces off against Quirrell over the philosopher's stone; Katniss defeats the Hunger

Games, Bilbo faces off against Gollum—which they defeat in order to return home forever changed—Harry returns home, but has a newfound inner strength as a wizard; Katniss returns to District 12 an unlikely champion; and Bilbo returns home, just in time to save his belongings from auction and live an eccentric life in the Shire. The monomyth makes up nearly half of our Hollywood blockbusters, hundreds of thousands of books (fiction and nonfiction), and is often the retroactive frame through which we tell stories about ourselves. I tell a story of being bullied in grade two and, after receiving support and guidance from my brave and emboldened uncle to stand up to my bullies (the mentor, also a key component of the hero's journey), I am able to stand up for myself.

The monomyth also has societal and cultural force as it guides our nationalist doctrines, our queer activisms, and even our relationship struggles. Therapists use it as a frame through which to push clients toward self-discovery; Trump used it to justify global calls to war. The monomyth, like other storytelling apparatuses, frames and creates the world around us and, in so doing, it actually *makes time*, particularly the sort of time that literary author Jeanette Winterson describes as a lie: *time as a straight line, time as a singular present, time as a known history, and an unknown future.*[13] When we think of storytelling we think of tall tales, myths, fabrications, and fables. But what if all stories are time-tellers, time-makers, history producers, future creators? Every storytelling trope has material uptake as it frames the past, future, and present in different ways. Sometimes these frames are irregular, multiple, and complex, and sometimes (more often) they are linear, progressive, and cumulative. In each tale, we take a journey to an elsewhere and, in so doing, we construct a present as a somewhere.

Stories are not just our access points into the worlds of fantastic beasts and imagined lands, because everything we write or speak is a form of storytelling, whether philosophy, science, cultural anthropology, or narrative. This means that all of our processes of writing and telling play a role in the making of time. This is a central component of the work ahead: the fact that we all tell stories and, in so doing, *make time*. In claiming that we are time-makers I mean simply that there is no outside of time. There is no grand clock that marks the passage of days; there is rather a relational passage by way of complicated entanglements of time, meaning, and mattering. Likewise, there is no outside of the story; our worlds are only and always the weaving together of the variety of memories, experiences, and anticipations that make up our own storied embodiments. We tell these stories as linear, but they are actually living presents: thick temporal stretches forward and backward that bring meaning, possibility, and hope to present experience.

One of the most legislative modes of telling stories (outlining an argument) is through chronology, particularly the teleological chronology, as the hero's journey demonstrates.[14] So, for example, in a course introducing students to feminist philosophy, I start with Christine de Pizan, one of the first documented feminist philosophers, and work through Mary Wollstonecraft, Emma Goldman, Simone de Beauvoir, Betty Friedan, Lucy Irigaray, Marilyn Frye, Donna Haraway, and others from the mid-nineteenth century. In the last week of class I rush through contemporary philosophers—and by contemporary, I mean scholars from the 1990s to the 2010s. We debate first-, second-, and third-wave feminism; we talk about the heterosexual matrix and oppression; and we only have time to dip our toes into contemporary feminist thinking for we are rarely able to spend luxurious time in the present.

This method of history-making, philosophizing, storytelling tells the same story over and over again:

1. For centuries women were absent from the realm of philosophy, although Plato said some feminist things once upon a time;
2. Women who were able to get any of their thoughts into print were rich, white, or had rich, white, and scholarly lovers/husbands;
3. Women finally made it into the philosophy books when they started fighting for personhood; and
4. Once it really hit the airwaves, feminist activism, philosophy, and theory fit themselves into a series of waves: first, second, and third. Today we are in the fourth wave? Postfeminism? Postmodernism? We won't know until the era has passed.

In a text that is about a living present, such methods of storytelling are a bit out of step with my overall aim and so, to honor the life of a living present, I enlist a diffractive method of storytelling. One could liken it to Foucault's genealogical history of the present, whereby we are tasked with the project of telling time through historical and contemporary mechanisms of power; a diffractive methodology, however, is much more unruly.

Diffraction is a scientific term, which indicates the way that waves bend and change when they reach or pass through an obstacle—called a diffraction grating—but it has also been enlisted as a methodological term.[15] Sidestepping the process of "critique" that characterizes modern philosophy, diffractive readings shift our focus toward the production of new theories, and the development of alternate ways of understanding a changing political and social (and postmodern) climate.[16] In the context of telling alternative histories, this hesitation around "critique" references the tendency to use critical narrative in order to mark a shift in thought or tradition. For example, the canonizing of the first, second, and third waves of feminist philosophy relies inherently on the arguments that each wave supersedes or overcomes the previous: that is, second-wave feminism fought for representational equality, where women fought for equal rights through the mechanism of having access to the same things that men had access to, being represented in the same spheres (voting rights), and occupying roles otherwise withheld from them. This equality was gained through women maintaining the behaviors and values that their male predecessors held, including doing away with their "epithets of weakness."[17] Enter third-wave feminism, and suddenly we are questioning the rules of the game itself. Why is it that women's equality requires the debasement of *women's behaviors*? Why must power, success, and strength be expressed by rationality and masculinity? Third-wave feminism's success is its critical stance in relation to both second- and first-wave feminism as it worked to question the norms of gender that led to woman's secondary status in the first place. It is precisely this axis that supplants the narrative of the "waves" at all; just as the monomyth relies on overcoming adversity, the story is juicier when there is a conflict.

A diffractive method takes an alternate path as it looks for unruly overlaps. Take for example the event of two pebbles dropping into a still body of water. The disturbance in the water around each pebble will produce a series of ripples that will progressively move outward and the ripples from one stone will eventually overlap with those of the other, producing an additional pattern from the differences in amplitude and phase between the wave components. In science, this overlap is called an interference or a diffraction pattern, and in our work, here, the diffraction pattern is precisely the unchronological overlaps and disturbances between modes of thought, memories, philosophies.[18] To illustrate diffraction at work, we can layer Mary Wollstonecraft's *A Vindication of the Rights of Woman* (1792) and Simone de Beauvoir's *The Second Sex* (1949). The relationship between these two authors is often simplified to a first/second-wave chronology, when, instead, a diffractive lens finds a compelling story about how centuries of female scholars have interacted with (whether intentionally or not) the prestige of scholarly husbands and lovers in order to make cracks in a male-dominated realm. Wollstonecraft's anarchist-scholar husband William Godwin contributed to her tale by publishing a graphic and detailed biography of her after she died of septicemia following childbirth, while Beauvoir's fame was often linked to her lover Jean-Paul Sartre. The overlaps between Beauvoir and Wollstonecraft are apparent, but it is their relationship with the interference patterns that gives us food for thought: Wollstonecraft and Beauvoir lived two hundred years apart and in the time between their lives, women achieved emancipation in the United Kingdom and France (as well as many locations within the Western world). Emma Goldman famously paid tribute to Wollstonecraft in 1910 ("Mary Wollstonecraft: Her Tragic Life and Her Passionate Struggle for Freedom"), while also acknowledging that "Mary's own tragic life proves that economic and social rights for women alone are not enough to fill her life, nor yet enough to fill any deep life" and yet Wollstonecraft and Beauvoir were each judged on their failures to abide by common expectations of marriage and so-termed feminine duties.[19] As well, both were denied legitimate standing as "philosophers" within their lifetimes, and were awarded such accolades retroactively and by way of fierce defense from their later readers. This is the story that is interesting to me as a feminist writer in the early twenty-first century. It is a vertical and diffractive story that takes the overlaps and interferences to reveal the sociocultural and economic factors that were and continue to constrain feminist thought.

Diffraction becomes a method of reading ideas and insights through one another, and of attending to relations of difference between them, including "how different differences get made, what gets excluded, and how those exclusions matter."[20] Contrary to apparatuses of reflection, such as mirrors, which produce faithful images of objects, apparatuses of diffraction mark the differences and divergences of overlapping waves. If we loop back to Wollstonecraft's and Beauvoir's diffractive waves, we can imagine that their shared experiences of fighting for space within male-dominated spheres amplify their overlapping efforts, while at the same time, divergences between their work illustrate precisely how "different differences get made" and how those differences have lasting impact. For example, Beauvoir's most well-known text, *The Second Sex*, was originally translated by Howard M. Parshley, a zoology professor who was asked to edit and abridge the text as he went. The outcome was a text that scholars have criticized for almost seventy years as it is vastly different from Beauvoir's original monograph. In particular, Beauvoir's distinct existentialist philosophy was often rerouted through watered-down and inaccurate concepts. Existentialist terms such as "authentic" or "pour-soi" were translated as "real" and "her true nature in itself" respectively, translations that grossly misarticulate Beauvoir's meaning.[21] Beauvoir's trials with translation demonstrate a framing effect on her work, contrary to Wollstonecraft's original use of the English language, and thus offer an alternate jumping-off point for explorations of what constitutes "philosophy," and how gender (and language) intersects with such definitions.

It is not only waves that exhibit diffractive patterns, but also matter—that is electrons, neutrons, and atoms. This discovery shifts the study of phenomena, indicating that diffraction experiments can be used to learn either about passing *through* the diffraction grating, or about the grating itself.[22] Like the interferences between waves, the use of a diffractive methodology within philosophy can read the *ripples* (the connections and divergences between theories), or the *disturbances* (the pebble itself, or rather, the question, context, or "cut" of the storyteller), and each of these demonstrate the way that practices of knowing *themselves* have consequences for what will count as a theory. With Beauvoir and Wollstonecraft, we may dredge up the dropped pebble to recognize that I, as the one making the "cut" or choice on what to discuss, dropped a pebble into the relational readings of both of these historical figures. I am interested in the fact that both were read alongside male counterparts and that this is a common trope throughout history. If you, the reader, were to drop a pebble into the pool, you would inevitably read an alternate overlap, as you would bring your own interests and background knowledge to bear on the dropped pebble.

It can be argued that reflexive processes already recognize that the observer/investigator/theorist acts as an instrument in the construction of evidence, but reflexivity "still holds the world at a distance"[23] by remaining fixated on the relationship between an observer and a representation (an outcome) rather than seeing a relationship between an observer and an object. It assumes there is a distance between entities, or some purity surrounding an individual object, when, in fact, there is no such thing. Every practice of representation has an impact on the objects of investigation; every engagement with an object is predicated on an entanglement between I and other that is always already at play.[24] Consequently, a diffractive methodology is a form of engagement that puts us in touch with phenomena over facts; becomings over things. Through diffraction, the goal is not only to "put the observer or knower back *in* the world (as if the world were a container and we needed merely to acknowledge our situatedness in it) but to understand and take account of the fact that we too are part of the world's differential becoming."[25] We too are part of the making of meaning.

At this point, diffraction starts to feel a bit esoteric, but in fact, as it is mobilized, it feels more akin to a method that Ahmed describes in her recent *Living a Feminist Life*. Ahmed talks about bringing feminist theory home to the everyday experiences of living, working, and learning as feminist killjoys, as willful subjects, as diversity workers. As such, the subjects of our feminist lives are our memories, the relationships we have with our teachers, our choices of television shows, and we are as responsible for building feminist worlds as our worlds are responsible for building us. Ahmed writes:

> It is the practical experience of coming up against a world that allows us to come up with new ideas, ideas that are not dependent on a mind that has withdrawn (because a world has enabled that withdrawal) but a body that has to wiggle about just to create room.[26]

This is the home of diffraction-as-method, and it is the dusty adage of the personal-is-political, a phrase that we feminists are more than familiar with, and yet continue to keep at arm's length. For example, Anglo-American feminist theory has done a great disservice to the actual experiences of trans women through engagements that have used the concept of "transgender" as a theoretical tool and not a subject of empirical analysis. Such a practice works to marginalize trans people, both through its failure to attend to the political and intellectual priorities that they have self-determined and through its systems of knowledge production, which delimit the terrain of trans scholarship. In a frank appeal to future efforts, Viviane Namaste writes, "Simply put, Anglo-American feminist theory would be well served by actually speaking with everyday women about their lives."[27]

Namaste's argument is specific to trans women, and bears repeating for its precise focus, and so, in recalling her work, I hold both the specificity of her argument and its wider application to the work that we do as philosophers and theorists, alongside one another. In the pages that follow, Namaste's challenge inspires me to talk to real people about their lives wherever I can. This takes place through reading research studies about queer youth coming out on YouTube, reading news articles about water shortages in First Nations communities, and drawing in creative and autobiographical texts in order to make room for voices (including my own) to speak and diffract alongside the theory.

A Path for What Lies Ahead

The *living present* shows us that time is the product of materialities, stories, connections, and concepts. It does not preexist the worlds in which we live, the systems of communication and time-keeping through which it is read. The living present is not an abstracted theory, but an indication of a transcorporeality, whereby rather than thinking of the human body as a distinct, autonomous entity, the concept of transcorporeality reveals that the human is "always intermeshed with the more-than-human world"; the human is always "inseparable from 'the environment.'"[28] Engaged not only with a present of transcorporeality, we are also transcorporeal *living presents* or *time-bodies*, where time-bodies stands in as shorthand for the reality of being embodied time-makers. Time-bodies are produced by an infinite number of interrelated entities in the future and the past and are also producing an infinite number of interrelated entities. We make time at the same time that we are recipients of the temporal worlding of millions of other time-bodies. As will be demonstrated extensively in the pages to come, even the stories that we tell are actants in the making of time and the co-creative process of becoming time-bodies.[29]

The apparatus of the living present is applicable to all matter of theory, practice, and understanding, but I am most interested in the living present as it enables us to dive into a variety of stories that have been told about gender, sexuality, culture, and nature. These stories are "timescapes" or multidimensional concepts of time as relative to the observer or *storyteller*. Although the topic of each investigation (whether it is queer theory or climate change) comes to the surface as a key character in the narrative, the force of the engagement is less about the topic than it is about how we have told stories about the said topic, including how we construct meaning and materiality through the stories that we tell—and likewise, how the stories that we tell are lines of flight that have infinitesimal impacts well beyond the conscious "I."

The task is thus to unsettle the fierce linearity of our stories about history, particularly as they impact our political movements, theories, and daily choices. We tell stories about the past as though they have hard edges, and so understand a present as an effect of historical causes. The consequence of this is that we often feel held captive by both the past and the future—a cause-and-effect paradigm that limits freedom in its articulation of "fate" or "well, it's always been that way." If we unsettle this model, we can start to see the openness of the future, the embeddedness of the past, and are able to recognize the absolute responsibility we have as stewards of the present. Put another way, if we "thicken" the present moment to include multiple pasts (and multiple futures) we are invited to act with a deepened level of accountability to all possible timelines.

The work ahead describes time as the unfolding of matter-in-action. By this I mean that time is not quantified by minutes or hours, it is not some *thing* that we can point to or measure, nor the container that gives life direction and causal force. Time *is* storytelling, bodies-in-motion, phenomenal entanglements between bodies and ideas. Time is made in events, in conversations, in the stickiness of past memories and our hopes for the future. To make this case,

I draw on a variety of stories about time, ranging from fiction to philosophy, and from pop culture to quantum theory. This includes diffractive retellings of stories about time within Western philosophy, queer theory, and Indigenous philosophy in Chapter 1, "Telling Time: From Deleuze to Heraclitus and from Queer Theory to Indigenous Ways of Knowing." These stories demonstrate the force and impact of various time-tellings in not just our theories, but also in our lived experiences.

Chapter 2, "The Living Present: A Co-Creative Conversation between Deleuze and Winterson," dives into the living present by way of a collaboration between Jeanette Winterson's *The Stone Gods* and Gilles Deleuze's *Difference and Repetition*. For Deleuze, the living present is one frame of a tripartite understanding of time that also includes the pure past and the eternal return, and together these syntheses provide key readings into the duration, becoming, and difference of time as it operates in our lived environments. For Winterson, the fluidity and contingency of time has always been a central force in her literary work and the synchronicities between her novels and Deleuze's philosophy lend to rich explorations of the relationship between fiction and philosophy.

Chapter 3, "Quantum Materialism: Bringing Time and Matter Together in a Feminist Future," explores new feminist materialisms alongside quantum theory. More than ten years after Karen Barad published *Meeting the Universe Halfway*, the quantum feminist text par excellence, there are still gaps in the uptake of this phenomenal onto-ethico-epistemology. In fact it is the temporality of a *quantum materialism* that I am interested in, not only as it reveals itself in the entanglement between science and feminism, but also in its echoes of Indigenous philosophies. It is through these diffractive collaborations that I see potential for the work of co-creative and decolonial projects which start from a place of entanglement, rather than a place of opposition.

Chapter 4, "'An Erratic and Uneasy Becoming': Queering Time, Reworking the Past," employs a somewhat rhetorical telling of my own process(es) of coming out, in order to demonstrate that although queer time operates to destabilize monomythic progress narratives, it is complicated by coming out practices. By stretching the coming out narrative to include repeat performances, Two Spirit practices of *coming in*, and the complexities of giving account of oneself as transgender, the living present demonstrates that coming out is an agential timescape that is always already embedded in not just a cultural-historical lens, but in material objects and emotional archives. This chapter also draws on the concept of univocity in order to explain a deep entanglement between humans, objects, text, as they comingle in our stories, theories, and day-to-day experiences.

This has uptake for queer praxis in that it expands upon our obsession with the identity categories that both strengthen and plague queer communities and activisms, while exploring the sameness of being that is always the other side of difference.

Chapter 5, "Thick Time: Echoes of the Anthropocene," reads the living present alongside current discussions of the Anthropocene, the posthuman, and ultimately the anticipatory academic discourse surrounding climate change. Ultimately, we are well beyond the hope of "purity" or rather a magical future (or past) outside of a messy, devastating, and, oftentimes, hopeless present. The lack of progress-oriented politics that is central to the living present reminds us that we are always "in the middle of things." There will be no end to climate change just as there was no beginning. What really matters is our ability to better understand our complex and multiple present accountabilities within an otherwise incomprehensible process of change.

Chapter 6, the final chapter, "An Ethics of Entanglement," grounds this work in a thick, durational, understanding of time, especially our own temporal forces as "time-makers" in each and every word, act, or deed. Through questions such as: What hold does the future have on the present? How does matter act as a memory? And what is the use of a living present for political and social projects? I explore an ethics of entanglement whereby we are not bound to any sense of right or wrong, but rather to our univocity, that is, our embeddedness in the making and unmaking of all entities around us. In particular, this chapter draws on contemporary research on epigenetics as it has been discussed in relation to intergenerational trauma within Indigenous communities in Canada.

It is a growing and unfortunate trend to pay lip service to new feminist materialism's indebtedness to Indigenous philosophies without engaging meaningfully with the content and I am as much to blame as anyone else. However, in this book, I attempt to do away with hand waving, by weaving Indigenous contributions, theories, philosophies, stories, and questions into every chapter. Also in every chapter is my attempt to identify the theoretical and practical outcomes of using a living present as an apparatus of understanding, for the living present is much more than a philosophy; it is something that enables us to better approach a problem, foregrounds the vast historical context of a present moment, and gives us the space to really think strategically about the future. Through the frame of the living present, we may all better understand our accountability as time-makers, time-bodies, whether through our theoretical arguments, storytelling, the memories that haunt our present choices, or the force of our individual expectations and anticipations of the future on present actions. A living present provides more than methods of "waving at," "reading differently," or "thinking anew," and instead actually represents processes of time-telling and time-making. Thus, it is through the living present that we can approach questions of rights, politics, community organizing, and a changing climate in ways that effectively move us toward multiple models of accountability and action.

1

Telling Time: From Deleuze to Heraclitus and from Queer Theory to Indigenous Ways of Knowing

We inhabit time as fish live in water. Our being is being in time. Its solemn music nurtures us, opens the world to us, troubles us, frightens and lulls us. The universe unfolds into the future, dragged by time, and exists according to the order of time.

—Carlo Rovelli, *The Order of Time*

As I complete this manuscript in March of 2021, the entire world has been in the grip of the Covid-19 pandemic. If ever there was an event that brought us face to face with the irregularity of time, it is the global speeds and slows of a powerful virus. In some ways the last year has been dreadfully slow, time all but stopped in my hometown of Saskatoon, SK, for the months of April and June, 2020 when restaurants, schools, and businesses closed down. Streets felt eerie without traffic, grocery stores were desolate with their empty shelves and parking lots. In other ways, time has flown by as the signifiers that mark and stretch time (summer festivals and events, the movements of leaving the house at scheduled times) have dissolved for some, amplified for others. Days and weeks run together in a strangely anticipatory climate as we have pushed "pause" on so many parts of our lives, while still living in a world that is moving faster than ever around us.

With her characteristic precision in both philosophical and political climates, Claire Colebrook's "Fast Violence, Revolutionary Violence: Black Lives Matter and the 2020 Pandemic" snaps back at the timelines of the Covid-19 pandemic. She demonstrates their implication in racisms, sexisms, and other modes of "slow violence" as it is enacted through systematic discriminations and exclusions that occur "gradually and out of sight."[1] As it applies to the pandemic, Colebrook explains how in the United States, the virus's higher prevalence rates within non-white communities play out alongside increased border and immigration controls. Effectively, the pandemic operates to give speed to many slow violences that have been here all along.

Not unlike the reach of the 2017 women's marches, alongside an amplification of Tarana Burke's 2006 hashtag #metoo, the Black Lives Matter movement was reignited by the slowest eight minutes and forty-five seconds many had ever witnessed in the devastating and merciless murder of George Floyd on May 25, 2020. In each of these cases, particular "events" represented tipping points for public outcry. Floyd's murder was a tipping point for Black Lives Matter, while Trump's inauguration ceremony tipped the scales of a misogynistic and destructive election campaign, spilling into a global women's march movement that is estimated to have included 673 marches of more than 7 million people. Each event *contracts*, that is, recalls and relives, centuries of slow violence against racialized communities, against women and feminized people, ensuring that we are in the thick of these histories; the power of their lineages still hurt and haunt us as we work to build futures of freedom and justice. As other chapters in this book will describe, time cannot be extracted from the lived bodies and environments upon which it is inscribed. Bodies that have breasts, testes, and those that have both. Bodies that are tall and white, nonbinary and brown. Bodies that use wheelchairs to move and bodies that use technological devices to hear. The intersectional subjectivities that make up each unique "human" are entangled with our memories, our hopes for the future, our understanding of ourselves.

So what is *time*? Is it the measurable period of an action or event? Is it relative to the observer? Is it entirely an illusion—merely a childhood security blanket that we cling to in order to avoid the chaos of timelessness—or is it a grand clock that moves us ever-forward, never backward. In any formation, time is utterly fascinating and endlessly complex, having captivated writers, thinkers, scientists, and creators for centuries. There has been a lot of querying about time going on as of late, whether regarding our obsessive time management in an age of more and more complicated notions of productivity, explorations into the speed of change and its impact on knowledge production, or as a central piece in the call for Indigenous sovereignty.[2] In the face of the contemporary breadth and span of such queries, some have stated that we are in a "temporal turn," but I am not sure this is accurate. The entire corpus of Western philosophy betrays a fascination with time, whether that fascination is with metaphysical or concrete time, and so it seems as though time's *turn* has been here all along.

Taking up some of these twists and *turns*, this chapter tells time through a variety of frames—classical physics, quantum physics, ancient philosophy, queer theory, and Indigenous philosophy—by asking the following questions: What is time? What does it do for us? This chapter sets the stage for many of the chapters to come in its exploration of a variety of ways of talking about and theorizing time but, more importantly, it demonstrates that our theorizations of time are themselves part of the very timelines through which we are shaped and understood. A caveat here is the absolute struggle I experienced in telling these stories outside of a linear frame. We are all intoxicated by causal narratives, and I am just as susceptible to the lure of a happy ending as anyone. Instead, my strategy has been to read out of step, to layer stories in new ways, and to bring divergent histories into conversation with one another through unique enactments.

Is Time Absolute or Is It Relative?

The living present, as outlined in Deleuze's *Difference and Repetition*, tempers all of my own engagements with time, whether philosophical or physical. Bringing philosophy "to life" so to speak, I have lived its thesis daily since first encountering the living present's fluid movement forward and back. The living present is actually only one of three Deleuzian syntheses of time, each of which serves as a unique contraction of past, present, and future. The second synthesis of time is the pure past (or memory), which operates on the present in order to make the present *pass*, while the third provides the possibility for the new or an undetermined future through the caesura: the cut between the pure past and a novel future. Discussed at length in Chapter 2, the three syntheses operate simultaneously, all informing the concept of the living present, and illustrating the ways that *time* is given life through the activities of remembering, storytelling, predicting, and anticipating. Most significantly, the living present demonstrates that there is no time-as-container within which we *have* experience; rather we are ourselves created and in turn create the world through these temporal processes, through lived experience. Also important is that these processes are *passive*; meaning that rather than understanding time as a series of selective, agential, or active associations, wherein our conscious selves peel back through the rolodex of memory to pull out the bluest or shiniest card, our memories and predictions are largely unconscious (we may say to our rolodex: "show me a plumber" and it spits out the smells of our childhood basement flooding during a historic rainstorm). Our memories, in this model, are governed as much by our bodies (the fingers that instinctively know how to translate words to keys to screen) and environments (the pink bar of soap that recalls my grandmother's bathroom sink from thirty years past) as they are by our consciousness.

So upon confessing my bias, I am still set to attend to a much wider landscape of time and few are more famous than Albert Einstein's General Theory of Relativity, published in 1915. Einstein monumentally shifted our understanding of time from that which happens outside of us, or *to us*, to that which has changing properties, relative to the position or experience of the observer. Einstein's special theory of relativity demonstrated that, on a grand scale, there is no fixed frame of reference in the universe; there is no house that holds our cosmos together. Instead, everything moves *relative* to everything else and, in the case of space and time, we cannot even think about space without also thinking about time. Building on this, Einstein's General Theory of Relativity argued that, rather than separate entities, space and time make up one continuum (or a fourth dimension) called space-time. Space-time is best described through a curved or "warped" grid, where any mass or large object will distort space-time by forming a gravity well around the heavy object. Think of a layer of fabric tightly stretched across a room and then imagine placing a bowling ball in the centre of the fabric. As the bowling ball sinks toward the floor it pulls the fabric with it, bending the "space-time" around it. Planetary orbit, then, is the result of the sun bending the fabric of space-time. The Earth travels along this bend, just as the moon travels along the Earth's bend in the space-time continuum.

Long before Einstein literally curved space and time, Western science believed the closed Universe model developed in Isaac Newton's *Philosophiæ Naturalis Principia Mathematica* (1687). Newton's world relied on absolute space and absolute time where each was bound to quantifiable, natural laws. This meant that the universe was fixed; it *was* the house that held our world together. Newton built his science upon the works of Galileo Galilei, and of course Galileo is infamous for his daring critique of scientists and astronomers before him, who for centuries looked up at the heavens and saw the sun and stars move across a static sky that belonged to Earth. Galileo fought for one of the most *revolutionary* discoveries in the world of science: the discovery that the Earth was *not* at the centre of the Universe.

For Galileo, the scene looked very different: he saw gravitational movement around Jupiter and other planets, he saw the stillness of the night sky alongside a moving, orbiting Earth. Such a reorientation cost Galileo his freedom, but transformed our concepts of space and time from things relative to our environment to things that are independent from their environment.[3] And so, building on Galileo's work, Newton's famous claim that "absolute, true, and mathematical time, of itself, and from its own nature, flows equally without relation to anything external" made time into an absolute entity; space became an absolute terrain and both precipitated a scientific system that turned natural philosophy on its head and ushered in our modern understanding of science.[4] This enabled society to measure, predict, and study both space and time in a much more rigorous manner and, through Newton's "container" model, both served as receptacles for movement and extension; this means that he supported the spatialization of temporality or the separation of subjectivity and temporality (whether I am seven years old or eighty, whether I perceive it quickly or slowly, time ticks along at a steady rate, because it is outside of me). Such a shift precipitated the invention of that object to which we slavishly submit ourselves for daily guidance and measure: *the modern clock*.

It is no great proclamation to state that the majority of our Western apparatuses of time-telling limit understanding to an external counting-of-moments. The clock is heralded as one of the most profound inventions of all time, with roots as far back as 2000 BCE. The invention of the pendulum-powered clock took place in 1656 by Christiaan Huygans, but before that there were sundials, water clocks, timesticks, and obelisks to track and measure time's passing. While the time-telling of the sundial relies on the movement of the sun alongside a carefully crafted spherical scale, the mechanical clock captures time within a self-propelled apparatus. Following its invention, the mechanical clock garnered ownership over the passage of time, and thus began to direct the activities of the day. Today the hands of the clock, now more often a digital screen, have masterful control over our activities. I know that when my alarm goes off at 7:00 am, I have two hours before I have to begin work. I know that when the clock strikes 10:15 that there is no *going back* to 10 am to quickly catch up on the fifteen minutes I have missed.

Today, elementary school textbooks cite Einstein's General Theory of Relativity as the "true" account of space and time (space-time)—it having superseded Newton's substantivalism (and relationalism in its historical form); the mechanical clock, however, has maintained Newton's absolute universe. We never look at the clock and say, "It's 1:30 pm, but for my aunt who lives in Lake Louise, which is 5,449 feet above sea level, time ticks faster, so it might be 1:31."[5] Rather, the clock remains our North Star and, with it, we perceive time as fixed, constant, and external to us. We are all *governed* by the force of the clock's ticking hands and as they move ever-forward we rush, fret, agonize, and plan.

But what does it mean to move from a model where time is described in terms of motion to one where motion, movement, and change are described in terms of time?

In the tradition of Western philosophy, this query has often been answered through two unique philosophies of time, namely relationism and substantivalism. Relationism shares a history with Heraclitus, Aristotle, Leibniz, and even Einstein and argues that time is not a thing in itself, but rather emerges from events; there would be no time if there were no events to mark its passing—my passage from age six to seven is marked not just by the birthday party, but also by every experience, event, and instance that takes place, each instant adding to the marking of a year. Substantivalism, on the other hand, is Newton's piece de resistance, as he argues that time exists independently from any measure or mode of counting; the yearly calendar is just a map of a grand clock in which we move, play, and age.

Time in Ancient Greece

> I know well enough what [time] is, provided that nobody asks me; but if I am asked what it is and try to explain, I am baffled.
> —Augustine, *Confessions*

Heraclitus's (540–480 BC) famous anecdote that "one cannot step twice into the same river, nor can one grasp any mortal substance in a stable condition, but it scatters and again gathers; it forms and dissolves, and approaches and departs"[6] has inspired centuries of nonlinear prophetics about the ever-changing nature of time. Heraclitus tells a tale of change, subjective-time, movement, and flows, as his starting point was the dynamism of the natural world (the river that coursed and flowed, the movement from hot to cold, cold to hot), and he heralded time as the signifier of unending change.[7] Significantly, Heraclitus's ever-changing river was not an open-ended multiplicity, but rather a symbol of the most pervasive law of the natural world: *change*. Change was his inner harmony, the only thing he believed capable of corralling a multiplicitous world into order; change constituted Heraclitus's sense of time.[8]

Throughout all of his (very sparse) works, Heraclitus tried to break away from the beliefs and ideas of his contemporaries. For example, at a time when philosophers were attempting to explain the natural world in very logical and rational ways, Heraclitus held such logic in contempt. He wanted to wake his readers from their slumbers, criticizing them as lacking comprehension and sleepwalking through life: "But of this account, which holds forever, people forever prove uncomprehending, both before they have heard it and when once they have heard it. ... The rest of mankind [sic], however, fail to be aware of what they do after they wake up just as they forget what they do while asleep."[9] Heraclitus's distaste for the works of his own contemporaries reveals itself in his affinity for change, movement, and flux. In fact, he is often acknowledged as having generative force in the creation of the modern-day concept of *becoming* as Nietzsche writes that Heraclitus "will remain eternally right with his assertion that being is an empty fiction."[10] With an eye toward becoming, then, Heraclitus refrained from solidifying the subject, instead setting forth a relational universe; remember that you can never step into the same river twice, for the river is not just made up of millions of moving water droplets, but it is also continually reconfiguring its location and its boundaries via the eroding riverbank, the deer that drink from its shorelines, and the soils that disperse and compact at its riverbed. The becoming of the river is an acknowledgment of not just the case that time is change, but also that identity is itself change.

Aristotle (384–322 BC) plays a supporting role to Heraclitus's time-tale, further linking time and change in his argument that time is the "number of change in respect of the before and after."[11] This means that time is the means by which we measure change; so, for example, when we observe the orbit of the moon or the movement of sunlight along the spokes of a sundial, the time that passes between point A (where the gnomon of the sundial casts a shadow at 6 am) and point B (where the shadow is cast at 6 pm) makes up the units that measure the passing of a day: a change from morning to night. If the gnomon's shadow stayed in one place, there would be nothing to measure. Time would stand still. Note, however, that Aristotle did not equate change and time, arguing that time is not the movement itself, but rather the medium through which we can transcribe movement into measure, ensuring that time is the mathematical complement and not a force in and of itself.[12] Aristotle's link between time and measurement framed ancient physics right up until Newton's (and Galileo's) temporal realism finally edged it out of the textbooks.

Aristotle also describes time as the *counting* and, in many ways, as reliant upon the count-er (i.e., the rational human soul/mind capable of counting), a factor that thickens our telling of Einstein's theory of relativity earlier in this chapter. In addition to empowering the human *counter*, Aristotle empowers our objects of counting—the calendar, the sundial, the clock—with significant power, as the external measures that identify time's passing. Undoubtedly, the power of our objects of counting remains to this day as we fixate on the hands of the clock, and obey the pages of the calendar in structuring our lives.

Heraclitus and, to a lesser degree, Aristotle, are both interesting here due to their anticipation of Deleuze's philosophy of becoming. Heraclitus's transformative river foreshadows the endless flow without origin of becoming, while Aristotle links change and becoming through potentiality and actuality.[13] Writing that bronze matter is imbued with potential and that in that potential exists change, Aristotle claims that while bronze has the potential of being a statue, it is not the bronze in itself that represents change—these two expressions are not the same thing.[14] Instead, change is a sort of "pure" process distinct from the actuality of either the bronze matter or its outcome, such as a statue. Take another example: if we imagine a freshly baked chocolate cake, we understand it as an entity unto itself. But if we backtrack to the ingredients used to make the cake—cocoa powder, flour, eggs, sugar, and oil—then we are to understand the cake as an actuality that relies on the cake-potential of the separate ingredients. In fact, the ingredients are becoming-cake, even as they sit in their respective containers within the cupboard. The piece that makes Aristotle's argument more interesting than merely an explanation of the parts (ingredients) that make up a whole (cake) is that the potentiality (the becoming-cake) exists apart from the cake itself. Once the cake is baked, its ingredients are no longer potentialities—they are actual chocolate cake. The ingredients as becoming-cake are pure potential only in their unfinished state. Like later philosophies of becoming, Aristotle's discussion of potentiality resists a world where all parts have definite outcomes, and instead enables a relational world of *possibilities*.

Now, remember how any story changes, dependent upon the hero? If we switch our protagonist from Heraclitus to Parmenides, we tell a very different story about time. Rather than viewing time as that which is related to change or motion (whether held in the mind or the units of movement), we instead have a story of static objects and fixed measures. A skeptic of sensory knowledge, Parmenides argues against a shifting and changing world, stating that there is no such thing as change. Reality is singular and fixed and therefore the passage of time is an illusion. Parmenides's student Zeno (490–430 BC) used his famous paradox of "The Arrow" to argue that although we may be inclined to perceive the flight of an arrow as movement through time, such an understanding relies on our apprehension of the arrow as having been at a different point in the past than it is in the present.[15] Likewise, such an understanding relies on the anticipation of the arrow's movement to a higher point in the sky in the near future. Zeno argues that all we know of the arrow's physics is the position it occupies *now* and, furthermore, that it only occupies a space equal to its own size at any given *now*, which would indicate that each "now" is the arrow at rest and not representative of true movement. Zeno's world relies on reason alone; the senses are unreliable witnesses. Given that change can only be conceived of through sensation (visual apprehension of an arrow moving through the sky), Zeno claims its falsity.

Likewise, Plato (427–347 BC) can be layered atop Parmenides and Zeno as he argues that time is representative of permanence rather than change. Plato's famous claim that "time [is] an eternal moving image of the eternity which remains forever at one" supports his argument that the eternal ideas were ultimately nontemporal, but that *time* is an absolute entity, not unlike Newton's substantivalism with respect to space and time.[16] Consequently, our common concept and use of *time* came into being as a result of our apprehension of the said movement: "the sight of day and night, and the months and the revolutions of the years have created number and have given us a conception of time, and the power of inquiring about the nature of the universe."[17] Quite different from Aristotle's time-as-the-measure-of-movement thesis, Platonic time *is* movement (of celestial bodies) and, as movement, it exists outside of human apprehension, counting, or understanding.

Although not necessarily a cogent addition to stacked philosophers of substantivalism, I want to drop a pebble into one more pool: St. Augustine (354–430 AD). Like Plato, Augustine was suspicious of the workings of time, and so together they amplify the statement that "the past and the future *are not* (now), so they are not real"[18]—prioritizing the present and rational apprehension in the same way that Zeno does through his mistrust of sensory perception. That said, Augustine had a penchant for the soul and brought a finite substance of time from the exterior to the interior in his argument that time is a phenomenon of human consciousness. Augustine started by locating each expression within the present: "a present of past things, a present of present things, and a present of future things."[19] Together, these activities enact the processes of memory, direct perception, and expectation, all of which serve as dimensions of human consciousness. While Aristotle (and Plato, for that matter, though for different reasons) may have mapped the movement of celestial bodies to record the passing of months and years, Augustine argued that the mind exacts all temporal movement through a dilation of these three processes, processes that engage and overlap in relation to a given request or need: "I can take out pictures of things which have either happened to me or are believed on the basis of experience; I can myself weave them into the context of the past, and from them I can infer future actions, events, hopes, and then I can contemplate all these things as though they were in the present."[20]

By bringing the internal world of human consciousness into play, Augustine changed the parameters of our temporal musings. In fact, he mirrors some of the processes of the living present: a reaching backward and stretching forward in order to garner meaning and understanding within the present. Despite sharing Zeno's reliance on the rational mind, he allows for an apprehension of futurity such that the "now" of the arrow may still include a "present of future things" whereby the observer could dilate the present movement to include an anticipation of the arrow's dip back to Earth after reaching its crest in the sky (as per gravity). Needless to say, Zeno would not have bought into this projection. In fact, Augustine's philosophy of time lives in the overlaps and amplifications between substantivalism and relationism, Parmenides and Heraclitus, Plato and Aristotle. That said, his limitation of time to human consciousness undergirds the location of time within the mind of the rational (male) subject.

Now, let's wind through substantivalism and relationism with respect to time once more. Take my memories of learning to ride a bike as a child. I distinctly remember the street (33rd St. W), the house we lived in at the time (a plain duplex—white on top and brown on the bottom), and the feeling of being scared and excited at the same time. We only lived on this street for a year or so, but I still travel past it regularly. Every time I pass by, I try to pick out the right home from the row of now-dilapidated buildings, and I think about how the busy street must have been much less busy back then to allow for kids to play safely. If the past is not *now* and therefore not *real*, is this recurring memory just a dream? Are my senses untrustworthy and my recollections merely fantasy? No, of course not. But there is still often an element of distrust surrounding memory. Augustine enables me to engage with this bike-riding memory through a present-moment-dilation that reaches to the past in order to collect data from the experience, data that plays on my present knowledge of bike riding, the recollection of BMX bikes in childhood, and the thick nostalgia that colors their recollection in the present day. All of this, however, would indicate very little about the "outside" world. Rather, they tell me about the parameters of my own self-consciousness, all of the memories encapsulated in the "now" that is my present.

If we thicken the timeline and pull Heraclitus into the conversation, we can imagine that each recollection of this bike-riding experience is another dip into the river. Every time I remember, the memory changes: sometimes I see it from the outside, sometimes I am the subject of the movement. Another time the bike transforms into the red banana seat bike I had as a ten-year-old, a few years, and many pedals later. The very act of reaching for the memory changes it, and yet, is this to say that the meaning behind is lost? Zeno is clapping his hands at this point. "See! Your memory is unreliable! How can we trust anything that morphs and changes at every step?" My changing memory easily begs for memory's falsity, the fictional memories that Akhtar and colleagues discussed earlier.[21] As I remember the bike-riding lesson, I recall a yellow BMX bike with training wheels; but is that because that was the truth of the bike I was practicing on? Or is it because five years ago my father told me that I once had a yellow BMX bike? If I shared this memory with my dad today, would he rewrite it entirely?

We may be tempted to agree with Zeno, in claiming that our senses are unreliable witnesses, and yet, it is the engagement with the tactile, the sensory, that plays a role in the "stickiness" of memory at all. "Stickiness," in this respect, references the degree to which a memory attaches and lodges itself in one's psyche. The very process of writing, remembering, and piecing through my childhood experiences of learning how to ride a bike has made the memory very sticky. It's close at hand in a way that it wasn't prior to this venture. I have added smells, color, and feeling to what were once just visual flashes. The interesting part of all of this is that acknowledgment of my impropriety does not mean that a particular memory should be thrown out. Instead it tells us about the intricate blending of emotion, the new, matter, and memory that frames my bike-riding beginnings. Such blending occurs for many of us when we experience new things, when we are afraid, or when we are surrounded by unique visual, tactile, or sensory cues and each of these components plays a hand in the making of memory and thus the making of time.

Returning to our philosophical time-tellers, it is clearly the Heraclitan story of movement, change, and becoming that has more influence on the project at hand, including a philosophy of relationism that refuses to recognize time as real in and of itself and instead tracks its *emergent* existence. Rather than sidling up to the substantivalist's linear calendar, a relational thick time is both the condition of possibility for temporal experience and the event(s) through which time can pass. That said, as with any story (be it an oral history, journal article, online blog, or children's book), the storyteller makes choices that affect all other parts. I have chosen to make certain cuts alongside other connections and my choices mirror those that others have made, and in other cases diverge. I could just as easily have begun with Henri Bergson to tell a story of duration and memory (see Chapter 2), or with the tracing of Earth's stratigraphical timelines as they construct eras of human and nonhuman life (see Chapter 5). Depending on the storyteller, we tell a distinct tale about a present temporality and, assuredly, we wind a new path with each "cut" we make, or each pebble we drop into the pool. The verticality of "thick time" stacks Heraclitus, Aristotle, Bergson, and Deleuze. Some likely partners, others not. In this particular stack, the slice might be change, movement, or becoming but we wouldn't be able to make a neat cut around the philosophies that accompany the terms. Likewise, we could stack Parmenides, Zeno, Augustine, and even Leibniz and collect varied slices of idealism, rationalism, and time-as-idea. The power of a diffractive method, then, is that were we to cut along different lines—say those that speak of memory (St. Augustine and Bergson) or those interested in potentiality or expectation (Aristotle, Augustine, and Deleuze)—our outcomes would be quite different from those I have traced here.

Now such a tale makes me curious: What does it mean to queer time in relation to these varied histories and configurations? How do we release time from its container or "closet" so to speak? Transform its movement in ways that trouble not only the tight lines around space and time but also around linearity, cause and effect? Although I take up queer temporalities in much greater detail in Chapter 4, they are relevant here as they diffract the stories that Western philosophy has been telling about time. It is precisely through the activities of *queering* time that scholars have been able to demonstrate the pull of the heteronormative timeline; that is, the expectation that one moves through childhood→adolescence→love→marriage→family. For queer subjects, not only does this linear path serve as both a physically and psychically legislating force, but it is also often impossible to adhere to, thus adding to its painful effects. Queer temporalities have provided rich possibilities for lives lived otherwise and, more specifically, have demonstrated that it is often those bodies that live outside of the dominant paradigms that have the most to teach us about transformative politics.

Queering Time

Similar to other disciplines, queer theorists are really into *time* these days and explorations are varied in scope and intent.[22] Some retell history, while others have crafted phenomenological tales about bodies-in-time. Some have engaged critically with futurity, and still others have troubled time's linearity through queer narratives and alternate timelines. Regarding the first of these, there is no shortage of queer reclamations of past musicians, authors, leaders, and artists in order to reveal lives long hidden. Such efforts to retell the past echo the work of the living present as they continually remake history in an effort to thicken the queer present. This demonstrates time as a form of *storytelling*, such that, through telling stories about our pasts, we are able to make queer futures that include an ever-growing cast of past contributors. Queer *time*, thus, gets longer and longer, while our queer present is ultimately afforded greater presence. That said, there is a danger to such acts of storytelling and retelling as methods of reclamation.

When I taught the undergraduate course "Gender and Popular Music" I regularly cited the jazz musician Billy Tipton, as an example of how queer scholars and cultural workers were reclaiming the lives of otherwise "closeted" artists. Billy Tipton lived as male throughout his life and career, only revealed to have been assigned female at birth after his death in 1989. Since then, Tipton has been the topic of many exposé articles and monographs, many of which shamelessly reveal private details about someone who had no interest in being exposed as such. The Tipton story clearly demonstrates not only the damage of reclamation activities as they inevitably enact a violence on a life lived otherwise, but they also illustrate that such retroactive "activism" ascribes a linear timeline to a life that does little more than solidify progress narratives about gender, sexuality, and coming out itself. Additionally, the concept and expression of being trans was very different in 1959 than it is in 2021, so to pluck Billy Tipton out of history, cast him as trans, and turn him into a spectacle is akin to the slow violence I spoke of in this chapter's opening pages.

The critique of progress narratives is peppered throughout this work and one way to resist its lure is to actually lean into the drag of the past, remind ourselves that our pasts are never as rosy and teleological as they are made out to be. On this front, Heather Love's *Feeling Backward* explores the experiences of shame, depression, despair, and paranoia that are often the forgotten stories within queer progress narratives. These "backward" feelings (feelings that stretch back) don't disappear just because we have gay-straight alliances in most Canadian high schools. Instead, they remind us to look back, paying attention to the ways that painful histories of being closeted, excluded, and invisible have far-reaching impact on the present. Such explorations do more than retell stories then; they draw out the emotional impacts of the experiences such that they affect the present. For Christopher Nealon, this "affection" is the result of material objects: queer artifacts, especially lesbian pulps and muscle magazines, including the ways that the veiled (and even imagined) references to homosexuality in such texts create a shared history that connects their readers across temporal fields. Nealon attributes this "call of the past" to the fact that we are "trained a little in hearing the call of homosexuality in analogies to secret, impossible affiliations" and so this training operates as the unconscious contraction of spoken and unspoken cultural cues that queer communities have long relied on to find places of belonging and recognition.[23]

It is difficult not to turn toward phenomenology in discussions of the "touch" and impact of the queer archives on the present. In fact, the argument that we are *time-makers* relies on an engagement with various types of human experiences such as memory, perception, and desire, as well as our orientation toward things as a process of *making* such things. The key is to stretch phenomenological explorations of the everyday lived experiences of gay and lesbian people to one that explores what it means to "'orient' oneself sexually toward some others and not other others," as Sara Ahmed attempts.[24] For Ahmed, our orientation toward things (people, objects, norms) is borne out of a preexisting horizon in which some things are "reachable" and others are not. As it applies to sexual orientation, Ahmed queries the unquestioned link between *sexual* and *orientation*, such that we take for granted the identifying function of the pair, but not the spatializing function of being sexually oriented toward one and not another. A queer phenomenology, then, over and above a phenomenology of queerness, shows us the way that our sexual orientation (as we are oriented toward) shapes the spaces in which we are and, likewise, the timescapes within which we find ourselves.[25] Of interest to a Deleuzian living present, the object (i.e., tables, lesbian pulps, rainbow flags) plays a significant role in Ahmed's account of orientation, further thickening Nealon's recognition that the artifacts of our (queer) lives are heavy with memory and meaning, and this meaning makes up the material of our experience.

What links all of these queer theories of time, including their ability to make inroads in terms of decentering dominant temporal narratives, is their relationship to the future. Despite very real efforts to "improve" the lot of queers everywhere, queer theorists have generally not had very positive relationships with the future.[26] Perhaps most pessimistic of all, Lee Edelman finds the future wholly suspect. Describing the force of the future as distinctly tied to the figure of the child, Edelman describes the child as the perpetual horizon of every "acknowledged politics, the fantasmatic beneficiary of every political intervention."[27] As the penultimate figure of purity and innocence in need of protection, the child has the concomitant effect of rendering *queerness* as the side that does not fight for the future of the child. Whether through the lack of queer reproduction or the absence of children from within queer politics, Edelman determines that queer subjects should refuse the child, along with hope and anticipation and instead embrace a queer negativity. This negativity circumvents the "reproductive futurity" that the child signifies and instead embraces a death drive or a politics that is not oriented toward a "better future."

To embrace a death drive is to have a certain degree of privilege and, consequently, the sacred child of the future is always already white. Racialized and queer kids sidestep the purity of the future, requiring and calling for alternate timelines, while demonstrating that Edelman's pessimism forecloses on the lives of many who do not have the luxury of choice when it comes to having hope for a better future.[28] This means that queerness is a "not yet here," but more interesting is the sustained absence of an anticipated utopia that is possible in such a suspension of outcomes.[29] Alongside J. Jack Halberstam's expert queering of the linear timelines of heteronormativity, which I will save for the critique of the coming out narrative in Chapter 4, queer temporalities have also graced us with a novel form of affirmative politics—a queer future not only without teleology but also without the feigned helplessness of pessimism.

Where queer temporalities serve the living present is precisely in their affirmative politics. Deleuze's and Guattari's philosophy of the "concept" as the creation of novel worlds is powerfully wielded by the works of queer feminists who see possibility in thinking and dreaming of political systems with equitable representation, or comprehensions of gender that do not rely on the language of the binary. Perhaps most fascinating in this regard is Elizabeth Grosz's sibling texts, which powerfully propose a new philosophy of time that begins, surprisingly, with Darwinian evolution. Darwin has long been a figure of discomfort for feminists, considering the role of evolutionary theory in justifying relations of domination and subordination between races and sexes.[30] However, Grosz argues that Darwin actually offers a biting critique of such hierarchies, and that, rather than supporting essentialist models of human nature, he provides an antihumanist understanding of biological dynamics. The key finding is that evolution is open-ended. It pushes biology forward, but that push ascribes to no teleological path.[31] While Darwin's theory of evolution has been used by modernists and progressivists in the hopes that it will enable humanity to be perfected along a certain trajectory, Grosz understands the anti-teleology inherent in Darwinian evolution to indicate that life is open-ended, and is involved in natural/cultural/sexual/social modes of self-transformation that have direct relevance for feminist theory. Under this view, evolutionary theory, then, provides a picture of what temporality *is*; that is, the active force that enables objects to come into existence: "The ongoing condition of becoming that enables even the universe itself to become."[32]

With this model we return to the familiar landscape of chance, adding randomness and accident to the mix in order to describe the ways that we are thrown into an unknowable future, largely "uncontained by the past."[33] This ontology of becoming, however, does not determine that subjects are parachuted into a world, but rather that they are co-creatively made into subjects (we are time-makers) and alternatively make the world into things, objects, and entities. This is a deepening of the phenomenological experience of not only being oriented *toward* an other (table, person, or text) that Ahmed speaks of above, but it is also a tipping point for the reciprocal *matter of time* in which such "things, objects, and entities" are also making us. For Grosz, such a project not only calls for a radical reworking of the daily allegiance to absolutist time, but it also calls for an alternative ethics that expand our frames of reference beyond the limited tools at hand. It is thus through queer theory's relentless reliance on the concept of *becoming* that we come to recognize that queer theory is always already *about time*. E. L. McCallum and Mikko Tuhkanen liken this to the move from a time of *Chronos*, or linear time, to one of *Kairos*, which they determine as the "moment of opportunity"[34]—or a sense of time that aligns with Grosz's argument for an open-ended and inventive future. Effectively, the moment of opportunity includes nonlinear kinship patterns, transforming the coming out narrative, shifting our habits so that they are more fluid, more flexible, and mobilizing a thousand tiny sexes in the face of the strict heterosexual matrix.

Each of these branches of queer theory makes time in different ways. We live in a thickened present where gay magazines are plentiful, but the 1950s "hetero" muscle magazines are built into the narratives of desire; they serve as a nostalgic gay *underground*. Queer reclamation practices tell us about our own desperate nostalgia for origins, lineage, while queer phenomenology attunes us to the closeness between our lived sexualities and desires and our transgressive orientations toward them in the face of other, more forceful and expected orientations. Finally, queer temporality's engagement with the future, whether from a Deleuzian lens (Grosz, McCallum and Tuhkanen) or critical lens (Edelman, Muñoz), indicates affective beacons of disruption and change, processes that invite us as bodies and scholars to expand our levels of engagement and to be accountable to the stories that we weave for they are always the very "stuff" of our futures and our pasts. The final time-telling of this chapter is in regard to Indigenous philosophies of time. What often goes unsaid and to which I will attend at multiple points throughout this text is the weight of our Western, Eurocentric, colonial pasts in shaping contemporary stories about time. I am far from the first to critique any newness of new materialism, but we

Western Europeans are fixated on our colonial tales, and so relentlessly reach for what is close at hand when time has been told as story, through oral histories of future, past, and present by Indigenous scholars, elders, and grandmothers for centuries.

Indigenous Temporalities: Storying-as-Time

> The past is real and present ... held in our memories and in the shape of the world. It is the ground of our being, its actuality, its particular substance. The future? The future doesn't exist. We must create the future by our decisions, our actions and inactions. Together with the place we live, we are cocreators of the world, bringing it into existence moment by moment.
> —V. F. Cordova, *How It Is: The Native American Philosophy of V.F. Cordova*

Imagine making snowballs as a child. Packing a tight ball and then rolling it through icy, sticky flakes to make it larger and larger. Imagine each layer of snow forming a new present, its matter adding shape and content to layers to come. Through this snowball metaphor, time is enacted by way of a universe *in the making*. Every present action shapes a novel future, and each movement is deeply implicated in every outcome. This description is from Indigenous philosopher, Viola F. Cordova. Cited as the first Native American woman to receive a PhD in philosophy, Cordova spent her scholarly career moving from university to university in both the United States and Canada. Cordova's movements were due to her self-proclaimed refusal to succumb to "artificial accolades" and the arcane expectations to publish just to publish, to teach just to teach.[35] But her movements also satisfied her philosophy of responsibility as they amplified her reach. Cordova helped to found the graduate program in Native American Philosophies at Lakehead University, she participated in the development of *Ayaangwaamizin*, an international journal of Indigenous philosophy, and she provided an annual lecture on the philosophy of science as it intersected with Indigenous environmentalisms at the University of Alaska. Like many other Indigenous philosophers from the mid-twentieth century, Cordova's medium was far less the written word than it was her oral teachings through lectures, teachings, dinners with students, and guest appearances in classrooms and so, after her sudden passing in 2002, her students pored over her unpublished writings in an effort to put them together in a collection of essays and stories.

The resulting collection, *How It Is: The Native American Philosophy of V.F. Cordova*, describes Cordova as "a challenging, chain-smoking, idea- and laughter-driven professor," noting that "students gathered around her the way elk come to hay in the winter, half-starved for ideas that can sustain them."[36] This specter of the inspiring, insouciant professor haunts a text that is ripe with short stories and poems alongside investigations into colonization and the limits of European philosophy. Cordova's philosophy of time is uncannily close to Deleuze's living present, though born of centuries-old Apache teachings. It is also vastly different from any of the philosophies of time that we have explored thus far, as she is refreshingly clear. Reminding me of the silver glint of Occam's Razor, Cordova, like many other Indigenous philosophers and elders, does not cloud her argument in complex riddles and dense argument. She is direct in her delivery and even still effortlessly in conversation with many known and unknown interlocutors. Layering atop Heraclitus's metaphor of the ever-changing river, and Barad's ripples of diffraction, Cordova tells her students in a lecture that their lives are just pebbles thrown into a pond. "And not just the pebble," she continues, "your life is the pebble and the water and the energy that moves the waves and the movement of the waves themselves."[37]

At one point in the text, Cordova describes Indigenous time as *merely* a measure of motion, invoking Aristotle. However, the "merely" is not to be missed here as "measure of motion" for Cordova is not the same as "measure of motion" for Aristotle as she describes it more aptly as the "measure of *relative* motion," wholly relative to *human beings.*

Now wait, doesn't this align with the problematic interiority of rational time? A humanism that posits man at the centre of the universe? Well, yes and no. According to Cordova, time, humans, and the universe itself are entirely co-created. So it is much more aligned with the entanglement of a living present whereupon each human being has a significant hand in past, present, and future, while also existing as a tiny speck within a much larger, heterogeneous whole.

Contrary to the Western European obsessions with progress narratives, Cordova's Indigenous time employs an infinite universe: an ever-growing (snow) ball upon which every present is layered upon a steadily growing past. The future is nothing other than the becoming of the ball, entirely indebted to the actions that bring each new present-made-past into being. This element of responsibility is central to the book at hand and Cordova shouts powerfully from the page: "I AM RESPONSIBLE. My actions in the world are not meaningless; they may be no more than a drop of water in an ocean, but at some point that drop triggers a deluge, or weather patterns, or myriads of other 'relative motions.'"[38] Many

Indigenous philosophers speak of the significances and consequences of past and present actions, as they fundamentally bring future universes into existence. Most notable is the seventh-generation principle from Iroquois philosophy, which teaches that any decisions we make or actions we take today should take into account their impact on the next seven generations. A thickened timeline par excellence, this principle stretches our timelines, calling us to be good ancestors to our future communities and lands.

As the seventh-generation principle and other teachings demonstrate, a significant element of Indigenous temporalities is their relationship to storytelling, or rather to time-as-storytelling. For Indigenous and queer scholar Mark Rifkin the practice of "storying," as he describes it, enacts a form of temporal sovereignty by sensationally investing the teller and the listener in particular places and times. Rifkin writes that the work of storying "can be thought of less as the act of telling a story than as the immanent dynamism in the ways stories move through the world, the kinds of qualitative relations they generate as part of producing collective experiences of duration."[39] This is contrasted with settler time, or the linear concepts of time that prop up modernity and that refuse contemporary status to Indigenous people—instead binding them to romanticized pasts and "traditional" knowledges and systems. It is thus through storying that Indigenous people are able to co-create contemporary timelines alongside and through settler time.

Juan Alejandro Chindoy Chindoy also describes time as storytelling, explaining that the memories of the ancestors of the Kamëntšá culture, an Indigenous people living in southwest Colombia, are stored and transmitted through the art of storytelling. This transmission imbues meaning on the lands and culture of the Kamëntšá people as "stories orient the meaning of life."[40] Chindoy Chindoy writes that the value of storytelling is often dismissed in European and North American cultures, as it is assumed to be only about passing along history and/or content. Instead, as Rifkin, Cordova, and Chindoy Chindoy each demonstrate, storying itself is an act of making time and making futures. The "story" is not just extractable from the storyteller, the listener, the room in which it is told. Storying is itself responsible for creating a future; its function is to create meaning in time.[41]

And so, what of the many stories about time that we have explored through this game of philosophy Jenga™? By following different stories about time, I intend to demonstrate the impacts of these stories on how we both understand and *live* time in the present. Furthermore, I intend to make clear the impact of the author's choice in telling any historical tale. I reiterate James Williams's guiding quotation: "We live as time makers, anything that exists is a maker of time."[42] Like many before and after me, I venture into a time-making process, and each pebble drop results in a new pattern of ripples. In fact, it is Einstein's overthrowing of a Newtonian Universe that illustrates this process most clearly in the world of science and philosophy alike. Einstein's Special and General Theories of Relativity made it clear that time is not the linear safety blanket that we are accustomed to. Instead, it is relative to both the observer and the position of the observer: there is no "right way" to tell the story. The key is that the criteria for my gleanings pull out different answers every time and this itself is a diffractive method. I travel along varied paths of time-telling, including both substantivalism and relationism, not to determine a winner, but to show the conditions of possibility that create such a belief in the first place.

Accompanying more dominant Western philosophical and scientific theories of time with queer and Indigenous philosophies demonstrates the depth and complexity of *time* as a political tool, serving as an effort toward memorialization, building a novel future, and a changing past. The speeds and slows of the Covid-19 pandemic include the upswell of the Black Lives Matter movement and its echo of its inception in 2013 following the acquittal of Trayvon Martin's murderer George Zimmerman. It also reinvents stories from QTBIPOC people which reveal racisms that perpetuate hierarchies within and through the very movements that seek to liberate them. We need QTBIPOC leadership in our countries and communities; we need Indigenous, anti-racist, and decolonized voices at our tables. I have no doubt that Indigenous elders, community members, artists, and leaders are surely laughing at our much-delayed, settler naivete, but there is no time to waste. There is no writing about queer lives or becomings, no feminist futures, no politicization of Deleuze without these compelling, rich, and powerful movements, and so to layer Rifkin, Cordova, Chindoy Chindoy, and others into the story is to further remind us of our human relationships with time and temporality, our co-creation with the Earth, the lodging of our bodies-in-space that has always been so, whether we are queer, Indigenous, Greek, German, or all of the above. With this thickened time in hand, Chapter 2 outlines the living present as a method of understanding that also eschews a dichotomous relationship between space and time. Through this, I hope to continue our project of both making time *matter* and showing that it is our entangled material experiences that themselves *make time*.

2

The Living Present: A Co-Creative Conversation between Deleuze and Winterson

Everything is imprinted forever with what it once was.
—Jeanette Winterson, *The Stone Gods*

Jeanette Winterson's *The Stone Gods* charts three different encounters between Billie (homo sapiens) and Spike (robo sapiens), two lovers who blur the boundaries between human and nonhuman, gender, and machine, across varying temporal sites. Early in the novel, Spike and Billie are on a ship that is traveling toward "Planet Blue," the new hope for a civilization that has destroyed its current planet Orbus. Billie has been solicited for the mission late in the game, so is learning of the plan mid-route. Spike tries to soothe Billie's anxiety about the project ahead by telling her that "this is a quantum universe … neither random nor determined. It is potential at every second. All you can do is intervene."[1] For Spike, an intelligent robot made up of metal, wires, and data, this prospect is exhilarating; for Billie, it is terrifying.

Moving forward, through, and back in time, Winterson's *The Stone Gods* folds in on itself; time repeats and rewinds, love echoes through technology and organism, and cause and effect become the evermore distant relatives of possibility and production. The novel's tone is apocalyptic as each of its three vignettes explore the theme of environmental destruction: the first and third through an imaginative future where humankind has exhausted the Earth's resources and has resorted to other means of consumption and control, and the second by traveling back in time to 1774 where "Billy and Spikkers" find themselves in the middle of British Captain James Cook's takeover and destruction of the lush, balanced ecosystem of Easter Island. Winterson's use of Easter Island refers to the factual Polynesian island of the same name. Also called *Rapa Nui*, Easter

Island is famous for its 887 stone statues, called "moai," which were created by its early inhabitants. For Winterson, these "Stone Gods" represent the humanist desire to master both time and nature, but there is a sense in which she is less concerned with a present moment of global crisis than with reimagining the stories we tell ourselves about what constitutes the past, what counts as progress, and what humanity means in relation to a vast timeline of the Earth's existence. In such an elongated existence, the time of human beings becomes just one moment among others. Displacing the reader's reliance on a linear narrative, *The Stone Gods* is self-referential; it trips over itself, gives away its own endings, and, at any given moment, it could be revealed that what we think is the future is actually the past (or the present, or an alternate timeline altogether).

Like much of Winterson's work, *The Stone Gods* expresses the co-creative relationship between meaning and materiality. She enlists the affective impact of physical objects and spaces as stewards of the story (the Stone statues, the unattached and yet animated head of Spike, again a robo sapiens, in Wreck City, Easter Island in 1774, an imagined "Planet Blue" that serves as an experimental haven and postapocalyptic home for human- and robo-kind). Winterson also introduces readers to the becoming of time, whereby time is a continuous process without beginning or end. "Planet Blue" (from the first vignette) has dinosaurs, monstrous gorillas, and many other creatures deemed prehistoric to Earth *c.*2007, but while Billie and Spike chart their colonial trek, their approaching ship accidentally directs an asteroid toward the new planet. Sadly, the asteroid's collision with Planet Blue changes the mission entirely as it sends the planet into an ice age, thus making it unviable for human colonization. The crew turns back to Orbus, but Billie and Spike stay behind to witness Planet Blue's impending ice age. As they themselves drift away, Winterson reminds us that the future is also the past as she imagines the future of Planet Blue post–ice age: "There will be men and women, there will be fire. There will be settlements, there will be wars. There will be planting and harvest, music and dancing. Someone will make a painting in a cave, someone will make a statue and call it God. Someone will see you and call your name."[2] As Billie takes her last breath and Spike's power runs out, Winterson lulls them to sleep: "Close your eyes and dream. This is one story. There will be another."[3]

Winterson's *The Stone Gods* winds through the same story in various timelines, and, yet, her approach is not merely circular: Winterson's stories are dynamic engagements with temporality and the past is continually reimagined in its present invocations. The metaphysical implications of such a move signals a Deleuzian living present that is never a static "now," but always a stretching between past and future as it contracts all past experiences and expects those yet to come. Consequently, like Billie/Billy and Spike/Spikkers, we are continually moving through time. We are layering feelings about signing up for a spin class upon haunting memories of that yellow BMX bike from our childhood bike-riding lessons, and using this pair to anticipate an outcome of dropping out of the class early; we are layering chapter one of *The Stone Gods* beneath chapter two so that when chapter two's Spikkers is human and male, we read him as trans. But is he transgender? Transhuman? Or both? And even more importantly, where lies the transition from one to another when there is no beginning and no end? A living present also includes processes that exceed our human bodies, including bodies of water, the stone statues on Rapa Nui carved out of solidified volcanic ash, insect bodies, robo-bodies, the systems of a city as it breathes its workers in and out from dawn until dusk. Each of these processes is temporal, not in its adherence to an externally imposed timeline, but in its own temporal *becoming*.

This chapter provides a defense of a living present as a *method of understanding*, both for day-to-day processes and for larger negotiations with community, culture, science, and history. The living present describes our ability to serve as *affective* time travelers and, in so doing, reveals our ethical responsibilities to our past, present, and future worlds. Although we will explore some of these entangled responsibilities here, subsequent chapters will describe the impacts and potentialities of a living present in greater detail. This chapter works through Deleuzian arguments that both thicken (*as a fine and continuous layering of memory, experience, and anticipation*) and deepen (*as a vertical, rather than a horizontal stretching through time*) our understanding of a living present. Of note is my reliance on Deleuze's typical method of working very closely with canonical philosophers, but then stretching their work to new places—a process he describes as "approaching an author from behind and giving him a child that would be his but would nonetheless be monstrous."[4] Such a process can easily be described as *diffractive* as it takes traditional texts in directions otherwise unthought. Think back to our example from the introduction of dropping two pebbles into a still pond (see Figure 2.1). The overlapping waves become a new mode of thinking, just as Deleuze's unique methods of analysis diffract traditional texts so that rather than trying to determine the "truth" of Kant's *Critique of Pure Reason*, Deleuze enlists it as a means by which to think about the concept of critique itself.[5]

Deleuze's diffractive readings of literature, music, and cinema test and prove his thesis that the arts are the creative venues through which becomings effect their environments.[6] Thus, not unlike Deleuze's explorations of Lewis Carroll's

Figure 2.1 Pebble Diffraction
Source: Photo 10129421 © Jin Yamada, Dreamstime.com.

Alice in Wonderland or Marcel Proust's *In Search of Lost Time*, Winterson's *The Stone Gods* serves as an entangled parallelism to the living present. We could imagine that Gilles Deleuze and Jeanette Winterson might have been friends under the right circumstances, sharing stories at a mad-hatter's tea party, where they playfully encouraged one another to travel through their respective projects (philosophy and literature) by a rhizomatic chariot rather than by GPS. Both seamlessly construct a living present in the stories that they tell, though their individual "time-traveling apparatuses" differ. Winterson's tools of time-travel include concepts of love, humanity, apocalypse, and the body, while for Deleuze, the concepts include becoming, difference, imperceptibility, and the nomad. Notably for both, even the "concept" itself is suspect as Deleuze circumvents our instinct to understand concepts as those that reflect ideas or general notions and instead as themselves agents of meaning. For example, Deleuze's concept of *becoming* engenders alternate modes of identity and being, while Winterson's concept of *love* clearly makes love, rather than defines it ("*Love is an intervention. … Not romance, not sentimentality, but a force of a different nature*").[7] Both authors instinctively conduct diffractive readings and tellings throughout their works as they resist mapping ideas, themes, and concepts to those that have come before, instead dropping pebbles of all sizes into various pools throughout their travels through time. With this in mind, we begin our time-traveling adventures with the "concept" itself.

The Making of Concepts

> [Philosophers] must no longer accept concepts as a gift, nor merely purify and polish them, but first *make* and *create* them, present them and make them convincing. Hitherto one has generally trusted one's concepts as if they were a wonderful dowry from some sort of wonderland.
> —Friedrich Nietzsche, *The Will to Power*

When approaching Deleuzian concepts such as becoming, duration, intuition, habit, difference, and then even past, present, and future, the linking thread is the fact that all concepts are spatio-temporal; all concepts refer to the relationship between matter, time, understanding, and being (becoming) but, in so doing, each of these concepts feels a bit like they are the great-aunt once removed from the concepts we are used to. Deleuze and Guattari regularly demonstrate that "concepts are not waiting for us ready-made, like heavenly bodies. There is no heaven for concepts. They must be invented, fabricated."[8] Such a claim reveals both the permeability of the concept (the ways that we can question, reframe, reuse, and transform concepts that we otherwise take to be "truths") and the historicity of the concept (such that all understanding requires a genealogy of the very terms that we use to chart our course). Deleuze and Guattari also claim that concepts belong to philosophy alone.[9] Rather than serving as an egotistical claim about the value of philosophy, it determines that if philosophy has any purpose at all, it is to create concepts (new ideas, connections, alternate orderings of reality). This is the third and most inventive function of the concept: it is a thing that *creates*. Think of the concept of love. Instinctively, many conjure up images of a man and a woman as a reflection of love. Every book that Jeanette Winterson has ever written has a philosophical and temporal engagement with *love* at its core, and *The Stone Gods* is no exception. As Billie and Spike wait for death on Planet Blue, they make love: "When I touch her, my fingers don't question what she is. My body knows who she is. The strange thing about strangers is that they are unknown and known. There is a pattern to her, a shape I understand, a private geometry that numbers mine. ... She is a stranger. She is the strange that I am beginning to love."[10] Seconds later, Spike grabs a screwdriver to remove her legs in order to conserve energy; the juxtaposition reminds the reader that Billie and Spike are indeed *different* species. Spike is the universe's first robo sapiens, and as much as we are desperate to read the lovemaking as a reflection of what we know, it is a transhuman encounter that exceeds our reservoir of ready-made definitions of love and lovemaking.

The concepts of *love*, and *sex*, then, become the force that *creates* connection between partners; they are the unlikely affection that Billie feels for the robotic head of Spike that she carries around in Wreck City at the close of *The Stone Gods*. This third meeting of Billie and Spike echoes their relationship on Planet Blue, but the environment is vastly different in the rough, lawless Wreck City that Winterson describes as a "No Zone": "no insurance, no assistance, no welfare, no police. It's not forbidden to go there, but if you do, and if you get damaged or murdered or robbed or raped, it's at your own risk."[11] Spike and Billie of Planet Blue are slick explorers, brought together by a mission to save a dying world, while the characters skirting the edge of Wreck City are renegades trying to make sense of a satellite signal from the past. Framing love as a wild possibility for same-sex and polyamorous relationships, for human and nonhuman, Winterson's *love* really is a Deleuzian concept. It enables what Claire Colebrook casts as the "power to move beyond what we know and experience [and] to think how experience might be extended."[12] Concepts as pure potential exemplify that as much as we try to contain and define them, they exceed our understanding. As much as we try to contain and define love, it always exceeds us.

We could also think of a concept as the canary in the coalmine that alerts us to the presence of a larger problem. For example, the thousands of pages that philosophers—and, even more so, poets—have spent agonizing over the concept of *love* rings a bell of strong affection, unrequited desire, irrational attachment and wanting. In a world where emotions and feelings generally do not take centre stage, many have tried to capture love as a concept we can make sense of, when really it is the canary signaling to us that *love* is the furthest thing from philosophy, common sense, or that which we can define and contain. Love is an opening up to the new and unknown world of an *other*: "*She is a stranger. She is the strange that I am beginning to love."*[13] The catch is, however, that philosophers are slow to admit the gas leak after they've developed a clear and distinct idea (concept). As Deleuze writes:

> Philosophers introduce new concepts, they explain them, but they don't tell us, not completely anyway, the problems to which those concepts are a response. … The history of philosophy, rather than repeating what a philosopher says, has to say what he [sic] must have taken for granted, what he [sic] didn't say but is nonetheless present in what he [sic] did say.[14]

Think back to the game of philosopher Jenga™ from Chapter 1 where Zeno takes the arrow of time and renders it immobile. For Zeno, motion is logically impossible because it cannot be perceived outside of the senses and so he is wholly suspect of change. If we are to follow a Deleuzo-Guattarian path, the more interesting question becomes "To what problem is Zeno's static time a response?" Why didn't he trust his eyes? His hands? The feeling of touch? What was it about the body and its greatest detectives (the senses) that made Zeno so afraid? It is no great leap to see that Zeno's fear of the bodily senses plays a role in the history of Western philosophy that has cast the body as the irrational "other."[15]

Rejigging our understanding of the "concept" is just one among many tricks that Deleuze plays on his reader and it is no surprise that there are so many Deleuzian dictionaries.[16] Each new concept opens us up to new events, processes, and ideas, activities that are very compelling for feminist, queer, postcolonial, and other sociopolitically oriented projects. At the same time, each concept is a bell, signaling the alarm on existing problems or gaps in thought.

Becoming-Otherwise

Take the concept of becoming, a term borrowed from Nietzsche and then adapted and reconfigured by Deleuze and Guattari, which has been stretched and thickened to include many other engagements with *being*. Today, becoming is a moving target. Its genesis has largely been through continental philosophy, but its productivity has been through its mobilization within queer and feminist fields where it provides hope for alternate world orderings, dynamic ways of being, and possibilities for social change. Becoming indicates a subject that is always and already exceeding the categories of self, or even gender. It is a subject that never truly *is*; a subject that is always in-process and so representative of freedom alongside an endless string of "almosts" and "not quites." *Becoming* has even had uptake in popular culture as the title of Michelle Obama's 2018 memoir, where it represents her life's journeys, standing in as a term representative of *to shine*, *to accomplish*, and *to inspire*. As much as becoming speaks to a future that exceeds our present, the lived experience of subjectivity-in-process is often neither welcome nor safe in a world in which *being*, more than ever, garners power, stability, and calm.

So what is this *becoming* really? What does it *do*? Deleuze's exploration of *Alice in Wonderland* tells the story of Alice falling down the rabbit hole to be presented with the dilemma of fitting her body through a doorway that is half her size. At this point she drinks a bottle of liquid that shrinks her down to the door, only to realize that she is now too small to reach the key, which she has left on the table above. Alice then eats a piece of cake, which shoots her up to the ceiling, turning not only the door, but also the table and key into tiny fixtures below. When reading *Alice in Wonderland*, we want to understand her changes in size as having happened *in time*, such that when one says, "Alice becomes larger," they mean that "she is larger now; she was smaller before."[17] We identify Alice as huge and Alice as tiny as distinct events taking place in linear time. When thinking in terms of *becoming*, however, the timeline shifts. Rather than thinking according to distinct events, becoming "does not tolerate the separation or the distinction of before and after, or of past and future."[18] Becoming eludes the present moment; Alice is perpetually mid-flight. She becomes larger than she was at the same time that she is smaller than she becomes. Such a proliferation of identities and movements places an emphasis not on coherence, sameness, or self, but on *difference*; an ontology not of *being*, but of *being-in-process* as we have discussed above.

Becoming is moving in both directions at once: "Alice does not grow without shrinking, and vice versa" and, furthermore, her becoming taller and becoming smaller do not occur in abstraction from the food and drink that accompany her change; much less the table, key, and doorway that are themselves becoming smaller/larger along with Alice.[19] As Alice grows, the key shrinks, both relational activities. In this sense, becoming constitutes more than an (anti)-identity claim; it expresses a temporality. Rather than thinking about time as a chronological counting of moments—sets of *befores* and *afters* that are progressively directed toward a future—becoming illustrates that time is a durational succession of change that apprehends any distinct "moment" or "present" as a becoming that is codeterminate with a live temporal frame. *"It is* never the beginning or the end which are interesting; the beginning and end are points. What is interesting is the middle."[20]

Duration and Difference

In *Creative Evolution*, Bergson writes that "duration means invention, the creation of forms, the continual elaboration of the absolutely new."[21] Duration refers to "pure time" or time that has not been limited by sets of minutes, hours, and days (i.e., time that has been spatialized, turned into a before and an after). This means that duration has no separation between present and past, whereupon we encounter a series of "presents" that happen and then move into the past. Instead, past and present are one and the same, operating together to create an organic whole. Bergson often uses the example of a melody to illustrate the flow of duration. Think of the notes of "Twinkle, Twinkle, Little Star": CC, GG, AA, G. Were we to play the second "A" in the melody (the lingering sound of "star"), we would instantly spatialize the note, turning it into a thing at a particular time. On the contrary, when we apprehend the melody as an interconnected whole, it is the rhythmic organization of all of the notes together that makes up the experience of music.[22]

In this way, duration is inventive; it is the "continuous progress of the past which gnaws into the future and which swells as it advances" for even though time is layered (remember again our figuration of "thick time" from the introduction, Figure I.1), Bergson supports the forward momentum of time.[23] It just happens to be a forward movement that also builds upon and changes the past in an infinite number of ways. Now does this mean that we can change the past? Simply put, no. I cannot rewrite history to make my undergraduate degree in Philosophy a degree in Physics, but I can shift my understanding of the past through present and future activities. For example, imagine I start my melody of "Twinkle, Twinkle Little Star" on an "E" note. The fingering for the melody would start flawlessly: "EEBB" and then as I reach for the next few notes "CCB" the entire tune takes an ominous turn. The movement from B to C is a half-step, rather than the whole step between G and A of the original tune, so as we sing "little star" we fall into a minor tone. Suddenly the children's melody is not so joyful and the durational time travel in this moment is the recognition that my hand has fallen to the wrong starting point; it reminds me of my childhood lessons in music theory and gives a retroactive grimace as I cast a negative shadow on the first note played (the point at which I went astray).

Thinking durationally involves a radical shift in the belief in direct causality between past and present. We think that there is some virtual comprehension of the whole that precedes the musician's writing of the symphony, rather than recognizing the spontaneity of creating the melody. Often, the writing of music is far from a plotted, mathematical process, and instead it is somewhat "inspired." Fingers reach for familiar and unfamiliar sounds; the eardrums vibrate at varying frequencies as instinct and skill come together in the creation of an unanticipated tune. Duration therefore criticizes the retroactive way in which we explain the past through the belief that present judgment proceeds from past cause, or rather "if the melody pleases us, it must have been planned out in advance."[24] This unidirectional flow of time attributes cause to effect, rather than recognizing the function of duration as an open-ended thickening and stretching of the time of the present.

So how do we loosen our shackles of cause and effect? We do it through intuition. Divorced from its common understanding as a knowing sensation or instinct, Henri Bergson describes intuition as the immediate and internal apprehension of temporality. It is contrasted with intellect, otherwise intent upon determining facts and data about *things*. The intellect limits us to a binary, or habits of thinking in terms of quantitative difference, rather than qualitative difference. For example, a quantitative, intellectual approach thinks about a melody as a succession of particular notes—CC GG AA G—while our intuition of the notes is qualitative; we perceive it as "Twinkle Twinkle Little Star." It doesn't matter that we don't hear the whole piece, as the few notes are enough to contract our sense of the familiar sound (and in the case of such a well-known tune, we only need the rhythm of the first four notes to contract an entire song).

Now, for any readers of Deleuze, it is easy to see the overlap between Bergson and Deleuze. Duration appears both implicitly and explicitly in Deleuze's conceptualization of being as constant movement and variation, and intuition-as-method lends itself to Deleuze's discussions of immanence, where immanence is the immediate, inherent apprehension of reality that all individuals experience. However, Deleuze (with Guattari) builds upon Bergson in critical ways, most notably by turning Bergson's "difference-in-kind" into "difference-in-itself" and by extending the intuition of duration to foreground our previously discussed concept of *becoming*.

Just as Alice was becoming-tall and becoming-small at one and the same time, *becoming* indicates that all identity is in-process. There is no "self" at which we will one day arrive; we are always becoming-woman, becoming-animal, or becoming-otherwise. And although Deleuze and Guattari often define becoming in the negative, writing that "becoming is certainly not imitating, or identifying with something; neither is it regressing-progressing; neither is it corresponding, establishing corresponding relations,"[25] the uptake of the concept is in its subtlety of definition such that becoming is a verb; it is an action, a movement. The difficulty in providing a positive explanation refers to the fact that the term is *active*, engaged in ongoing metamorphosis and unable to be fully represented by a determinate definition. Becoming is "pure change," in the same way that duration is "pure time," and rather than aligning with a systematic and definite definition, it—like many Deleuzian-Guattarian-Bergsonian concepts—remains open-ended.

Becoming, duration, intuition, and even the Deleuzian "concept" each signal distinct relationships between identity and time, or rather a view of time as the force that denies a stable identity. Contrary to the belief that one can fit oneself into distinct categorical identities (she is a Caucasian woman; he is an African Canadian man), becoming sidesteps such categorization. Not surprisingly, becoming has had significant impact within feminist, queer, and postcolonial projects, particularly for its role in troubling the categories (or concepts?) of identity we are used to. Even concepts such as "heterosexual" or "homosexual" are stagnant and our reliance on them limits our ability to understand diverse sexual practices. Rather than relying on definitions that emphasize coherence or sameness (i.e., *she* is in a relationship with *he*. That looks like heterosexuality—they are *straight*), *becoming* places the emphasis on *difference*. Put into play, this can look like querying the differences between asexuality and heterosexuality, or likewise between aromanticism and polyamory. Like the concept of the time-body, these diffractive paths encourage us to multiply our understandings of human connection, rather than to divide it. Part of the reason why a concept such as becoming-queer is so powerful is because of the concept of difference in-itself: for Deleueze, difference is an ontological difference grounded in nothing external.

How does this differ from common or historical understandings? Think about a piece of music and our methods of differentiation and description. When examining "Twinkle, Twinkle Little Star" we might differentiate it by saying that "Twinkle, Twinkle" is different from Beethoven's 'Piano Sonata No. 20' (Sonata in G) on account of genre. "Twinkle, Twinkle" is a folk song, while the "Sonata in G" is a Sonata. How do we know this? Because a Sonata has a classificatory structure: it has three main sections consisting of an exposition, the development, and the recapitulation and the Sonata in G fits into this form. On the contrary, the folk song is characterized by simple melodies and narrative lyrics. Given the plain and poetic structure of "Twinkle, Twinkle" and its history as a lullaby passed down through generations, it fits the genus of folk song. In this case, the difference between the two songs boils down to categorical or classificatory differences, or the degree to which they map on to a predetermined set of classifications, and it is precisely this mapping that vexes Deleuze the most. Every time we "map" one thing on to another, or search for similarities and differences through a representational frame (How does the Sonata in G mirror the Sonata form?), we turn difference into identity. We give novel becomings *form*; we fix them in place; we embed lives that are always in-process within set expectations. *Difference-in-itself*, or *pure difference*, is thus multiplicitous enactment; it is not enough to differentiate between folk songs and sonatas, for each and every so-called sonata is infinitely different from the next. Lumping them all within one category only serves to stagnate and limit the life of the melody.

It is not, therefore, the differences between a folk song and a sonata that define them as different "types"; it is *that they differ at all* that gives them life, or rather it is not the "differences which are and must be: it is being which is Difference."[26] This means that all there is is difference; there is nothing else we can "name" about subjects other than their unique difference-*ing*. We can easily see how this supports the durational becoming of "Twinkle, Twinkle Little Star" (our agential and multiple little childhood melody) but how does difference-in-itself extend our understanding of time?

In anticipation of chapters to come, the term "queering" has long been used to signify movement: the twisting, shifting, and transforming capabilities of those practices that seek to disrupt heteronormative models. Rather than focusing on named categories such as defining *who* constitutes a lesbian (as though there is a transcendental lesbian-ness to which all instantiations refer), or *who* constitutes a trans person, and therefore *who* is able to count as part of the genus "LGBTQ," the concept of *queering* helps us to see difference-in-itself as the particular *happenings*, *events*, and *becomings* in which singularities (what we want to call the "particular," "individual," "thing," or "identity") engage and emerge. Take, for example, the "L" in our familiar and ever-changing acronym. The concept "lesbian" comes to us from the Isle of Lesbos, in the Aegean Sea, where the Greek poet Sappho wrote lyric poetry about many things, including female lovers. Sappho lived during the sixth century, BCE, and was born into an aristocratic family. She was celebrated throughout Ancient Greece and was often called the "tenth muse" or the "Poetess" contra Homer.[27] For hundreds of years after she died, her poetry was praised because of its lyrical sophistication rather than its homoerotic undertones. Christian authorities in the Middle Ages still rejected her, however, from the canon of Greek philosophers/poets because of homoerotic content in her works. Due to this, much of Sappho's poetry has been lost and all we have is one poem that is relatively intact ("Hymn to Aphrodite") and a series of fragments.

It was not until the nineteenth and twentieth centuries that scholars began digging through the archives to reclaim Sappho, and to make a more direct link between her poetry about women and her sexuality. Hence, terms such as *Sapphic*, *Sapphist*, and *Sapphism* all came to signify sexual relationships and desires between women, and today Sappho is a contemporary icon of lesbian and queer culture.[28] Although my telling of Sappho is chronological, contemporary *queerings* of Ancient Greece are wildly entertaining, whether for the scholar of ancient poetry who is thrilled to see herself in Sappho's lyrics, or the nineteenth-century historian who gasped at the thought of "The Poetess" in bed with Aphrodite. In each case, "lesbian" becomes the concept that signals the problem of same-sex desire as it has always bubbled up in an otherwise heteronormative world, and we cannot tell a full story without the unique events and becomings that led to the term. That said, the import of pure difference reminds us that it is never as easy as taking the "lesbian" of today and mapping them onto Sappho's poetry of the past, but rather that we are to recognize Sappho's lyrics as themselves the becoming-otherwise of desire, love, and sexuality. Far from defining her as a lesbian, Sappho's desire for Aphrodite is precisely the passion that opens us up to the new:

> That man to me seems equal to the gods,
> the man who sits opposite you
> and close by listens
> to your sweet voice
>
> 5 and your enticing laughter—
> that indeed has stirred up the heart in my breast.
> For whenever I look at you even briefly
> I can no longer say a single thing,
>
> but my tongue is frozen in silence;
> 10 instantly a delicate flame runs beneath my skin;
> with my eyes I see nothing;
> my ears make a whirring noise.

> A cold sweat covers me,
> trembling seizes my body,
> 15 and I am greener than grass.
> Lacking but little of death do I seem.²⁹

The project of *queering* the ancient Isle of Lesbos, then, is a mobilization of "pure difference" as it sparks various lines of flight both for Sappho and for millions of others experiencing their "tongues frozen in silence" or the whirring in their ears in the face of desires that cannot be mapped on to knowable expressions. Such *queerings* bring forth many different ways of understanding gender, sexuality, and desire where rather than searching for representation or sameness, we embody difference as the making of sexual subjectivity.

We seem to have gotten away from duration in this radical new form of difference but, in fact, the key component of difference is that it is *durational*. My unique subjectivity as a queer woman, the difference or singularity that is my DNA, cannot be understood as a timeless constant—the same "me" that persists over time. Instead, I am an aggregate collection of moments of growth, new experiences, sensations, and ideas, and these moments do not merely *add* to some underlying core "self" but actually bring about the difference that is, in fact, also an "I." Thinking the ideas of difference and duration together, Todd May writes that "becoming is the unfolding of difference in time as time"³⁰— and I would expand this phrase to read: becoming is the unfolding of difference as duration. This is the becoming-woman or becoming-self that is always in-process, and whose relational, interdependent subjectivity is the furthest thing from a fractured, completely random self. It is not as though I am a new person every few moments, with no recognition of the past that I was a part of. If I think back to the memory I shared of learning how to ride a bike at age seven, I may be made up of entirely different beliefs, feelings, and even cells, having been in processes of becoming for thirty years, but the layers of memory and repetition are enacted every time I get on a bicycle, drive past the street where it all began, or speak of the memory to others.

With this example we enter into the realm of repetition, for a key part of Deleuzian temporality is that difference and repetition are two sides of the same coin. Much like Deleuze's *difference,* repetition is not to be understood according to its traditional meaning: as the recurrence of the same. To sit down at a piano and practice a piece over and over again is not to play the same thing, multiple times. Instead, each time I play through "Twinkle, Twinkle Little Star," I create the song anew. Repetition is itself a differencing such that repetition can never mean duplication or sameness, as though "Twinkle Twinkle" exists as a pure and ideal form somewhere. Instead the piece is a becoming: it is different every time, and it always represents a distinct event. Deleuze describes this process through the workings of a clock:

> Four o'clock strikes ... each stroke, each disturbance or excitation, is logically independent of the other, *mens momentanea*. However, quite apart from any memory or distinct calculation, we contract these into an internal qualitative impression within this living present or *passive synthesis* which is duration.[31]

If we think of the clock strikes as A, B, C, and D, there is nothing about strike A that expects, anticipates, or needs the strikes of B, C, and D in order for its existence as strike A, in-and-of-itself. Taken out of the context of marking the hour as the fourth, the strikes alone are arbitrary. It is rather their *durational sense* that gives them meaning. That is, when we hear the third strike, we stretch the sound to include the first and to anticipate a fourth (or a fifth or a sixth), and we don't only stretch the particular instant of hearing a clock strike, but we also stretch the experience to include our experiences of many past clock chimes, and many past presents of 4o'clock. As well, we blend the chime into a waning sun or a stomach's growl in anticipation of a 5 o' clock supper. This temporal stretching is what Deleuze calls *contraction*. I have already discussed my use of this concept in the introduction but, to expand briefly, a contraction means that any moment of sense or understanding is the product of our reaching into the past to instantaneously draw on all past experiences so that the past has a resounding effect on the present (and the future). When I ride a bike, I contract years of movement in order to push off without toppling; contraction is passive (not conscious) and embodied as I cannot employ the cellular habits when I am not seated on the bike. Back to the clock, it is through our contraction of the distinct strikes of the clock that we instantaneously "restore them in an auxiliary space, a derived time in which we may reproduce them, reflect on them or count them" and thus vocalize an understanding that "It is four o'clock."[32]

The common-sense way in which we turn the repetition of difference into the repetition of the same aligns with the way that we instinctively turn time into a spatialized counting: that is, we take the strikes of A, B, C, and D as four strikes of the same, a set that we count and understand as a quantifiable identity of 4 o'clock. My legs move up and down on the pedals and "riding a bike" materializes as a result. Becoming ensures that we see more than different "beings," "things," or "identities," and instead continue to hear the clock chime as the unfolding of different forces in a durational time—the bike ride as ever novel, never the same, but always a transcorporeal experience of body, machine, road, and weather. Through these examples we see that duration is the architect of both difference and becoming, and intuition the immanent becoming of difference itself.

Toward a Living Present: The Three Syntheses of Time

We are hardwired to turn difference and differentiation into knowable identities. We like definition and boundaries (knowing that Spike is a robot and *not* a human; knowing that Billie is a woman and *not* a man; knowing that the future is ahead of us and not behind us). But in order to embrace a living present, we need to break our boundary-making habits. Described as the present of retention and expectation, the living present is never a solitary "now," but always a stretching between past and future as it contracts all past experiences and expects those yet to come. This means that the present is thick with every past that contributes to its articulation or understanding (think of the instinctive bodily memories that made it possible for me to learn how to ride a bike), and likewise that the present stretches to the future through anticipation (pushing my foot down on the pedal anticipates a future in which the forward thrust has momentum, is received by the rubber pedal and translated through the chain and wheels of the bike). The living present shows us that these multiple processes are inextricably connected. They are comingled in each experience and each experience, in turn, is vertically stretched into an ever-thickening temporal moment. Deleuze's concept of time relies on three passive syntheses: the living present, the pure past, and the eternal return. These syntheses are passive because they do not rely on a consciousness that "plucks" memories out of the past or rationalizes causal outcomes; rather they are unconscious acts of gathering from both one's own physical and mental (and spiritual) experiences, and the materiality of the world around us. The three syntheses work together in the meaning and mattering of time, but each operates in distinct ways.

The first synthesis, the living present, is well illustrated by the bike-riding example as the experience draws not only on the muscle memory of my legs or fingers on the pedals and gears, but also on the mechanism of the bike itself. It lurches forward if I push too hard or topples over if I am too delicate. My body unconsciously memorizes, and commits to habit, movements that help and hinder my progress in the activity at hand. As with the example of the clock, habits constitute "our expectation that 'it' [the successive striking of the clock] will continue, that one of the two elements will appear after the other,"[33]—and therefore form the *material* of continuity. In fact, it is only because the present is a contraction of the past and the future that we experience a connection between strike A and strike B at all, or that I know to push my right foot down on the pedal while my left goes slack. We know that the chiming of a clock follows a certain form, has a particular character to it, and so are able to draw a connection between sounds that would otherwise be noise, just as I have a recollection of the lurching bike, the forward momentum that results from a contraction of past and future. This instantaneous stretch ahead and backward is Alice growing smaller and taller at once; this is the becoming that denies a stable identity, while ensuring that there is a subject, an "I" that persists. In fact, it is through the first synthesis of the living present that we have memory at all and, yet, Deleuze's living present relies on neither consciousness nor subjectivity, as he commonly denies any "self" that lies beneath: "We speak of our 'self' only in virtue of these thousands of little witnesses which contemplate within us: it is always a third party who says 'me.'"[34]

The habitual activities of the living present are not the product of a conscious (or subconscious) dipping into our past to find representations of present events and signs, nor are they reflective operation of the understanding. As a *passive* process, retention is the process by which "a whole series is drawn together in one stretch or duration."[35] We can imagine the adult hand that reflexively pulls away from a hot surface, while a child reaches toward the stove, not yet having lived through the present that will add this experience to her plethora of habitual contractions or the first-time piano player who struggles to find the "G" on ivory keys that have not yet become a familiar language. Habits constitute our expectation that a familiar song on the radio will continue and not end abruptly after the next note or that when we turn the page of a novel we will find a continued and cohesive tale. In fact there is "no continuity apart from that of habit … we have no other continuities apart from those of our thousands of component habits, which form within us so many superstitious and contemplative selves, so many claimants and satisfactions."[36]

As these examples demonstrate, a key element of the living present, including its related processes of duration, intuition, and habitual contraction, is that it is not limited to human-centered understandings or psychological processes that only take place in a human consciousness. Just as the preoccupation with human consciousness has tied us to modernist progress narratives, our understandings of *time* have bound us to a metaphysics of counting, calculating, and of living "in" a time that we apprehend through human reason (remember our thickening of the philosophical *timeline* from the introduction?). Instead, a living present applies to all organic, inorganic, human, and transhuman entities. *Everything* is made by way of the passive habits of contraction: "What we call wheat is a contraction of the earth and humidity. ... What organism is not made of elements and cases of repetition, of contemplated and contracted water, nitrogen, carbon, chlorides and sulphates, thereby intertwining all the habits of which it is composed?"[37] This stretching beyond and through human consciousness cannot be stated enough in an argument for the living present as method, for it represents the most significant diffraction of Bergsonian intuition. As described above, intuition is Bergson's philosophical method. It is the means through which we engage in an "integral experience" of the absolute uniqueness of an object, and is contrasted with processes of analysis or examination that break an object down according to known elements (the difference between plucking individual notes out of a melody and intuiting the absolute being of the tune itself).[38] As Deleuze weaves Bergsonian intuition into his philosophy of time, he ensures that at no point is the living present grounded in a human consciousness. The living present is inhuman (or ahuman, material, technology, alive, inert). It is, in fact, a durational intuition, but it need not be grounded in any human or animal (or even material) subject; it is instead the thick *embeddedness* of meaning and mattering as it moves and modifies all entities.

Deleuze's second synthesis of time is the *pure past*, and he writes that the present and future are always dimensions of the past. Now why do we need a second synthesis if the first already links past, present, and future in the living present? Although the living present is the process that makes time, it is a present that *passes*, and in order for the present to pass, there must be such a thing as a *pure past*. As Deleuze describes it, the pure past is not an inert substance, an archive into which the present moment passes and is stored until we call it to mind. The pure past is memory and the ground of time but, like habit, memory is not a psychological process, and is instead the whole of experience and sensation, a form of past-in-general that continues to act on the present through our passive "leaps" into the past. In this way, memory is the "being of the past" and any sense we make of the present at all is the product of its passing through the pure past through processes of contraction.[39] For example, when I place my fingers on the keys of a piano, I am transported back to my very first piano, which had a large brown splotch of paint on the "D" key that was next to middle "C." I also pass through my past of curt piano teachers who were always disappointed with how little I practiced. Just as I can never play the same melody twice, and instead create it anew each time, "repeating the past always transforms the past ... the past is as much in production as the present."[40] When

I sit down to play a musical piece that I played effortlessly at age fifteen and can only now pluck away at with one hand, my inability to read the notes contracts the many years that I failed to keep up with my previous skill and ultimately colors my piano-playing memories with a wistful and regretful hue, rather than the rose color they used to don.

Deleuze's third and final synthesis of time is the eternal return, a familiar term to readers of Nietzsche who wrote:

> What, if some day or night a demon were to steal after you into your loneliest loneliness and say to you: "This life as you now live it and have lived it, you will have to live once more and innumerable times more; and there will be nothing new in it, but every pain and every joy and every thought and sigh and everything unutterably small or great in your life will have to return to you, all in the same succession and sequence—even this spider and this moonlight between the trees, and even this moment and I myself. The eternal hourglass of existence is turned upside down again and again, and you with it, speck of dust!"[41]

This often-quoted passage describes the eternal return cyclically and as though everything that has already happened will happen again and there is really nothing *new* that is possible in the universe. It has also been interpreted to refer to a query into *being*; that is, into what kind of person would be able to will the eternal return of the universe. Would it be one who lived a "half-life" of fatigue and negativity? Or one who said yes to whatever life offered, who expanded their connections and possibilities at any opportunity? Deleuze builds upon this second understanding to discuss the eternal return as a future that is a dimension of the present and the past. However, diverging from Nietzsche, Deleuze defines it not as the return of the same but the eternal return of *difference*: "The subject of the eternal return is not the same but the different, not the similar but the dissimilar, not the one but the many, not necessity but chance."[42] At the most fundamental level, Deleuze's philosophy is one where things *cannot* repeat. I will never play a song on the piano identically to a time that has come before. To repeat the same is to deny the passing of time entirely and to turn matter into a frozen image of thought (or to drop to our knees in front of Zeno, crying that he was correct all along). Through the third and final synthesis of time, Deleuze therefore ensures that the future is always a "cut" between before and after. It is always a launching into the new, but a launch that is entangled in the present and the past. And since difference returns as the new and not as the same, time fundamentally moves from past to future, and not the other way around. As a result, the eternal return expresses the force of pure becoming in a way that neither habit nor memory is able to do, for it is itself the movement of diversity and multiplicity, of "difference and its repetition." The eternal return can therefore be said to express the constant becoming-otherwise of all matter as time.

Together the first, second, and third syntheses of time resist an ontology that grounds itself in human consciousness. They free us from the dualism between interiority/exteriority—time as inside or outside of us—and instead propose that time is the very making of matter, memory, and meaning. As James Williams's repeated refrain rings out "We live as time makers—anything exists as a maker of time" and as Jeanette Winterson pens on page after page of *The Stone Gods*: "Everything is imprinted forever with what it once was."[43] Ultimately, each minute, event, and vast contraction of time constitutes its own durational process, its own living present, which returns again and again in a differential repetition.

Now, it is easy to comprehend the contractions of a collaborative conversation, but how does this work in relation to inorganic matter? Think about the ivory keys of a piano. According to Deleuze, the keys (the wood, their coating, the connected levers and strings) would play an agential role in the creation of melody and it is not difficult to parse such a claim. I again remember the piano on which I learned how to play "Twinkle, Twinkle Little Star" and its anchoring brown splotch of paint on the "D" note. The result was that I never troubled to find my proper starting point—never accidentally turned "Twinkle, Twinkle" into a sad, minor key—until I had to play on an unmarked piano. Likewise, every piano played has a unique feel and weight to the keys, and such materialities undoubtedly change the flow, volume, and pace of the music. What this indicates for us is that time is both deeply material (integrated with multiple bodies, things, entities, and events) and is itself formed by passive contractions of habit. Time neither preexists the contraction of the melody, as a timeline on which we find distinct notes, nor is it the container in which a five-minute-long piece of music takes place; it is made by the duration of the notes themselves.[44] We could also think of this in relation to a tree: a tree that ages, grows larger, and decays is not acted upon by the passing of time, but rather making time through its movements and changes. In this way, matter itself is the force of time's passing and, consequently, Williams's "we live as time makers" includes tables, chairs, animals, and plants.[45] Existence is predicated upon the making of time, and each time-maker is part of a living present.

Each of the three syntheses—the living present, the pure past, and the eternal return—are equally important in understanding the living present as a method of understanding as each of these feed into one another and no full understanding of time is possible without their cooperation. However, in future chapters I blend all three into the living present, with this first synthesis subsuming all three processes in order to determine the *matter of time*; that is, the modes by which the present is multiple, not only in terms of its open-ended potential (the eternal return) and its thick durational memory (the pure past), but also multiplied by infinite singularities (people, ants, chairs, economic theories) as they are each not only expressions of a living present, but makers of time. Unlike Deleuze, I don't divvy up the past, present, and future into unique, though interrelated, processes, for they are all expressive, at all times, through the living present:

> When I move through simple notes of a song, I am anticipating the sounds of the notes to come at the same time that I integrate the ringing of notes that have come before in order to create a melody. Meanwhile my fingers travel imperceptibly as years of habitual, temporal contraction land in instinctive movements, textures, and patterns.

> When I write about Sappho I contract a memory of a trip I took to Greece six years ago with an ex-lover. We were warned that it wasn't dangerous to show affection publicly between two women, but that we should be cautious anyway. I contract a fabricated memory of Sappho on the Isle of Lesbos, living out and writing about her love for women and it both calms me (we have been here all along) and worries me (how many centuries will it take to be free?).

As these anecdotes relay, the imports of a living present are vast. On one hand, a living present resists a present that is a fixed "now" and so demonstrates that the time we experience as *present* is always a stretching between past and future, while, on the other hand, the living present provides a means by which to think time, progress, past, present, and future *differently* and therefore to imagine (and thus create) novel future relationships with matter, energy, environment, and sexuality (as future chapters will show).

This stretching of the living present ensures that with every stretch we retain the images, sounds, or experiences that were once present, but now are past. Consciousness, then, stretches forward and backward, in order to give an object *time* and, consequently, to move forward *in time*, remembering that the stretch itself is not conscious but rather the elasticity of the present itself. The living present is supple, flexible. It is less about the passage of time than it is a liveliness of an immanent materiality (i.e., it is not the case that "I" am consciously stretching backward and forward as I remember how to play "Twinkle Twinkle" and anticipate the sounds the notes will make, but rather that the stretch is limitless as my fingers move unconsciously, as my ears layer the sound of this piano atop the hundreds that came before, as my feet reach for pedals that aren't where I thought they would be, as the echo in the room causes notes to resonate in strange and unfamiliar ways).

The Living Present as an Alternative to Progress Narratives

The rich value of the living present as a diffractive method of understanding will be brought into view through many different examples in the coming chapters, but a companion theme to these discussions will be the underlying critique of progress-as-Chronos that the living present enacts. By this I mean that our operations of thinking about time as chronological before and after binds our available understanding to a feedback loop of cause and effect. Such a chronology orients us toward a set of goals that will remedy the travesties of the past and, in so doing, it remains fixated on the anticipation of a superior future. Such a future-oriented politics of temporality is problematic, not only due to its force and impact on the present but also its lack of freedom for the future. Adams, Murphy, and Clarke note the affective power of anticipation in maintaining such a perspective, describing it as "a regime of being in time, in which one inhabits time out of place as the future."[46] *Alice shrinks so that she can get through the door (and yet no one thought to ask why passage through the door warranted such heroic feats).* Though we need not be entirely critical of the function of anticipation, I remain concerned about the ways such a focus can form a totalizing orientation.

For example, modes of preparing for or speculating upon future events, whether in the realm of technoscience, biomedicine, or environmentalism, have the effect of bringing future events (and disasters) into the frame of the present moment. In this way, Adams and colleagues write that "the future increasingly not only defines the present but also creates material trajectories of life that unfold *as anticipated by those speculative processes.*"[47] Take for example the discourse surrounding new reproductive technologies. In "Disciplining Mothers: Feminism and the New Reproductive Technologies," Jana Sawicki writes that while fertility treatments, surrogacy, and genetic developments respond to infertility in increasingly adept and effective ways, there is a faction of the discourse that relies on the image of a future where there is *no* infertility as justification for procedures in the present. The result is that medical models and norms "isolate types of abnormality or deviancy, while [constructing] new norms of healthy and responsible motherhood."[48] Sawicki's argument that medical solutions to fertility issues will become the only methods of response, while other approaches will be ignored, illustrates the ways in which our anticipation of a future that views new reproductive technologies as the correct answer to the problem of infertility ends up working "*as if* the virtues of movement into valued futures are already known."[49] Interestingly, in Jeanette Winterson's postapocalyptic world, reproduction has been entirely moved to the lab—"women don't breed in the womb anymore"[50]—and scientists have figured out a way to stop aging at a certain point so all humans get "genetically fixed" once they reach their twenties or thirties and halt the aging process entirely.

The uncritical acceptance of the *virtuous* movement into the future is akin to modernist progress narratives (monomythologies) or "the conviction that history has reason, purpose, and direction."[51] Through its description as having emerged in unegalitarian, unenlightened times, "modernity" embodies the movement of continual progress. Likewise, the thesis that "humanity is making steady, if uneven and ambivalent, progress toward greater freedom, equality, prosperity, rationality, or peace" emerges as a condition for the possibility of successful human subjectivity.[52] Folded through Sawicki's critique of new reproductive technologies, this progress narrative links with the logic of "consumerism and commodification by inciting the desire for 'better babies'"[53]—and, in Winterson's tale, *better, younger, women*. The result is that such technologies are fundamentally perceived as themselves *better*, more *productive*, and as indicative of technological *progress*. For Winterson's citizens of Tech City, progress looks like no one growing old, no one decaying, and a future that is wrinkle- and sag-free. For Sawicki, locating the problem of infertility within women's bodies means that new reproductive technologies can feed neoliberal constructions of time as a linear and cumulative movement *forward*, and buttress the disparagement of women's bodies that we have endured for eons.

The force of the neoliberal progress narrative is also in need of a *queering*, as it is precisely a temporality of futurity that anchors our current neoliberal politics and processes or rather that the social and political forces of capitalism, whiteness, heteronormativity, and nationalism are structured by their reliance on teleological progress narratives that maintain an acquiescence to the future.[54] To contrast this, there is a long history within queer theory of reimagining temporality outside of a heteronormative future of childhood→adulthood →marriage→children→middle age→retirement → death.[55] While this trajectory may indicate the assumed course of development and growth for most, for many subjects (queer and otherwise), movement through time has often taken a different path, as we learned in Chapter 1; for Edelman this path calls for a refusal of reproductive futurity, or a refusal to obey a future that hinges on the figure (and reproduction) of the Child.[56]

Others have explored queer time in regard to an elongated adolescence, such that while Western cultures map maturity according to a distinct trajectory from adolescence to adulthood, the queer experience can take aberrant paths. Coming out at twenty-nine can result in knee-jerk movements "back" to the insecurities of youth. Friends and family may suddenly disappear, requiring the development of new kinship patterns.[57] Another example is found in the North American "It Gets Better" (IGB) campaign. IGB prides itself on "[inspiring] people across the globe to share their stories and remind the next generation of LGBTQ+ youth that hope is out there, *and it will get better.*"[58] But critics have poked holes in IGB's imagined future. As one blogger writes, "The gay promise failed me. I went from being ostracized by my straight classmates in high school to being ostracized by many white gay men in an urban gay enclave."[59] In effect, IGB relies on the bootstrapping humanist narrative of the hero's journey, or the autonomous man who struggles through persecution (the requisitely painful teenage years of the queer youth) in order to reach an adulthood of wholeness, progress, and freedom from constraint. Unfortunately, the bootstrapping narrative is a neocolonialist myth, available only to those who occupy, or have access to various modes of privilege and power. Through questioning these preexisting chronologies of maturity, queer temporalities trace the diversity and richness of queer subcultures, thus retelling and reimagining the time of a stretched-out adolescence, rather than directing ourselves toward a predetermined future that casts a particular net of maturity and expectation.[60]

Now, it is not ridiculous to hope for a future that is different, a future where queer youth can attend high school without fear, or where reproductive technologies make it possible for two women to contribute genetic material to their shared child, or even for Billie and Spike to fall in love and live happily ever after on Planet Blue. Although there are problems with the myth that we can *progressively* reach a particular space and time of liberation and freedom, there is merit to the complexities of "hopefulness," "imagining the new," and "wishful thinking" that have been invaluable for feminist theorizing and political feminist projects.[61] Rebecca Coleman and Debra Ferreday have written about the ways that "hope," like anticipation, operates as a potentiality, an interpellation into the future that *acts* on the present.[62] Though hope is arguably just as dogmatic as anticipation, its act of leaping into an unknown future reminds us that "feminist visions of the future *have not* been realized in the present."[63] In fact, a feminism that is to be anything more than critique *must* be deeply and productively infused with an optimism that we are not doomed to live out the same injustices, discriminations, and violences *for all time*. We would do well to stop trying to reframe our existing political and ethical constructs and instead to imagine new ways of relating and being in the world. The key is to refrain from solidifying our hopes around what exactly a *feminist future* might look like, for this is where we slide into the static progress narrative. If we keep the future open-ended we are less likely to fix it to a fixed category or a predetermined classification. The potential of hope within this frame, then, is such that at the same time that it projects us forward, it recognizes the "persistence of the past in the present"[64]—or the fact that we are spurred on in the twenty-first century by injustices from the twentieth. For example, we are inspired by the famous five's work to bring about women's suffrage in Canada and their efforts to bring the Persons Case before the Supreme Court of Canada. Their story reminds us that social change is, in fact, possible.[65] Hope's potentiality is one of inventiveness; in hoping for transformed futures, we, as feminists, are creating such possibilities.[66]

So, how are we to embrace this hope, including its untimely-ness and open-ended-ness, without unwittingly subjecting ourselves to a paradigm in which the rational, human subject remains at the helm of time's passing? A living present shifts the focus on an open-ended future, ever so slightly, to include the affective power of the past and the present or, rather, cueing Winterson's time travelers Billy and Spike, we cannot think of their story as the cumulative journey of autonomous individuals to a *future* in which we will finally access the knowledge needed to fix our *past* mistakes, and respond to our *present* environmental problems. *The Stone Gods* refuses to provide a sequential tale of cause and effect and instead it skips around on itself; it reminds us that by thinking in duration we can never fully mark the future as *future*. To this end, there is a scene late in the novel where the Billy of Wreck City finds the unfinished manuscript of *The Stone Gods* on the London Tube, presumably the copy that the reader is presently reading. She writes:

> I was traveling home on the Tube tonight and I noticed that someone had left a pile of paper on the seat opposite. ... *The Stone Gods*, said the title. OK, must be anthropology. Some thesis, some PhD. What's that place with the statues? Easter Island? I flicked through it. No point starting at the beginning—nobody ever does.[67]

The novel's reflexivity ensures that the reader is never fully able to determine the chronology of the narrative; a piece (or manuscript) is always left behind.[68]

Curiously, one of the most compelling moments of Winterson's *The Stone Gods* is also the most subtly presented, as Billie and Spike of the third tale are trekking through the rough Wreck City while navigating the all-powerful MORE, a global company that took over as the universal leadership after a world war ravaged everything on Earth. This time, Spike is just a robotic head, the first ever developed, and Billie carries her around in a sling after having scooped her from the lab. In the closing pages of the novel, Spike is able to interpret a message dated sixty-five million years prior. The message says very little but includes one line of programming code for a robo sapiens.[69] Suddenly a timeline crystallizes as the reader remembers Billie and Spike freezing to death on the newly discovered Planet Blue. Dinosaurs trampled around them as the whole planet started to freeze over. Could it be that Billie and Spike of Wreck City are occupants of Planet Blue—the home they call Earth—sixty-five million years after the residents of Orbus destroyed their own planet and attempted to colonize a new one? *My drive for order suddenly tries to turn Winterson's multiple temporalities into one timeline.*

But I resist my well-worn habit; the three vignettes of *The Stone Gods* must be read in reverse, out of order, or even horizontally, as if they are taking place simultaneously in presents that could have been. It is the reader that applies the temporal logic that anticipates a future and constructs a past. And it really is much more interesting to let go of my expectations for a coherent narrative so that each vignette is a living present, with a multiplicitous timeline that is stretched to include the effects of that which has not yet happened and to reimagine a past that has already been lost.

To Dream a Future

I enlisted Jeanette Winterson's *The Stone Gods* as a beacon for a living present. The central characters, Billie and Spike, are the star-crossed lovers who find each other across time, sex, gender, race, and technology, lending to the quasi-Nietzschean view that life is the eternal recurrence of the same. However, as it plays out, Winterson adeptly illustrates not the return of the same, but rather a temporality that is fundamentally one of difference and repetition. History repeats itself in *The Stone Gods*, but each repetition differentiates the one that came before. As a result the novel tells us that we can never properly predict, speculate, or anticipate what the future will hold, at the same time that we must look deep into our presents and our pasts in order to make sense of those things that we think we know. Deleuze describes this dual process as that of always creating and always forgetting. On the one hand, we are always participants in the creation of a world that is otherwise—and this is not a spontaneous, mystical activity; it means that the examples of queer rights movements, becoming-lesbian and becoming-queer, have force in future configurations of partnership arrangements and modes of sexual subjectivity. Holding the pages of Winterson's cyber-feminist-narrative between my fingers compels me to rethink the trajectory of a story, to imagine ways of writing and thinking that don't rely on a *beginning* and an *end*. On the other hand, we must forget those identities, representations, and reflections that we cling to—to begin from an assumption that heterosexual and homosexual constitute distinct and divergent *identities* is to argue for rights based on beings who are fixed in time. Were we to forget these identities, we may be able to multiply our understandings of the changing subject, we may begin to imagine differentiations not based solely on sex or desire, but rather on the connections and possibilities that are afforded by one's material engagements with the world.

Thus, Winterson's epithet that "everything is imprinted forever with what it once was" is as much an ode to the living present as Deleuze's *Difference and Repetition*.[70] We can extend both texts to show that everything is imprinted forever with its own futurity, its own becoming. In many ways such an immense stretching of time indicates that there can never be anything purely "new" in the abstract, disconnected sense of being purely original, void of ties and conditions: each new becoming has a duration that contracts the past virtualities from which it came. And yet, it is important that we don't mistake this for a metaphysics of determinism, a sense that we are bound to our pasts and fated to our impending futures. If we understand memory as the passive contraction of the whole of the past and, further, that this contraction influences, transforms, and recreates the living present in a manner that returns as difference and becoming, then there is a vast opening to even our own undoings. We are unable to remain fixated on being as a knowable identity and instead are stretched to comprehend the dynamic responsibility afforded by the living present. And this is precisely why it is so important to open up collaborative lines of flight between Deleuze, literature, feminism, and queer theory. The thick time of the living present shows us that we are all time-makers: we are the passive syntheses of habit, memory, and chance as they make and unmake the world around us. The living present constructs new feminist futures at the same time that it rewrites the stories and events that we take to be feminism's past:

> *Here is a moment in time, and my choices have been no stranger than millions before me, displaced by wars or conscience, leaving the known for the unknown, hesitating, fearing, then finding themselves already on the journey, footprint and memory each imprinting the trail: what you had, what you lost, what you found, no matter how difficult or impossible, the moment when time became a bridge and you crossed it.*[71]

Rather than unraveling history, such a living present reveals a past rich with potential, a realm of possibility to which we are accountable but not bound.

3

Quantum Materialism: Bringing Time and Matter Together in a Feminist Future

We can hardly talk about quantum theory at all unless we find stories to tell about it: metaphors that offer the mind purchase on such slippery ground.
—Philip Ball, *Beyond Weird*

The question of how we should relate to that which we cannot control is still up for grabs, and as this question has become displaced, along with the wilderness, into the ocean deeps and the depths of space, so feminists must follow.
—Mette Bryld and Nina Lykke, *Cosmodolphins: Feminist Cultural Studies of Technology, Animals, and the Sacred*

To the extent that our work relies on and makes assumptions about the nature of the past and present, and to the extent that all radical politics is implicitly directed towards bringing into existence a future somehow dislocated from the present, our very object and milieu is time.
—Elizabeth Grosz, *The Untimeliness of Feminist Theory*

On October 24, 1927, twenty-nine physicists from across Western Europe met in Brussels, Belgium, for the fifth International Solvay Institutes for Physics and Chemistry. The guest list included all of the big names in physics: Albert Einstein, Neils Bohr, Erwin Schrödinger, and many others, with attendees ranging in age from twenty-five to sixty-nine and representing countries from Denmark to Sweden. One woman made the list, the acclaimed Marie Curie who sits stoically in the front row of the famous photo of the attendees (see Figure 3.1).

Chapter 4 will discuss the Deleuzian significance of the "event" in much greater detail but, assuredly, this gathering was a Deleuzian event in all of its affective glory. Of course at the time, no one knew they were about to

Figure 3.1 1927 Solvay Conference on Quantum Mechanics
Source: Benjamin Couprie, public domain, via Wikimedia Commons.

make (and break) history, but there is a mythic quality to the gathering, particularly as it is described as the birth of quantum physics. This photograph is sometimes described as "the most intelligent photograph ever taken," as, in addition to the monumental content of the gathering, seventeen of the twenty-nine attendees had already won, or would go on to win, Nobel Prizes in either physics or chemistry. Today everyone is interested in quantum physics: feminists, scientists, philosophers, queer theorists, not to mention bloggers, journalists, and authors. It is clear that the mysterious, unknowable landscape of quantum theory/physics/mechanics has captured our imaginations in curious and fascinating ways and we are far from getting any reprieve from the endless mystery it continues to offer. In a lucid account of quantum mechanics, Philip Bell outlines a number of the most popular principles within the field:

1. Quantum objects can be both waves and particles.
2. Quantum objects can be in more than one state at once: they can be both *here* and *there*, say.
3. You can't simultaneously know exactly two properties of a quantum object.

4. Quantum objects can affect one another instantly over huge distances: so-called "spooky action at a distance."'
5. You can't measure anything without disturbing it, so the human observer can't be excluded from the theory: it becomes unavoidably subjective.
6. Everything that can possibly happen does happen.[1]

How can things be in two places at once? Is every possibility actualized or is everything actual also a possibility? Many of these claims will be familiar as they have easily become the famous conundrums of a burgeoning field caught somewhere between math and *magic*, but I quote Ball at length here because his argument is that quantum mechanics actually says none of these things. He argues that each point is misleading and, as such, potentially does more harm than good. That's not to say that Ball determines any of these wholly *untrue*, but rather that they are interpretations of theory given in a world that does not yet have language for its subject.

Take, for example, the claim that quantum objects can be both waves and particles. Expressed as the wave-particle duality, this claim resulted from experiments which demonstrated that sometimes matter behaved like waves, while at other times it behaved like particles. This was a huge blow to the Newtonian universe that, as we remember from Chapter 1, relies on fixed and measurable entities: that is, rocks are made up of millions of particles, while sound travels through waves. To see matter behave like both particles *and* waves puts a great deal of classical science in question and contributes to the "spooky" or "weird" tenor of quantum physics. Ball argues that this claim mistakenly makes us think that quantum objects change properties, they move from wave to particles depending on the situation. Instead, he invokes Einstein to argue that the focus here shouldn't be on the behavior of quantum objects, but rather on the interpretation, including the fact that we lack both language and understanding to accurately account for the phenomenon. Rather than showing us weird behavior of matter, the wave-particle duality shows us that the concepts with which we are familiar—particles and waves—are inadequate in describing the behaviors of quantum objects and effects.

Ball's argument caught my attention primarily because it is a sentiment long-expressed within feminist philosophy and theory. Audre Lorde's resounding call for transformative politics in "the master's tools will never dismantle the master's house" lingers here as a reminder that we have great work to do as feminists, community leaders, and as citizens of complex worlds, in bringing about the *feminist futures* we long for.² Ball's pithy criticism of contemporary quantum mechanics, then, prompts us to think about the impacts of our present theories on our future world-making. Will we ever understand quantum time given that we still use and live the concepts of classical physics? Will we ever be able to grasp intersectionality through a durational frame as long as race, sex, and gender represent singularities in subjects?

Quantum physics represent far more than a new *physics*, or a new way of measuring and understanding the basic building blocks of our world. Quantum physics offers an entirely different view of *reality*.³ This is precisely the thrill that rippled through feminist and queer scholars upon encountering Karen Barad's groundbreaking account of the relationship of quantum physics with feminist theory and philosophy in *Meeting the Universe Halfway* and, like Ball, Barad argues that in focusing on the waves and the particles in the wave-particle duality, we miss the larger impact of the experiment. Where Ball still determines that there is some entity called a "quantum object" that we have yet to understand, Barad demonstrates that there is no quantum "object" mysteriously waiting for discovery; instead the uptake is that the experiment is itself a phenomenon: an entanglement of the object, the efforts of measurement, and the observer.⁴ There is no meaning outside of this entangled relationship and, similarly, Barad recognizes that this "phenomenon" represents a future understanding of reality we have yet to grasp.

Like many topics of inquiry within this book, quantum physics is nothing *new*. By this I mean more than the fact that it was developed nearly one hundred years ago, and rather that the theories that uphold quantum physics are embedded within Indigenous philosophies and knowledges, as well as beliefs, theologies, and philosophies that have been circling the globe for centuries. As quantum theory whets the appetites of scientists and scholars alike in the twenty-first century, it echoes a past where Europe's top physicists stubbornly did everything they could to avoid the conclusions (openings) that quantum physics ascribed. In fact, many of the theory's greatest namesakes valiantly sought definitions that were much more coherent than quantum physics will ever allow. Desperately trying to disprove their own discoveries, such efforts were geared toward the development of a "Theory of Everything" (TOE), something that would reconcile quantum theory and Newton's laws of science so that physicists could return to the safety of a grand design. Even Einstein, especially as he aged, sought a TOE in his "unified field theory," a theory that would bring classical particle physics and general relativity together in a unified description of the universe.

Like the lure of progress narratives, the TOE offers comfort, but the more that physicists, scientists, and philosophers explore quantum theory, the more obvious it becomes that a unified theory is impossible. In fact, I would argue that quantum theory offers hope precisely because it is so unbelievable. Somehow questioning the very fabric, time, and space of the universe has opened doors for unthought futures, for revitalizing stagnant pasts, for imagining great and vast possibilities. As a result, this chapter takes a path already traveled to explore new feminist materialisms and quantum physics. I aim to shed light on a theory at the edge of chaos, demonstrating that it is *time* that makes the link between feminism and science, by following links between Einstein, Braidotti, and Deleuze, between Bergson, Barad, and Bohr, in order to illustrate the "new reality" that feminists, queer theorists, and Indigenous philosophers have always already been crafting. There are an infinite number of contributors and interlocutors to this story and so I acknowledge that the practice of framing is the only predictor of meaning. In this case *time* is the diffraction grating that we need to build ourselves alternate tool kits. By linking temporality with new feminist materialisms, we are able to mobilize novel methods of communicating and understanding one another and therefore are able to participate in the work of building braver futures.

On the Material (Re)turn

There is a wonderful temporality to the concept of the "turn." As it is used within the humanities to signify a new branch of theory, it illustrates that we are always turning, moving through the linguistic turn, the performative turn, the iconic turn, the posthuman turn, the *temporal turn*. Some have been quite critical of the "turn" of phrase, due to implications that it creates fixed boundaries between one particular mode of thought and practice and another, or that it solidifies linear beliefs that one mode of thought can overcome the past. But I see it more as a continuous cycle, where to "turn" is to shift the dial slightly to the right or to the left within a continuous, connected loop. Every turn is much more a series of *(re)turns* than anything else as each is deeply indebted to its multiple pasts. Where would the performative turn be without the keen discussions of the power of language and speech acts as developed in the linguistic turn? In this framing, the "material turn" then represents a novel *movement through theory and matter*. Much more than a new theory or philosophy, the material turn is a unique and significant way of bringing such entities together in a manner that is, in fact, as old as the hills.

Sometimes called neo-materialism or critical materialism, other times new materialism or feminist materialisms, and outside of feminist arenas, noted under the banners of speculative realism, object-oriented philosophy, and object-oriented ontology, "the material turn" shifts the way that we understand and examine *matter*. Involving a variety of cross-creative and co-creative readings between physics and philosophy, biology and feminism, it has really been feminist and queer theories that have generated the greatest impact in the field. For this reason, as well as my denial that anything can ever really be called "new," I am most comfortable calling the field feminist materialisms. Feminist materialisms are often framed as a response to the "linguistic turn," the product of not only an analytic tradition of structuralism and philosophy of language, but also continental projects of post-structuralism and postmodernism—attributed to Jacques Derrida, Judith Butler, Julia Kristeva, and Michel Foucault, among others—as they emphasize the role of language and the social in the construction of meaning and knowledge. Of course post-structuralism has been invaluable as a means of destabilizing binarized biologies of gender, sexuality, race, and ability, but it has also maintained a world of ideas and representations that is not only endemic to continental philosophy and social theory, but also to feminism.

Consequently, the material turn is indebted, in part, to Barad's statement that "language has been granted too much power."[5] On the one hand our postmodern feminist identity politics, as intensely constructivist, has turned gender, sexuality, race, class, and ability into abstract categories, many of which fail to transcend their dualist legacies, while, on the other hand, feminist materialisms question even Butler's theory of performativity such that it makes matter passive to the speech act, rather than an active force in the engendering of the gendered subject.[6] For example, the coming out event, which will be discussed at length in Chapter 4, is never only a "speech act," a verbal utterance-thus-making of a queer *self*. It is always also a series of movements, inflections, modes of dress and behavior as they both intersect with and destroy preconceived beliefs. Of course, the famous drag act of performativity draws on expressions well beyond discourse in order to demonstrate the *making* of gender within a post-structuralist milieu, but we continue to miss the nuance of the material turn when we imagine that a human *actor* dons an outfit and thus makes an identity, or likewise that a cultural system of meaning and classification predetermines a nation.

This is deeper than discussions of the over-conscription of the subject, for it reveals that we have always been wrong about subject formation and thus have always been wrong about matter. It is precisely because it is so widely read that the particularly humanist bent of Butler's work restricts embodiment to an acting human subject, rather than acknowledging the "dynamic life of which that subject is an effect."[7] As it applies to Butler's *Gender Trouble* this means that despite the incredible impact of gender performativity and its work in terms of disconnecting sex from gender, culture from biology, what we have to do now is find the lost material body (and its clothing and piercings and cars and computers) that has been widely overwritten.

In an illustrative interview between Butler and Vicki Kirby, Kirby poses the following question: "There is a serious suggestion that 'life itself' is creative encryption. Does your understanding of language and discourse extend to the workings of biological codes and their apparent intelligence?"[8] Creative encryption refers to medical research that tracks the activities of bacteria as they are confronted with antibiotics. The bacteria effectively conduct code-cracking and encryption capacities that allow them to reinvent themselves and so, with this in mind, Kirby argues that our continued reliance on the nature/culture binary (whether we are Cartesian or post-structuralist) restricts any full account of the *nature of nature* in such an operation.[9] Butler's response is a reminder that it will always be impossible for the human to adequately and completely capture a world "out there." She claims "I am sure that encryption can be used as a metaphor or model by which to understand biological processes, especially cell reproduction, but do we then make the move to render what is useful as an explanatory model into the ontology of biology itself?"[10] This line between metaphor and ontology, though slight, enacts a distancing from matter or the *material*, despite the fact that Butler does address such things in great detail. In *Bodies That Matter*, Butler takes up much of the criticism of *Gender Trouble*, including its disavowal of the body, as she writes that the debate between constructionism and essentialism misses the point of deconstruction. She spends a great deal of time illustrating the lived entanglements of sex and exploring the deep relationship between history-formation and the materialization of the body. These arguments demonstrate that such grand swipes only reveal the force of exclusion and erasure as they continue to inform our dichotomous attempts at thinking about subjectivity at all, and so I draw on this delicate conversation between Kirby and Butler to illustrate the ways in which we all write, think, and act within very particular material contexts. That we would zero in on Butler's failure to provide a theory of materiality in *Gender Trouble*, *Bodies That Matter*, or any other text, is in fact, an entirely wrongheaded critique. It asks the wrong question to the answers that Butler has productively provided not only to queer theory, feminist theory, and community activism, but also to new feminist materialisms, as her work is the diffractive ripple (the condition of possibility) for our questions about the power of the text.

We would do better to recognize the manner in which early queer theory showed us the ways that sex and gender are material in word, deed, and expression. In so doing these traditions offer us a form of temporal materiality—the performative repetition-as-subject-creation that again provides a productive point of departure, rather than a frame against which we should rail. We can then redirect the conversation from a familiar mode of critique to a diffractive methodology. Just as Kirby follows the ripples of our having taken the distance between nature and culture to be a given in the first place, we can be wary of the ways in which our familiar post-structural and linguistic framings endorse the fact that "it is in the nature of Culture to unwittingly take itself for Nature."[11] We are so intent upon *not* conceiving of nature as linguistic, communicative, and reasonable that we ignore the many ways that *nature makes culture*. Consequently, Kirby's own provocative conditions of emergence include Derrida's "there is nothing outside of the text" as a starting point, rather than as an adversary.[12] Our studies of language, discourse, and text may be less about mapping an exterior "nature" than they are about revealing the expression of entangled subjectivity that can never be extracted from the story. That is, they may reveal that nature *is* creative encryption: processes of code-cracking that intelligently and agentially reinvent themselves in every moment. Kirby's proposal is that the line be rewritten as "there is no outside of Nature," a turn of phrase which enfolds Haraway's naturecultures in its collapse of the dualism that so often frames our contemporary imaginings.[13]

Calling for *matter* to play a central role in epistemological, ontological, and ethical projects, the material turn documents the radical interconnectedness of things and ideas. This interconnectedness extends to the fact that we cannot fully understand our own environments and experiences without also understanding the effects we have on those things (whether people, plants, highways, or animals) around us, and, concurrently, the effects that such "things" have on us. By collapsing the binary between the real and the representational, these materialisms take up the task of investigating "life itself" as the *affective* capacity of matter.

Is There Such a Thing as "Life Itself"?

Less about some mysterious essence of "aliveness" or "pure essence," the concept of "life itself" is about examining the effects of bodies and organisms as they integrate with ideas, politics, and ideologies. Nikolas Rose's *The Politics of Life Itself* brought the phrasing to the fore, investigating how biopolitics and practices of *biopower* have changed the way that we understand the human in relationship to biology and new technologies.[14] Thanks to Foucault we recognize that biopower is not only about *power over bodies*, but also about the complicated mechanisms by which we control, police, subjugate, and order bodies and populations.[15] It has been the means by which eugenics and forced sterilizations have taken place, but it has also been the driving force behind preventative medicine and public health initiatives. Each of these operations relies on the goal of protecting and managing *life*, above all else, but the key is that *life* is not indiscriminately protected. Biopower protects a specific type of body, it evaluates what is and is not an acceptable life, and it anticipates a future population that is shaped and defined by the loaded terms of "health," "vitality," and "well-being."

Biopower also helps us to distinguish between a molar-level understanding of the body, with its visible and tangible limbs and organs, and a molecular biopolitics where life is now imagined as "sub-cellular processes and events."[16] In other words, biotechnologies (and their biopowers) have ensured that "life" is no longer some sort of "natural life" that we can examine, classify, and pathologize, nor is it a healthy equilibrium to which we can return. By molecularizing our identities into genetic codes and turning health into a manipulable cellular configuration, biotechnologies have effectively "[changed] what it is to be human";[17] otherwise "natural" processes are now deemed to be one possibility within a range of possibilities such as reshaping the aging process through hormone replacement, or reconfiguring sexuality through Viagra.[18] Such technological advances have meant that the very definition of life is changing and, thus, biotechnologies are much more than answers to health problems and instead themselves technologies of life. These examples demonstrate that our world is already a combination of social-cultural-science-matter and such a world relies on a view of material-as-subject, rather than object. Just as many of our theoretical "turns" fail to account for their pasts and futures, the material turn is a misnomer, as we have been material all along.

Let's look at an example: there are long-standing absences of potable water in many First Nations in Northern Saskatchewan. Places like Clearwater River Dene Nation have had a boil water advisory since 2006, while White Bear First

Nation has had an advisory since 2011. In 2010, the United Nations passed Resolution 64/292, which indicated that access to clean water and sanitation were human rights. The UN called on international aid organizations to engage in the provision of clean and affordable drinking water in developing countries. They also called on developed countries to ensure that they were meeting this right in their own nations. When we look at the Canadian context, aid organizations such as WaterAid, WaterCan, and WaterKeepers spend millions of dollars building wells in developing nations and, yet, as of 2021, we still have sixty boil water advisories in First Nations communities. Given that there are 634 recognized First Nations communities in Canada, it means that nearly 10 percent of these are without potable water.

This is a colonial tale, as the right to water is granted to white settlers, city dwellers, the affluent, the recognized, and this is also a tale about racialized misogyny, as Indigenous women shoulder the burden of environmental racism in Canada and around the world. Unfortunately, the Canadian government was quick to enact the neoliberal savior narrative as, on July 2017, Carolyn Bennett, Canada's minister of Crown-Indigenous Relations, made an announcement that the Canadian government was investing 9.2 million dollars into the water system at White Bear First Nation.[19] This followed on the heels of Prime Minister Trudeau's promise to eliminate all boil water advisories in Canada, and so the White Knight (Trudeau) rides in with a gift that is already a human right of the White Bear First Nation's residents and, in so doing, ensures that the gift of progress and "development" remains in the hands of the Crown.

Despite it being a "human right," water is not an inert substance. It is not a "thing" to which we can lay claim, ownership, occupation. Water is embedded in every living, growing being. Water pummels the rocks that line our shores, it is "air" for creatures of the sea, it can destroy an entire city in one tsunamic wave. Water is our lifeblood and we are always already *wet* with our own watery embodiment. In *Bodies of Water*, Astrida Neimanis describes this entanglement: "Blood, bile, intracellular fluid; a small ocean swallowed, a wild wetland in our gut; rivulets forsaken making their way from our insides to out, from watery womb to watery world: *we are bodies of water.*"[20] There is no separation between bodies-and-water, and so any conversations about access to water are transcorporeal conversations. For residents of White Bear First Nation, water is a privilege, not a right. It costs money, it takes time, it requires planning and upkeep. Water also shapes relationships and well-being as its absence has the impacts of dehydration and sickness, while its presence is a sign of racism and exclusion. We do not need to rely only on examples from new biotechnologies in order to understand the affective power of matter, for we *are* only and ever made of matter, *and land, and water, and air.*

And so, by shifting of our understandings of matter, feminist materialisms refer to the politicized water that is absent from White Bear First Nation, the metal arms of a wheelchair, the skin, bones, and sinews of the human body, the long ring of a piano note. Not all of these are historically considered "material" in the sense of being understood as objects with distinct mass and volume but, in this case, all of these are material entities, operating with, alongside, and through one another as they *make* the event of the ongoing boil water advisories at White Bear First Nation, or the Solvay Gathering in 1924. It is not only the chalk scratching across the surface of a chalkboard, or the heavy jugs of water hauled home every night that comprise intensive sites of contact in these events in time, but also the flashes of insight upon solving a physics equation, the despair upon having to boil water every night in order to bathe one's children.

I trust that it is no great leap to understand the material impact of a piece of chalk, scraping against a chalkboard, but what about the materiality of ideas? Given that feminist materialisms so directly critique the linguistic turn, and even post-structuralism with its inability to know that which lies beyond the text, there is understandably an absence of explicit focus on the value of *thought, thinking, text,* or *words,* though of course no *text* or *theory* can supersede its medium. Among other valuable points of collaboration that I have previously outlined between feminist materialisms and Deleuze, this is precisely a point where a productive opportunity arises. Returning to Deleuze and Guatarri's discussions of both *becoming* and of philosophical *concepts,* it is the case that becoming is itself an expression of agential realism. Likewise, the concepts of becoming-woman, becoming-animal, becoming-otherwise, becoming-immanent, all refer to the active forces of identifications, revelations, and expressions in creating novel and temporary subject positions. Understood as nothing other than a becoming-flow, the activity of *becoming* reminds us that there is no fixed system of interpretation or knowledge production, no fixed language or thought, but instead an ongoing process of meaning-making whereby ideas and thoughts are borne out in the expressions, movements, and embodiments of the self, and vice versa.

I'm sure some may argue that I am oversimplifying but, in many ways, *becoming* easily expresses Barad's intra-action in motion through its indication of the potentialities of philosophy, science, and art as they actively alter the material environment through their very instantiation. For example, think about a study exploring the link between the presence of queer characters on television and public tolerance surrounding diverse sexualities. It is not the case that the study only produces an analyzable data set, but it actually creates a public reality that reflects this link. The act of study enacts a *becoming-queer* of both television and popular culture, and of course it is not only research practices and analyses but also the act of thinking *itself* that creates new modes of existence: *thinking creates life* and, like becoming, such a process is definitively temporal.

Consider another example: the success of the women's rights movement throughout the twentieth century. The women that spoke out against sexism, misogyny, and phallocentrism not only revealed the false normativity of a male-dominated society but, in so doing, they also created a women's history that did not exist prior. The texts of Mary Wollstonecraft and Christine de Pizan were dusted off and read according to the influence they had on the present; a history of lesbian desire was discovered in the writings of Sappho, as discussed in Chapter 2. Through the speeches, actions, readings, and *thoughts* of burgeoning feminists, entire worlds were brought into being, worlds that forever changed the lived experience of generations to come. So, if Deleuze and Guattari make the case that philosophy is an active and productive means by which to *affect* the environment—to *think* life into being/becoming—then feminist materialisms embolden the realization that the act of *thinking* is effectively material entanglement in its co-creation of embodied pasts, futures, and presents.

Now it bears clear mention that explorations of the "life" and "affect" of thought, water, or the agential chalk and ideas of a gathering of physicists lends toward vitalism. "Vitalism" refers to early nineteenth-century beliefs that "there must exist a life principle that (sometimes) animated matter, which was not itself material."[21] Taken up by Hans Driesch as entelechy (borrowed from Aristotle, and indicative of an intensive life force) and Henri Bergson as *élan vital* (an elusive vital force that acts on matter), early vitalists sought to determine that which was unquantifiable and unpredictable in matter's movements and creations.[22] Though this is not specifically the "vitalism" to which today's feminist materialisms refer, this tradition (particularly Bergson's philosophy) remains pertinent to discussions of the *what* of matter's being, and a much more problematic history of vitalism contracts Nazi Germany's doctrine that there were more and less "vital" forms of life (and thus, of humanity). Demonstrating biopower's awful reach, this doctrine of vitalism was used to justify the abduction, containment, and killing of those deemed "less vital," thus contributing to quite negative castings of the term vitalism.

It is not this framing to which I refer, but I acknowledge that all language is already thick with its own past, and so vitalism is haunted by this uptake. Less a reason not to use the term than it is the reminder that all language has power, it is how that power is taken up and directed that matters. Given his reliance on univocity, a frame I will discuss in greater detail in Chapter 4, Deleuze denies any hierarchy or quantifiable difference between not just species, but *life* itself, and so does not align with a vitalism that evaluated one life(force) as compared to another. However, concepts such as duration and the living present, both draw out components of the Drieschian-Bergsonian project in their attunement to intensity and becoming. In fact, Deleuze highlights the vitalism of his own work with his statement that "everything I've written is vitalistic, at least I hope it is."[23] Some have taken this to mean that Deleuze aligns with Bergson's *élan vital*, but I don't agree. In the sentence prior, Deleuze writes that "there's a profound link between signs, life, and vitalism: the power of nonorganic life that can be found in a line that's drawn, a line of writing, a line of music. It's organisms that die, not life. Any work of art points a way through for life, finds a way through the cracks."[24] Through this it is clear that for Deleuze, "vitalism" is not bound to human life, nor to biopower. It transcends the human and nonhuman, organic and inorganic matter so that Deleuze's vitalism is much more in line with his use of *affect*, as the impact of a singularity that extends well beyond itself.[25] As instances of becoming, *affects* are liberated from their makers the minute they are expressed: a piece of art has uptake that entirely diverges from its intentional creation, a piece of music evokes emotion not contained in the score. Importantly, Deleuze and Guattari indicate that there is no elusive force abstracted from and/or acting on matter as a vitalist force but, rather, matter is itself affective, as determined by feminist materialisms.

Vitalism has played a key role in various feminist materialisms as Jane Bennett references an intrinsic vitality of matter in order to contrast beliefs that matter is passive or inert.[26] Recounting the findings of the National Institutes of Health's 2001 report on stem cells, Bennett notes that although there is scientific agreement that adult stem cells are found throughout the tissues of a human body, it is not agreed upon that embryonic stem cells exist within the embryo prior to their extraction.[27] What this means is that rather than following more common physiological and mechanistic understandings of the human body, whereby embryonic stem cells would originate within the embryo, there may be a vitalist process taking place outside of the assumed incubator; that is, embryonic stem cells may not actually exist *in* the body prior to their extraction. To be clear, this still is not the vitalism that Bergson or Driesch spoke of. Bennett's vitalism is neither entelechy nor an elusive acting *force,* but rather a vital materiality. Drawing in yet another vitalism, Bennett updates Spinoza's *conatus* as the practice in which "each thing [*res*], as far as it can by its own power, strives [*conatur*] to persevere in its own being."[28] Bennett indicates that thing-power is not held by the human body alone, but instead by *every body*: "Even a falling stone ... 'is endeavoring, as far as in it lies, to continue in its motion.'"[29] In this way, inanimate and nonhuman bodies (a dead rat, a bottle cap, a rock) all operate to flatten the hierarchies between animate and inanimate, human and nonhuman. The thing-power of inanimate objects (or assemblages of inanimate objects) are in fact *actant* forces, a term borrowed from Latour.[30] Interestingly, the actant is neither subject nor object, but rather it is an *intervener*; it is a catalyzing force that makes things happen solely upon its happenstance location. The actant, then, is a differentiated substitute for *agent*, our familiar, and much more "subject-centered" term, as Bennett's project is to make vertical hierarchies between types of matter horizontal.[31] The actant, then, requires no prime mover, no human actor, and so the falling stone is affective without need for causality or reason and, likewise, the absence of causal force does nothing to hinder the impact and affectivity of its movement (whether it moves a mile from the wind of a barren desert, or a millimeter in the contraction of stone and heat into a diamond over the course of more than a billion years).

It seems that if matter is to be agential, that is, engaged in movement, force, intensity, it needs to be *passive* in its action lest it risks teleological or even causal force. Colebrook makes a case for passive vitalism that is valuable here as she tempers the mystical, animating, spiritedness of vital matter in a way that brings it to bear on our lived experiences of everyday interrelatedness. Vitalism's passivity is akin to the second synthesis of time's memory, whereby processes of recollection, triggering, forgetfulness, and embodied memory occur in every moment, without necessary agential force. As it applies to the life force of matter, a passive vitalism needs no prime mover, no teleology, and has no quantifiable measure; it just *is*. It strikes me that this is the lynchpin in understanding vitalism as an affective life force, over and above a value-laden *élan vital*. Passivity ensures the absence of a prime mover and thus of a grand overarching theory determining any sense of "good" and "bad," and thus represents a crucial ethical differentiation.

Even more interestingly, Colebrook criticizes "becoming" through her case for passive vitalism. She writes that the concept of becoming—as it has been enlisted within queer theory and operationalized in our philosophical texts—does little more than "repeat ... a highly traditional and humanist sentiment of privileging act over inertia, life and creativity over death and stasis, and pure existence or coming-into-being over determination."[32] Such a critique contracts our earlier discussions of the weight and influence of the monomyth, our narratives of progress and overcoming. The critique is not a rejection of the concept of becoming but rather a moment of pause regarding its misinterpretation and misuse, for Colebrook argues that *becoming* has become the normalizing force par excellence: "It has always been the case that anything resistant to dynamism, fruition, creation, and a flowing forth of open and productive life has been demonized as a death or inertia that tarnishes life from the outside."[33]

The *vitalism* of inanimate and animate matter, then, is not about realizing and actualizing the self, the subject, the object, the idea, or about a moment whereby matter flourishes into presence.[34] Instead, becoming always bears a "capacity to annihilate itself, to refuse its *ownness*," and passive vitalism resists a world in which "life" is determined to be a normative value.[35] This means that we must draw in inorganic matter, non-agential forces, and all that refuses conscious meaning or organization, even including capacities of death, extinction, stillness, and immobility, in the same frame as our familiar adjectives of movement, progress, and the new.

In a clear delineation between the active vitalisms that have maintained the practices of biopower and human domination of the nature and the passive vitalisms that characterize the materialities of thick time, Colebrook describes the difference with reference to Deleuze and Guattari:

> Vitalism in its contemporary mode ... works in two opposite directions. The tradition that Deleuze and Guattari invoke is opposed to the organism as subject or substance that would govern differential relations; their concept of "life" refers not to an ultimate principle of survival, self-maintenance and continuity but to a disrupting and destructive range of forces. The other tradition of vitalism posits "life" as a mystical and unifying principle. It is this second vitalism of meaning and the organism that ... dominates today. The turn to naturalism in philosophy, to bodies and affect in theory, to the embodied, emotional and extended mind in neuroscience: all of these maneuvers begin the study of forces from the body and its world, and all understand "life" in a traditionally vitalist sense as oriented towards survival, self-maintenance, equilibrium, homeostasis, and autopoiesis.[36]

The difference is slight, but profound. It directs our attention to the relationality of matter (agential entanglement) over the vitality of matter (individual agency) and, furthermore, it reveals a familiar gender bias at work, even in our new materialist imaginings such that orientations toward survival and self-maintenance rely on the vitality of an active *man*, as compared to the passivity of *woman*, as each has been systematized. A passive vitalism pulls not only "man" from the center of the story, but also "homo sapiens" from the authorial seat. "Life itself" is not a grounding concept, nor is it our north star, but rather a univocal *materiality* that is human and nonhuman, organic and inorganic. A passive vitalism is still creative, unbounded, and intensive but, as anti-teleological, it distracts us from our addictions to causal hero and Columbus paradigms or, as Patrice Haynes describes it, a passive vitalism, as the lens of entangled materiality, demonstrates that "life need not always live."[37]

Ultimately we are reminded that matter has *always* been a lively condition of experience and it is *already* there in our theorizations, experiences, and theories. Likewise, water has always been a condition of life and is already there in our racisms, sexisms, colonialisms, and nationalisms. Through these developments it is clear that, in fact, there is no such thing as "life itself" in the sense that "life" constitutes a unique entity. Sexism has always been a condition of science and it exists in not only the absence of women within the field, but also in the solitary presence of Marie Curie in the "most intelligent photo ever taken." Thus, feminist materialisms draw in much more than a return of "real bodies" to philosophy, Rose's "politics of life itself," or Braidott's "ontology of presence after so much postmodernist deconstruction" and instead support an onto-epistemological shift in understanding.[38] This means that life is an entanglement of time, matter, space, and interpretation, and that the life of matter includes mutual interdependencies that share reflexive relationships of force as they move, create, and influence one another. This swaps out the unknowable "real" for immanence—wild "nature" for agential realism—and consequently serves as a sensibility about the world that begins from the place of always already being entangled in a vital materiality.

Returning to a discussion of matter's agency, then, we know agency as the capacity of an *agent*—read: independent, conscious, human being—to *act* in a world. Taking into account the crucial and thoughtful separation from problematically vitalist accounts of matter, feminist materialisms reveal the agency of passive vitalism in the concept of "agential realism." Agential realism refers to the entanglement of meaning and mattering outside of the conscious human subject and it is here that feminist materialisms truly take a "quantum turn" as we begin to explore modes of thinking, being, and becoming that really do imagine and therefore create a new reality.

Quantum Reimaginings

In 2012, I had the good fortune of attending the International Feminist Materialisms Conference at the University of Copenhagen, just as new feminist materialisms were really gaining ground in Europe. Karen Barad's keynote lecture "Re-membering the Future: Material Entanglements and Temporal Diffractions" electrified the packed theater, while some of the field's greatest contributors accompanied, including Cecilia Asberg, Astrida Neimanis, Vicki Kirby, and a wealth of eager graduate students who are now seasoned scholars in the field. We were treated to a tour of the Neils Bohr Institute, still an active research facility at the University of Copenhagen and, as we wandered through Bohr's Memorial Room and the old archives, I remember how strange it felt. An international group of queer and feminist theorists poring over physics equations that maybe only one or two of us understood. We were captivated by the pull of quantum theory on our feminisms, caught up in the echoes of past experiments and debates as we crowded into the old lecture theater where Bohr once taught his students. To this day, I marvel at the experience. It has lodged itself in my memory as an event of theoretical growth and expansion, an unforgettable demonstration of the affective power of our material environments in participating in and creating both our ideas and our actions.

I am a philosopher, not a physicist, and so my engagement with quantum theory is couched in the modes of thinking and reasoning within which I have been trained. That said, quantum physics truly feels closer to philosophy than it does to the algebra I remember from tenth-grade math class. The wave-particle duality I discussed in the introduction to this chapter was one of the founding mysteries of quantum physics as it threw the classical world of physics into question, but many other "weird" theories, as Ball describes them, have added to the allure and confusion of quantum theory. Of primary significance to the exploration of time and a living present is the concept of quantum entanglement. Quantum entanglement refers to the phenomenon whereby separate objects (or systems) are said to impact one another instantaneously and at a distance, a process otherwise called the EPR paradox, after its authors: Albert Einstein, Boris Podolsky, and Nathan Roson. The EPR Paradox surmises that if two independent systems, system A and system B, interact with one another for a period of time, the two systems will ultimately become correlated with one another. Further, they determined that measurements done on one of the systems would be reflected on the other, even after the period of formal interaction.

So, imagine there is a scientific experiment being conducted on Earth and the same one is being conducted in a space station. The EPR Paradox would indicate that the two systems are able to share properties and so it is understood that the processes of system A are being transmitted through space to system B. But, in fact, there is no time travel taking place and this is another of the quantum principles that Ball finds very misleading as it assumes that system A and system B are individual entities to begin with, when, in fact, they are not. Einstein once described this movement as "spooky action at a distance," but Ball indicates that there is no "spooky action" and, instead, system A and B are parts of the same phenomena. They are representative of a process of correlation whereby the expression, principles, and behaviors of each system cannot exist apart from its counterpart.

Quantum entanglement is no longer just a thought experiment as scientists have proven out the EPR paradox in many lab environments. In fact, physicists at the University of Glasglow released the first ever photo of entangled photons in 2018 and it continues to be at the crux of developments within quantum mechanics as a whole. And so, pulling in our thesis that time is a living present then, it is apparent that quantum entanglement supports this thesis in that time is the movement of increasing entanglement or correlation: the effects of a past as they anticipate/create a future.[39] As it is mobilized within feminist materialisms, Barad's concept of agential realism directly extends the thesis of quantum entanglement to all interactions. This means that in addition to having co-creative relationships between various "quanta," or subatomic particles, there are also co-creative relationships between particles and thoughts, ideas and molecules, time and space. Agential realism indicates that practices of knowing, such as the sciences, philosophy, social sciences, or even learning shapes and colors, play a key function in shaping our world and likewise that such practices of knowing would not exist without being deeply entangled within corporeal and material relationships.[40] Through this, all entities (phenomena)—matter, human, nonhuman, discourse, nature, and culture—are actively involved in one another's co-construction, not unlike V. F. Cordova's co-created universe as discussed in Chapter 1.

Like Einstein, Barad works to explain interaction on a scale for which we don't yet have language, and so she describes the process by which agential realism occurs as *intra-action*. Whereas the latter refers to the interactions of individual agencies (still interconnected, but distinct, system A and B transmitting information), the former looks at the ways in which these distinct agencies are themselves formed through their engagement. Intra-activity is a foundational interaction between entities, whereby individual entities cannot be said to exist as things-in-themselves and instead only find meaning or expression through their connections and entanglement with other entities. This means that meaningful units of analysis are no longer "the table," "the water molecule," "the human," but rather the construction (or meaning-imbuing) of the table as a surface on which to place one's work. More importantly, this event of tablemaking is not merely a product of my placing things on the table, but instead the differentiating instant of my and the table's interaction with one another such that singularities only emerge from their intra-action. Intra-action is the entangled comingling whereby my flesh is soft as it rests on the hard table's surface, and hard as it swings through the air in a wide arc. Likewise, this very book is the product of agential realism as the words that I type are as much a product of the table on which I choose to work, the old laptop that is a bit too slow, and so delays my stream of thought and changes the narrative, and the books that surround me in stacks—books whose smells and marking I am familiar with, books that I reach for without even looking, for I know the size, color, and texture of their covers as I anticipate the words within.

The now idiomatic Baradian quote that "*matter comes to matter* through the iterative intra-activity of the world in its becoming" continues to act, not as a directive but as a method for thinking about the onto-epistemological consequences of agential realism.[41] That is, if the very being of my body—of my cat's curious nature, of my computer's irritating buzz—is an intra-active phenomenon, then my understanding of these entities must change. Barad's argument for agential realism is grounded in careful explanations of the actual physical relationships of atoms, molecules, and wave patterns, but I do not need physics to know that my cat is a vital expression of "life" and that her life intra-acts with mine in many different ways at any given moment. Thus the claims of feminist materialisms—that matter makes worlds and experiences, that both being and knowledge are contingent upon our entangled materialities—are not greatly refuted. These claims are rich, compelling, and, dare I say, *common sense*. The *real* work of feminist materialisms, particularly within feminist contexts, is in terms of what these "naturecultures" can *do*. This is why I close this chapter by identifying methods and enactments of feminist materialisms, including the particular epistemic paradigms that are opened up through their relationship with quantum time, and the continued potentialities of the field for future feminist, queer, and decolonial work.

(Re)turning to the Whole

In Canada, "Idle No More" took shape seemingly overnight.[42] It spread quickly as round dancers overflowed into the corridors of our shopping centers in the days before Christmas, as outdoor drum ceremonies punctuated freezing temperatures in city centers, and as our virtual airspace filled with photos and stories of people young and old, in jingle dresses, traditional Indigenous headdresses, and goose-down parkas. On January 5, 2013, First Nations, Métis, and non-Indigenous allies gathered at Kingsway Mall in Edmonton, Alberta. Documentation of the event shows a sea of bodies with clasped hands moving in a circular pattern as they sing "you're in Indian country now, see our tipis, see the pow wow, see our children running around." As I watch the YouTube video that a friend of mine compiled of the event, and I let these words come to bear on this scene, the steady, rhythmic round dance speaks volumes. It brings Indigenous ways of knowing to bear on sharp political commentary; it links to everyday experiences of the land and community in drawing attention to diversity; and it effortlessly distills the living present, with its anticipation of the future and its echoing of the past, into a way of life. The bodies and voices of those involved echo a history of self-determination and healthy everyday life, which intersect with a history (and a present) of colonialism that continues to act on our future and therefore cannot be forgotten. The temporality of this moment is intra-active as it demonstrates that institutionalized racism and neocolonialism are still very much in operation in Canada and the echo of the round dance is a reminder that we cannot absolve ourselves selectively of past harms. The body remembers, and not only that, but these memories and contractions of the past are the very makings of the present, and engenderings of that "novel future" to which we are so directed.

This narrative echoes Rebecca Adamson's note that Indigenous understandings are based on the "interconnectedness and interdependence of all living things—a holistic and balanced view of the world. All things are bound together, all things connect."[43] Thus, any environment, whether a round dance, a forest, a virtual classroom, or a community meeting, is a living being, deeply interconnected to its surrounding beings, and capable of forming new relationships and realities. Further similarities between feminist materialisms and Indigenous philosophies reveal themselves through their parallel references to quantum theory. Barad draws on quantum physics to illustrate the scientific physical "proof" for agential realism, while Adamson cites quantum mechanics as indicative of the forms of atomic co-constitution that are central to the experience of life. Indigenous knowledge (IK), as it has been used by (and against) Indigenous communities in North America and Australia, refers to many diverse sets of understandings about how to relate ethically to the world, ranging from one's treatment of the Earth, to the value of art practices, to the methods of building systems of communication, economics, and politics, understandings that resonate with feminist projects intent upon constructing ethical modes of "being and doing" in a postmodern world. These knowledges have framed the ethico-onto-epistemologies of Indigenous cultures for centuries: "The interdependency of humankind, the relevance for relationships, the sacredness of creation is returning as a fact of life. It is ancient, ancient wisdom."[44]

We have long made the mistaken assumption that meaning and knowledge can be found and crafted by studying and understanding *people*, *things*, *histories*, and *discourses*, when, in fact, meaning is the product of the encounter itself. The collision of Indigenous ceremony (round dances) and Western capitalism (shopping centers throughout many Canadian cities) constituted the Idle No More encounter, and such an encounter contracts centuries of encounters between European settlers and Indigenous peoples. Any attempts to write a detailed, well-researched, "neutral," history of what took place and what was said during early contact between European settlers and First Nations people in Canada will never actually get at the effects of this contact. The phrase "history is written by the winners" is deafening here. It not only reveals the one-sidedness of any historical narrative, but it also shows that it is not enough to say that we can access the "other side of the story" and then put the two together to create a valid account of what really happened. The entanglement of meaning and mattering means that there can never be *a narrative* of colonial contact, just as there won't be *a narrative* of Idle No More. Any attempts to solidify and codify affords little agency or identity to Indigenous people and continues to enact a violence on the contemporary understanding of the relationship between Indigenous and non-Indigenous Canada.

Likewise, through agential realism, we no longer understand agency as an attribute or intentionality of the human will; it is not something that someone has, but an enactment—not a *thing*, but a *doing*. Applied to decolonization practices, rather than understanding the goal of self-determination (which is often a topic of interest within conversations about First Nations, Métis, and Inuit communities and their agency in Canada), as being able to choose one's own form of governance, healthcare, and legal proceedings, "agency" in such a project is the activity of the "cut" itself as it makes particular choices and forms of self-determination available. Each cut is the product of larger material arrangements that include, among other things, the fact that self-determination is something that is "given" or "granted" and not always already in process; the parameters that surround funding provisions for such "self-determination" (or that it must be given through funding at all); and the issues around which self-determination is granted, compared to those for which it is not. All of these factors contribute to the effects of the encounter and the cuts that are enacted not by human beings alone, but by the material, social, and discursive arrangements with which we are entangled.

Indigenous and Native American scholars write that life, or an ethical life, is both the acknowledgment of, and the expression of, acting responsibly in relation to the infinite relationships one has with one's physical and metaphysical environment.[45] Gregory Cajete discusses Native science as a "*creative participatory process*" such that science isn't the act of studying nature and finding facts and conclusions; it is the process of intra-acting with other entities and in that intra-action creating knowledges, values, and meanings that have lives of their own.[46] The metaphysics of radical intra-connection—or more simply, a belief in the agential interconnectedness of the land, human beings, and animals—is enacted through natural laws of interdependence that are part of ancient, contemporary, and future wisdom.[47] There is no linear time when it comes to radical intra-connection for all encounters are entangled, all times one whole made up of millions of correlations.

When it comes to exploring and fully investing in the resonances between Indigenous philosophies, science, and philosophy, it is perhaps more problematic that we require a particular scientific, philosophical *rigor* in which to understand such forms of intra-action. Indigenous philosophy is often communicated in an entirely different way from Western discourse. It is framed by myth, oral storytelling, sometimes by way of images, and, oftentimes, these modes of communication are belittled and not taken seriously. They need to be rewritten, redefined, and translated through the language of Western discourse. My discussion of Chindoy Chindoy and Rifkin's explorations of time-as-storytelling from Chapter 1 demonstrate that the planes of dialogue, contact, and communication within Indigenous philosophy diverge from other theories and understandings of temporality, but the key is that if a "new reality" is our goal, we need to crack away at the effects of historical cuts that have been made between what counts as knowledge, what counts as philosophy, what counts as science, and how these cuts have maintained divisive Western/Indigenous, subject/object, norm/other dichotomies.

Through a deep, sustained, and also very contemporary engagement with entanglement, matter, and a living temporality, Indigenous philosophies of interdependence have *been here all along*.[48] That is, while we of the Western world are scrambling to find ways to configure our human relationships with each other, with animals, with ideas, and with the environment, we miss the thick time of geographically situated knowledges that have negotiated these relationships for centuries. If we look at the diffractions between vitalism and agential realism, between a philosophy of becoming and Indigenous knowledge, between quantum mechanics and feminist materialisms, we may find tools to shift in the way that we understand each other and we might be able to co-create the language that we need for this new reality. More importantly, we may find tools to deterritorialize the hierarchical models that we are accustomed to relying on in any intercultural conversations. For we are in dire need of alternative means of looking at social structures, our relationships with one another, and our human relationships with the environment, and I sense that these alternative means must be transdisciplinary collaborations if they are to fully address the limits of our existing frameworks, frameworks that have restricted our ability to engage with that which is at the limits of our understanding. Thus our work as feminist activists and scholars becomes the transformative tool not only for revealing normative social, cultural, and epistemological constructions, but also for *making* new realities.

4

"An Erratic and Uneasy Becoming": Queering Time, Reworking the Past

Queer time is a bushwhacked path, a sled's shaky trail, a web of continual reinvention in many different directions.

—Lila, "The Pace of Queer Time"

I came out when I was nineteen. But I have been coming out ever since. Now seventeen years later, I still tell a coming out story. I remember the day, I remember the phrases I used. I remember breathing in nervously as I sat on the stairs of my mother's well-worn wooden deck. *And yet*, that moment, the one I have marked as *the* event was not my first utterance of a queer self. It was neither the most difficult, nor the most vulnerable. It was just one event among many others, events that occurred before, after, and an event that is occurring right now.

In an interview with Raymond Bellour and François Ewald, Gilles Deleuze declaratively states that the *event*, used as a philosophical concept, is "the only one capable of ousting the verb 'to be.'"[1] The coming out *event* enacts precisely this movement: it is less an utterance of a queer self, of *being* queer, than it is a *becoming*, and, as a becoming, the event is a doorway into understanding the living present as it forms and frames our lived experiences of sexuality, gender, and desire. In recent years, we have seen a proliferation of identity categories such as pansexual, demisexual, aromantic, gender fluid, genderqueer, ace, polysexual, demi-gender, and many others. This proliferation really does seem to mobilize the "thousand tiny sexes" that Deleuze and Guattari, as well as Grosz, called for so many years ago and in order to really benefit from the multiplicity of becoming *otherwise*, we would hope that none of these identity categories solidified around subjects.[2] We hope that they would remain open and changing as they continue to contract and expand through new experiences, lovers, expressions, and needs. Unfortunately, this isn't often the case. Within queer communities we continue to fight for rights to medical care, rights for legal partnerships, and equitable representation in social and public society, and, within many of these frames, reliance on the queer *being*, or *subject*, still feels (and is) very necessary to our political aims.

We may characterize these approaches as either identity-based or as based on sexual and gender fluidity. Identity-based arguments link rights and benefits to people's identifications as gay or straight, for example, and such a model bolsters a fixed understanding of gender and sexuality that doesn't allow for movement through and between such expressions. This reminds me of a change in the Saskatchewan Human Rights Code in 2014. Despite clear arguments from individuals and community organizations to include gender expression as protected grounds, alongside gender identity, the Saskatchewan Human Rights Commission only included gender identity.[3] In the years since 2014, every Canadian province that underwent similar legislation change included both gender identity and expression as protected grounds, as did the federal government on June 19, 2017 (Bill C-16). Today Saskatchewan is one of only three provinces and territories that does not include gender expression (alongside Manitoba and the Northwest Territories). By not including gender expression, Saskatchewan's Human Rights Commission aligned with a rights-based discourse dependent upon particular categories, instead of providing protections that extend to more fluid and transitive expressions of gender. Lo and behold! We are back to the drawing room table in 2021, drafting briefing notes to argue for the addition of gender expression as protected grounds within the Saskatchewan Human Rights Code.

The coming out event is a unique occurrence within this terrain, as it is both a performative enactment and a pre-weighted confession within a specific cultural and social context. Coming out is always already marked as an utterance of *being* and our fixation on the coming out event, coupled with this formation, ensures that it serves as a rite of passage, a boundary-making practice that forms the before and after, and the lines between gay and straight, bi and queer, trans and cis, self and other. When I uttered the words "I'm gay" I located myself as a disparate point in relation to the matrix of compulsory heterosexuality and forever changed the place I occupy in the world.[4] My use of the coming out narrative here is directly connected to its passé status within queer theory and philosophy while, at the same time, the coming out event continues to have large uptake within the media, social sciences, and my lived experience as part of various 2SLGBTQ communities.[5] Coming out, thus continues to enact a degree of temporal *drag*, a concept familiarized by Elizabeth Freeman in *Time Binds*.

Referencing the pull of the past on the present, temporal drag is the way in which past experiences within the queer community can issue a sense of delay to the present. In some cases, this drag is productive as it reminds the present to pay heed to the memories, experiences, and knowledges already formed. On the other hand, it can cause the past to stick in places where it should otherwise be open to change. Despite the speech act of "coming out" having been criticized as a boundary-making politic within queer theory (as we will see below), it is a prevailing narrative in queer and trans cultures and subcultures. Coming out is a story (and not a monolithic one) that we tell about ourselves, our relationships, our worlds and, in so doing, it adds to the systems of knowledge that in turn make queer bodies and subjects.

This chapter demonstrates the ways that the living present provides an apparatus through which to explore queer politics without identity—queer and trans subjects without progress narratives—and to look at queer subjects (all subjects) as only and ever the product of material temporalities.[6] I draw on Jasbir Puar's description of these material subjectivities as assemblages, where she writes that "queerness is not an identity nor an anti-identity, but an assemblage that is spatially and temporally contingent." Likewise, Gloria Anzuldua calls subjectivity a river, a process that "needs to flow, to change to stay a river—if it stopped it would be a contained body of water such as a lake or a pond," and I call them time-bodies, or the material-temporal world-makings of bodies, stories, and experiences.[7] My engagement overlaps with these scholars, at the same time that it overlaps with a journalist from *Autostraddle*, Dory from *Finding Nemo*, and focus group participants talking about being Two Spirit. Through blogs, movies, storytelling, community-based research, and the personal anecdotes of leading queer theorists, I stretch the category "philosophy" in order to support my thesis that being is a multiple, non-specious, becoming. As time-bodies, we are embedded in the thick temporalities of the worlds that we inhabit, worlds whose boundaries are only ever applied retroactively. This embeddedness is the instigator for knowledge, ethics, culture, *life*, and thus necessary parts of the story we tell about time.

If we are to stretch "a thousand tiny sexes" backward and forward in ways that *dis*-identify, and *de*-stabilize the queer subject we must also engage with questions such as the following: How do we balance the legitimating force of identity with the creativity and self-determination of our practices of giving account of oneself? How do we tell stories that resist rather than restrict? And how do we live queer lives that make more than history, but rather make new and undetermined futures?

As a framing narrative, coming out enacts the creative self-determination of giving an account of oneself, while on the other hand it belies a monomythic narrative of overcoming inauthenticity and both of these are important to subjectivation. Consequently, it is through the concept of the time-body or the Deleuzian (non)subject that I am able to foreground a thickened, entangled sense of queer time through which we are better able to explore the nuances of lives lived and lives told by gender and sexually diverse people, including the role we all play in the making of novel (queer) futures.

Queering Space/Time

> I would like to be able to attribute my turn to temporality to a rigorous reading of Freud, Marx, or Hegel, or better still Kant, or to a deep and powerful reading of queer history, but in fact most of my ideas come to me in less recognizably scholarly ways. … I am in a drag king club at 2:00 a.m. and the performances are really bad, and some kid comes onstage and just rips an amazing performance of Elvis or Eminem or Michael Jackson and the people in the club recognize why they are here, in this place at this time, engaged in activities that probably seem pointless to people stranded in hetero temporalities.
>
> —J. Jack Halberstam, "Theorizing Queer Temporalities"[8]

As I discussed in Chapter 1, there has been a flurry of material in relation to queer temporalities—or as a freelance writer from the well-known feminist-queer online blog *Autostraddle* states: "queer theorists talk a lot about time. Or rather, queer theorists talk a lot about 'temporality,' which I understand as a pretentious way to say time."[9] This sentiment echoes Halberstam's quote above as each reminds us that although the philosophy of time is dense and complex, *time* is one of the most intimate things we will ever know. To bring up the topic of *time* is to inspire a chorus of eager and interested voices all singing a shared refrain in twelve-part harmony. We know time because we fight it and revel in it every single day. We race time, we luxuriate in time, we cry over time, laugh over time. Not a *moment goes by* that is beyond the reach of time's thick net and so, easily, we are captivated by *time* and all its curiosities of future-past-present, yesterday-today-tomorrow. Today, queer temporalities expand well beyond the academy as various queer writers, bloggers, and artists are taking their own bites out of the topic, but my own obsession with time started with an interest in architecture and spatiality (*just a pretentious way to say space, as Lila from Autostraddle* might say) as I explored texts on space and embodiment as they accomplished the necessary work of reframing and reclaiming queer spaces within the time of gentrification and progress.[10] My interest followed academic movements as scholars also moved from queer geographies of space and place to temporality.[11] If we are to trace the theoretical move from space to temporality within queer and feminist philosophies, we can imagine that, in many respects, this move is recuperative (making up for heteronormative and patriarchal absences), but it must also be cumulative (as spaces change over time, layering welcome signs over past exclusions).

Today, time and temporality are much sexier than space and place, though no more important in an entangled spatio-temporal frame. Of course, time is material as well, but it is much easier to let our feet slip off the ground when talking about time than it is when we are talking about the physical spaces, objects, textures, and sounds that envelope us in lived space. We do well to explore the spatial wake of queer temporalities as they provide some of the thickening agents for our queer timelines and, in fact, when thinking about queer space, just as Halberstam's epigraph reveals, I am similarly more inspired by the random ruptures of lived experience, memory, and movement, as I have enlisted such anecdotes throughout this work.

I am reminded of a night, nearly fifteen years ago, when some friends and I darted into an unmarked alley in a small prairie city and scanned the side buildings looking for the local gay bar. There was a tiny rainbow flag projecting out over an unmarked door about halfway down the alley and it guided us through the darkness. We were too early to be greeted by the usual crowd of smokers, but we could feel the energy of the raucous crowd that would later fill the space with shouts and laughter. We were in pursuit of Diva's, the local gay bar in Saskatoon, Saskatchewan—which, in 2021, is still only able to be entered by way of a back-alley entrance (though today, the entrance is adorned by a lit-up rainbow sign, and its back-alley status is much less a precaution than it is a throwback). Like the "gay bar" of any city, *Diva's* is a unique environment and it occupies a cultural role that regularly swings between transgressive and capitalist, subaltern and normative, spectacle and liberatory. It shows us that *space is never neutral*, and further that, as spaces of alternate social and sexual orderings, *queer spaces* are evolutionary sites, or what we may call "heterotopias."[12]

Foucault first used the term "heterotopia" in the preface to *The Order of Things* in 1966.[13] Discussing the difference between heterotopic and utopic languages, Foucault noted that while utopic languages "run with the very grain of language" and permit tidy narratives, fables, and discourses, heterotopias undermine language by destroying the patterns and knowledges that we use to construct meaning.[14] Heterotopias "shatter or tangle common names.... [they] desiccate speech, stop words in their tracks, contest the very possibility of grammar at its source; they dissolve our myths and sterilize the lyricism of our sentences," a definition that easily reminds me of queer cultural practices such as camp and parody, or pastiche and bricolage, as these queer aesthetics pull together various referents and operate within communities and cultural spaces.[15]

In each case, the sidestepping that occurs demonstrates a space of alternate social ordering, which are also spaces of play. Foucault's more thorough use of the term in his lecture *Des Espaces Autres* ("Of Other Spaces") predicts the rising interest in space within theoretical circles where he states that "we are at a moment, I believe, when our experience of the world is less that of a long life developing through time than that of a network that connects points and intersects with its own skein."[16] Though his lecture long precedes the internet, Foucault foreshadows the sense of immediacy that is both afforded and created by such technology with indications that "we are in the epoch of juxtaposition, the epoch of the near and far, of the side-by-side, of the dispersed."[17] Through this, Foucault illustrates the contingency of spatial understandings to historical processes and knowledges, noting that *space too has a history*.

While Foucault did not himself discuss the subversive potential of the heterotopia, the concept of a liberatory physical/metaphysical space has long enjoyed a playground within both queer theory and postmodern philosophy.[18] Most focus on the fact that space is central to the construction and maintenance of identities and subjectivities and, in so doing, that spaces are saturated with relations of power and power-knowledge. In a short and sweet piece titled "Last Look at The Lex," Gayle Salamon demonstrates this saturation in her lament to the closing of the Lexington Bar in San Francisco. Just as my memories of Diva's are entangled with sounds, smells, and sights, Salamon describes The Lex through its physical reminders:

> One end of the vintage wooden bar is faintly pocked with a few indentations, haptic reminders of shots downed and glasses slammed the night the gay owners of the Eagle Tavern roared in on their bikes to pay their respects to the newly opened dive for dykes. At the other end, tinier circles and crescents, imprints sunk into the soft mahogany from a femme who danced atop the bar one night in her high heels.[19]

As a heterotopic space ripe with history and knowledge, the Lex was a shape-shifter for Salamon: "Living room and seminar room and organizing hall and art gallery and stage set. ... How one space simultaneously manifested so many different places was part of its particular magic."[20]

It is precisely these entanglements that make spatial (and temporal) investigations of queer spaces so valuable as starting points for investigations into the construction, creation, and surveillance of sexuality. The *marked* qualities of spaces such as Diva's and The Lex are particularly salient to queer communities. Whether through hushed whisperings from those in "the know" regarding a local queer hangout, the rainbow flags adorning the street lights on Davies Street in Vancouver, or the stamp of a queer signifier such as the pink triangle that used to mark Edmonton's Play Nightclub, queer spaces are not "normal" spaces; they are doors that open upon worlds where gender and sexuality are central players, rather than outliers.

Heterotopias are also "slices in time."[21] They are places where one is able to break with traditional time, whether through the carnivalesque activities of a festival, the intermittent otherworldly times of vacation villages, or even the time of libraries, which Foucault describes as heterotopias of "indefinitely accumulating time."[22] This encourages the kind of vertical temporal slicing that we engaged with in the reading of Jeanette Winterson's *The Stone Gods* as Billie/Billy and Spike/Spikkers repeated themes in a vertical living present, adding complex layers of memory and history in each contraction. Returning to the back alley behind Diva's in Saskatoon—arguably more of a heterotopic space than the bar itself—it contracts a material past where the single rainbow flag represented a "need to know" privacy. The smokers that spilled out of the bar ducked into nearby alcoves in order to hide from view, and no one entered without a membership. Today, these safety/policing measures are replaced with huge crowds outside and inside the space and, although memberships are no longer needed to enter, there is a shared community history among patrons who remember this past.

While discussing queer spaces and heterotopias, I am also reminded of what constitutes a non-queer space. The physical queer site differs significantly from heterosexual spaces, places, and sites as generally the queer subject assumes all sites are *not* queer. We look for a sign, some symbolic message that we are welcome. This is often the rainbow, but it can also be a welcoming text, a pink triangle, a large "Q," or other components of the (private) cultural language that was developed as a safety mechanism for those on both the inside and the outside. Today, the barriers are not quite as heavy, as the growing popularity of "Safe Spaces" campaigns have helped us move toward more fluid, flexible, and queer-positive spaces, and any teacher, healthcare provider, dance studio, or storeowner can slap a safe space sign on a window or stick a rainbow sticker on their cash register to mark the space as "safe." Although such signs invite 2SLGBTQ people in, they still serve as indications that a space must be claimed "safe," rather than simply being so.

This is one of the many instances where time and space collapse upon one another. Safe space is dependent upon the past-present-future of spatial relationships including the materials (flags, books, art) present, while other times "safe" spaces have no rainbows or flags but are rather created through the presence of queer bodies. Think about sweeping movements to "turn a straight bar gay" that have taken place across North America. These events take place on short notice when queer folks swarm otherwise non-queer bars in an effort to take up space, increase visibility, and increase perceived safety and comfort of otherwise outnumbered 2SLGBTQ patrons. This mode of "coming in" to space is significant. It has uptake that is not explored within the queer "canon" but rather within Indigenous scholarship and cultural conversations.

In "N'tacimowin inna nah'": Our Coming in Stories," Alex Wilson describes the intersections of racism, sexism, and homophobia that Two Spirit people experience. Wilson shares an individual's story of attending a powwow where "safe space" was an event-in-motion:

> When the drumming started, I was sitting still, listening and watching. ... And then a blur flew by me and landed inside the circle of dancers that had formed. ... It was a two-spirit dancing as it should be. After that, more two-spirits drifted into the circle. I sat and watched, my eyes edged with tears. I knew my ancestors were with me; I had invited them. We sat and watched all night, proud of our sisters and brothers, yet jealous of their bravery. The time for the last song came. Everybody had to dance. I entered the circle, feeling the drumbeat in my heart. The songs came back to me. I circled the dance area, and in my most humble moment, with the permission of my ancestors, my eleven-year-old two-spirit steps returned to me.[23]

Wilson reads this story as one of coming in, rather than coming out, where coming in is "not a declaration or an announcement. Rather, it is an affirmation of interdependent identity."[24] As a culturally situated shift, Wilson notes that coming in is an act of empowerment; it enacts the process of understanding one's place within their community, family, and culture, alongside their sociohistorical position in a settler-colonial framework. In this example, it is also a temporal move as it contracts the speaker's youth, and a feeling of freedom that returns only through dance. I return to Wilson's concept of coming in at a later point in this chapter but, for now, the specter of the "safe space" in its variety of expressions continues as a valuable site for gender and sexually diverse people even though I remain curious about the public signification that "Queer Friendly Space" signs create. Will queer space always be *marked?* Will it always need to come forward as *safe?* We don't have answers to this yet, but within community spaces the safe space poster engages multiple readings at once: it is a welcoming in, a gold star of allyship, it shores up a past of unsafe space, and it is an indicator of straight and cis-guilt trying to make amends.

Marking space as safe or queer-positive is as much a project of acknowledging the existence of 2SLGBTQ and other gender and sexually diverse people, as it is an opportunity to think about bodies, beings, and becomings in new ways. Likewise, imagining a queer *time* serves as a rupture to our anticipated timelines. The repeated refrain throughout the scholarship is that queer time sits slightly askew of "heterosexual" time, and as such is able to reroute heteronormativity. Queer theorists have long criticized the overarching structuring of *life* as that which follows a heteronormative trajectory: childhood→adulthood→marriage→children→death. This largely utopic and definitively progressive path renders queer lives invisible in Halberstam's case, literally results in no future for queers, as a queer life is equated with negativity in Edelman's case, and doesn't go nearly far enough in terms of imagining a future where queerness is a collective potentiality in Muñoz's case.[25] The sidestep of queer time, with its elongated adolescence and its fifteen-minute "gay time" delay, thus offers room to breathe, grow, fail, and explore. Kathryn Stockton describes this delay as one of "growing sideways," whereby gay children have a propensity to grow astray during childhood periods due to complicated experiences of being invisible and uncertain. These growth periods include resiliencies, struggles, and unique motivations in a period that otherwise feels stagnant.[26] Stockton weaves the horizontal growth of queer children and adults together such that the two may share a lateral space of shared understanding and experience. This temporal contact zone creates kinship patterns that are also out of step with our familiar heteronormative progress narratives as they jump the timelines between adolescence and adulthood, and within queer communities we regularly see varied ages within social groups. What this has the potential to do is to collapse the heteronormative timelines by bringing intergenerational conversations about coming out, shame, isolation, desire, and expression to the fore.

That said, I am aware that the critique of the "heteronormative trajectory," as much as it impacts real bodies, is also an imagined path that is as limiting for heterosexual people as it is for queers. Anticipatory regimes of marriage and child-rearing (including that assumption that everyone can and/or wants to have children) wield heavy swords against any who don't abide by them—or those who engage with some access points and not others. Though they are referencing primarily queer subjects, McCallum and Tuhkanen's claim that "living on the margins of social intelligibility alters one's pace; one's tempo becomes at best contrapuntal, syncopated, and at worst, erratic, arrested" applies to all expressions of gender and sexuality (of which heterosexuality and cisgender are a part).[27] McCallum and Tuhkanen's sentiment echoes a line from Lila's poetic article about queer time where they share their experience of growing up without role models or images of what their little tomboy self could become. Lila writes, "My path forward never felt like a chronological progression towards a fixed point. But rather a whole lot of fumbling self-discovery. An erratic and uneasy becoming."[28] For Lila queer time is like a "self-declared snow day" or a chance to sidestep the clock-time of offices, norms, and expectations, because such things are not meant for us anyway. In this alternate worldly ordering—*this queer space and time*—there is less an urgency of critique than a sense of play, a slowing down and speeding up of our familiar narratives, and opportunities to dip into humor, playfulness, and the stolen time of a snowstorm.

Halberstam's *A Queer Art of Failure* is a rich testament to this queer levity. Halberstam pilfers cartoons, popular artists, and popular music for shiny and *affective* gems of language, art, and practice, rather than focusing solely on philosophers, feminists, and cultural theorists. For example, Halberstam dedicates an entire chapter to animated films such as *Chicken Run* (2000), *March of the Penguins* (2005), *Bee Movie* (2007), and *Finding Nemo* (2003), illustrating the ways that they revel in the childhood domain of failure, awkwardness, humility, and limitation.[29] Calling this genre "Pixarvolt," Halberstam argues that these films "make subtle as well as overt connections between communitarian revolt and queer embodiment."[30] The chapter itself hops the reader into a time-traveling device, compelling me to go back and remake all of those childhood memories: Might I attribute my love for revolution to *Toy Story*? My interest in feminist materialisms to *Bee Movie*?

For example, Halberstam explores *Finding Nemo*, an animated film about a father-and-son clownfish who are separated from one another when a fishing boat scoops little Nemo up in its net. Marlin, Nemo's father, is terribly timid, having already lost his partner to the sea, and so sets off, rather reluctantly, on a wild adventure to find his son. Luckily, Marlin has help from his friend Dory, a quirky and delightful angelfish (queerly voiced by Ellen DeGeneres), who has no short-term memory. Throughout the film, Dory easily steals the show (even securing her own sequel, *Finding Dory*) and Halberstam conducts an analysis of Dory's remembering, forgetting, looping back, and looping through as an ode to queer time. In particular, Dory's short-term memory loss troubles generational logic through the rupture of forgetfulness. As queer subjects and makers-of-queer-time, we may want to forget the past in many cases, rework or throw out tradition, and rid ourselves of the uncomfortable parts in order to start fresh, to build new traditions and relationships. This stretching toward futures unknown contracts patterns of kinship that have always been different within queer familial groups, as people whose families have disowned them are adopted by others, or friends develop ritualized gatherings around holidays and other "family" times. Of course such kinships also create a sense of belonging and a temporal drag as they bring past into present through memory and nostalgia, and Halberstam's discussion of *Finding Nemo* documents the chosen "queer family" that many of us build from friends and communities. In this case it is the Nemo-Marlin-Dory trio as the father-son trope of Nemo and Marlin are endlessly disrupted by Dory's queerness:

> [B]ecause of her short-term memory loss [Dory] actively blocks the transformation of Marlin, Nemo, and herself into nuclearity; she is not Nemo's mother substitute nor Marlin's new wife, she cannot remember her relation to either fish, and so she is forced, and happily so, to create relation anew every five minutes or so.[31]

The queer family here is not bound to the sexuality of its components, but rather an indicator of its *queering* of the imagined heteronormative trajectory that expects man-woman-children. The queer family, then, far exceeds this definition and can include all range (and number) of parents/mothers/fathers/children/siblings/niblings/friends.

One of the queerest elements of *Finding Nemo* is Dory's inability to support the linear storytelling motif. The absence of short-term memory ensures that her timeline is characterized by fits and starts: "Dory's ... odd sense of time introduces absurdity into an otherwise rather straight narrative."[32] As well, Dory's forgetfulness and time-triggers also show us the passivity of memory as she often (literally) bumps up against objects, other fish, or visuals that trigger contractions of her long-term memory, and long-ago past. These moments exemplify the passive contractions of the past and anticipations of the future that the living present enacts, demonstrating, not that we are oblivious to what's ahead, but rather that we are comingled with our spatial, relational, and temporal environments at all times. Dory's durational comportment shows us explicitly what a disconnected subject really is or, rather, *how a disconnected subject really lives*. Further, Dory's unpredictable timeline is characteristic of what coming out actually looks like for queer people, as it follows multiple, disconnected, disparate, and years-apart paths. I am reminded how in addition to coming out eighteen years ago, I came out last year at a cocktail party when a stranger my partner and I asked to photograph us couldn't understand why we didn't also want our friend to join us in the photo. When we smiled and told her that we were partners she became hysterical with embarrassed glee, as though she had happened upon the greatest exhibit at the zoo and was trying desperately not to look.

Halberstam's playful, humorous work, echoed in Lila's *Autostraddle* piece, and lived uproariously in queer cultures, whether through drag, queer comedy, queer performance artists, or parody, is unfortunately quieter within the academic terrain of queer theory than it used to be. Has irreverence gone out of style? Has it been replaced by a "serious" queer canon? Halberstam's humor is always a reminder for those moments when we take ourselves too seriously. It reminds us that these are our own ridiculous, complicated, and messy lives after all and, if faced with a choice, very few of us would choose to watch *Citizen Kane* over *Finding Nemo*.[33] So what of the coming out event? I find it to be both a line of flight and a yardstick used to measure queer identity formation within our social, medical, and cultural systems.

Come Out, Come Out Wherever You Are

Doctor: "How long have you felt this way?"
Dean Spade: "Does realness reside in the length of time a desire exists?"

—Dean Spade, "Resisting Medicine, Re/Modeling Gender"

After my "coming out" event occurred, I went back and reread the past: all of those best friends that I liked too much, those short-hair phases. "Ah yes," I said, "I have been queer *all along*." "Ah yes," my audience said, "I always knew that about you." For my ex-boyfriends, it confirmed the fact that we didn't work out; for my female friends, it was an opportunity for them to locate themselves within my adolescent trajectory of desire. Every retroactive reading was part of a desire to give an account of oneself, to be able to read one's life as intelligible, as consistent, and the communal uptake of my coming out illustrates the interconnectedness of my story with those closest to me. They wanted it to be their story too. They wanted to understand me and, in so doing, understand themselves.

The performative work of the (coming out) speech act is its role in bringing about a sense of freedom, of admitting a truth long hidden. It is performative in the sense that the act is never merely a reporting, but always the act of "coming out" itself. Illustrating this, Sedgwick references a T-shirt that ACT UP used to sell in New York that read "I am out, therefore I am,"[34]—a visual statement that presents queerness as something which must be stated publicly, lest it does not exist. Our early queer theory texts such as Sedgwick's *Epistemology of the Closet* and Butler's "Imitation and Gender Insubordination," each discuss the way that the performativity of "coming out" is its making of an identity that reinforces and is reinforced by a heteronormative structuring of desire and subjectivity.[35] This process relies on the closet as "the defining structure for gay oppression in this century," and thus the act of opening that closet door is an ontological transference from oppressed to liberated.[36] Not surprisingly much early gay and lesbian activism was intent upon blowing open the closet and increasing the ranks of those that were "out." Activists encouraged closeted individuals to perform the necessary speech act, rallying: "What can you do—alone? That answer is obvious. You're *not* alone, and you can't afford to try to be. That closet door—never very secure as protection is even more dangerous now. You must come out, for your own sake and for the sake of all of us."[37] Some of these projects therefore relied on "outing" known LGBT individuals.[38] For example, activist Peter Tatchell, of the British activist group OutRage!, was a documented proponent of outing public LGBT figures, and well-known US gay rights activist Harvey Milk is also said to have engaged in the practice as a political strategy.[39]

It is easy to understand the desire for a world in which coming out is a thing of the past. However, the concept of "coming out" is exactly that which maintains the inside/outside binary. Our very identities are bound to our deliverance from inauthenticity and being out itself must "produce the closet again and again in order to maintain itself as 'out.'"[40] I remember a headline from 2013 documenting an athlete's coming out: "NBA's Jason Collins Comes Out as the First Openly Gay Athlete in Major U.S. Team Sport."[41] Never mind the numerous professional female athletes who had been out for years, our reliance on a world of "firsts" and "only" repeats itself ad nauseam in an effort to mark the "other" as an anomaly. In this case, the subjectivation of the speech act is threefold. First, it reinforces the value of the liberatory coming out narrative, while second it ensures that the queer subject is a rare creature and thus unthreatening. Its third function in this case is to buttress the heteropatriarchy that places female athletes under erasure and thus reminds us of the operations of gay male misogyny as they denigrate femininity in lesbian, hetero, trans, and other subjects.[42]

In instances of coming out as trans, the story diffracts. Though the confessional speech act still serves a liberatory function there are quite a few differences between coming out as trans and coming out as gay, lesbian, or pansexual/bisexual. In particular, through a study that involved open-ended interviews with nine trans individuals who shared their coming out stories, Lal Zimman teases out a difference between disclosure and declaration in both the interviews and their review of the relevant literature. Declaration refers to the initial act of claiming a trans identity and disclosure refers to the act of sharing one's transgender history after transition.[43] As per the narratives of the research participants, Zimman indicates that the language of declaration aligns very closely with the sociocultural role of "coming out" among LGB people, whereby it represents that momentous act of freedom in breaking down the closet door. However, the linguistic act of disclosure differs from the coming out narrative as it does not serve as an act of sharing a long-held truth about oneself. Given that most trans people don't see the gender they were assigned at birth as a fundamental and true self, there is no "giving an account of oneself" that takes place in the disclosure of a transgender history. Instead it is a (sometimes forced) contextualization of a lived experience and can often be a very private narrative. The act of disclosure can thus have the impact of undermining a trans individual's lived gender, particularly in cases where they are not visibly trans, and where their audience is unable to resist the lure of cisnormativity. Not only that, but due to the entrenched monomythic force of coming out, audiences repeatedly expect trans people to submit to a public narrative of struggle and transformation, an expectation that is not shared by audiences of LGB confessionals.[44]

Of course, the differences here *matter*, as they remind us that speech acts are performative and so "I am a lesbian," as a performative utterance of sexuality, often has the effect of orienting the speaker toward an other (woman), while the phrase "I am trans" orients the speaker in different directions depending on its function as a disclosure or declaration. In the case of the former, the speech act contracts a past that may or may not include various transition activities (such as taking hormones, gender-confirming surgeries, name and pronoun changes, etc.), while the declaration speech act, in Zimman's case, anticipates such activities taking place in a future timeline. To speak of coming out, then, is to diffract the closet around gender as well as sexuality and to pay heed to the differences between and through these various modes of subjectivation.

Such a complicated terrain still straddles the worlds of naming, visibility, and self-identification. Are we reaching toward a queer future where there is no "in" or "out"? Are we paying heed to the power dynamics, vulnerabilities, and hierarchies that contribute to any one individual's navigation of sexuality, gender, and "in-ness" or "out-ness"? It seems as though "outing" projects were exuberantly naive in their assumption that a simple speech act could flip compulsory heterosexuality on its head (just as we have wrongly assumed that equal representation will somehow do away with patriarchy). Today, thirty years later, coming out is still a queer dance between the sacred and the profane. We ask, "Are you out?," of new friends, we slide fingers in and out of a lover's hand depending on the street, and we navigate an inside/outside world where the cold nakedness of an unplanned confession creeps in every time a new acquaintance assumes heterosexual or cisgender identity.

Applying a novel lens to an old story, Wilson's use of coming in reads the coming out event as a Western phenomenon where, rather than serving as a "declaration of an independent identity," coming in is a process of circling back, reclaiming, reinventing, and redefining one's roots and communities.[45] From a temporal standpoint, the coming out/coming in comparison resonates with Mark Rifkin's concept of "settler time" and its differences from Indigenous temporalities. Recognizing settler time as the linear, progress-oriented time that we have discussed at length in this project, Rifkin indicates the colonialism of such a timescape as it expects all others to adhere to its path. Within Canada's colonial history, this proves particularly troubling, as Rifkin is suspicious of attempts to craft a shared timeline between settler and Indigenous communities:

> The positing of inherently mutual participation in the unfolding of time—itself imagined de facto as a line reaching from the past toward the future—contributes to the adoption of a standard model of development in which non-Euro-American conceptions and experiences of time appear as deviations that are transitioning toward a dominant framework.[46]

As we have seen throughout the history of philosophy, any concept of a "natural" time renders non-Western modes of living and understanding time as mythic or storied perspectives, thus stripping them of any role in questioning the linear timelines that govern most Western systems. Wilson's *curving* of the time of coming in, so that it is a circular rather than a linear process, expresses an alternate timeline to what Rifkin describes as settler time, but the key uptake is not that it represents a deviation from the norm, an alternative to colonial time, but rather that it becomes one among many possible heterogeneous temporalities. Rifkin calls for the temporal sovereignty of Indigenous people to create, remember, and participate in a plurality of timelines in order that settler time loses its grip on the present moment—as it is lived by settler and Indigenous people.[47]

As we continue to think about the temporality of the coming out/coming in experience, we can return to Rifkin's rich discussion from Chapter 1 regarding the role of storytelling in creating and remembering the plural timelines of Indigenous people. The *storying* activity of coming in operates to generate everyday relationships between teller and listener, or subject and community, askance of the settler timelines that view coming out as an inside/outside phenomenon. In this way, coming in resonates more closely with philosophies of becoming, as its circular, interdependent form refuses the beginning and the end of the story and instead engages in the making of Two Spirit identity as a place and time of belonging.

With this enriched sense of the storying work of coming out (coming in), the Deleuzian *event* takes up the case. Remembering that the event is more than a "happening," an "occurrence," a locatable entity (that day in April 2000-whenever that I came out to my mom), and instead becomes a potentiality that is "actualized in particular circumstances,"[48] we see that the event cannot be abstracted from what led to its emergence, nor from what it creates. The event is never merely one component in a linear timeline—that is, I spoke my queerness at nineteen because my latent homosexuality had been there all along—and instead, every event ruptures a chronological timeline. This means that the coming out event, though embedded in a preexisting context, has a life of its own, it is a line of flight, pure potential that provides as much opportunity to change the future as it does to transform the past.

Now, there is an important nuance to this understanding of the event for on the one hand we can follow the event entirely, determining its historical preparation, path, and decomposition, while on the other we can entangle ourselves in the event, living in it as a *becoming* and thus "[growing] both young and old in it at once."[49] Through the first path we have the opportunity to trace the event: there was this one time in grade two when I had just cut my hair short. I walked into the girls' bathroom and the older girls gasped and shouted, "There's a boy in the bathroom!" Though it is an entanglement of gender and sexuality, the moment represents a transgressional root and I have returned to the memory over the years and rolled it around in different ways. At first it was deflating; I was ashamed for having been called out so publicly. But as I began to tell the story as an opener while teaching intro women and gender studies classes, it became a badge of honor, my childhood act of rebellion.

But let's try another path. Let's grow young and old in the coming out event at once. As I utter these words I anticipate a future where I am a queer woman living in a world that has no boundaries and no need for a coming out speech act. At the same time I anticipate a moment, two minutes ahead where I am awkward, nervous, I don't know if my audience will be warm. I contract the bathroom incident from grade two, but also kissing a boy under a tree in grade six and being thrilled. I mourn the loss of a heterosexual self, a self that supposedly had a clear and predetermined path, but I am nearly delirious with the anticipation of a queer life and the thought of meeting other queer people one day. I am also rushing through every lesbian, butch, dyke, gay man, queer hero, I have ever seen on television or in the movies (very few) and trying to locate myself within this thin and stereotyped cultural imaginary. I am thinking about what I should *wear*, how I should *talk*, what kind of music I should listen to. This wild temporal roller-coaster is a thick, vertical temporality, and it shows me that there is no "root" for my queer differentiations. Such things are always and only ever read retroactively and every retroactive reading trades in potential for the predictable (a limitless future for a gender-troubled childhood). It is in this moment of at once growing young and old in the coming out event that the materialities of memory come into clearest view: so many moments of my queer life are linked to the artifacts, sounds, and texts that existed as countercultural entities. Likewise, the story that Wilson shares of the powwow experience lives within the embodied experience of dancers moving, circles opening and closing, and the steady beat of the powwow drum.[50] The event is as material as it is temporal.

Rather than giving priority to coming out as a movement from the inside to the outside, or from artifice to authenticity, this unfolding of the "event" enables us to live inside and outside of its power. This means that my particular coming out, the one that for whatever reason I have marked as the "event," is not an axis point in my path of self-actualization and, instead, it is one "cut" among many. The particular speech act has as much presence today, as it did then. In fact, its presence has already grown exponentially the farther I get from that particular time; such is the matter of memory and the stickiness of telling a story again and again (see Figure 4.1). Rather than allowing the utterance "I am gay," "I am trans," or "I am pansexual" to fix us to any given umbrella of gender or sexuality, and thus allowing the event to be merely a causal force in my ability to live a

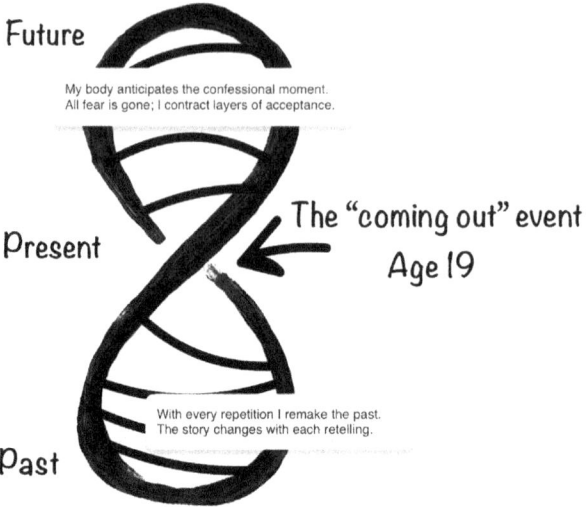

Figure 4.1 The thick time of coming out
Source: Author.

queer life, it is an opening up to this present in a way that lets me ask why I have marked that event as *the* event, and in so doing have overwritten alternate lines of flight as they serve as potentialities for becoming-otherwise.

Now, as indicated above, the coming out event is old news. It is a boundary-making story that has already been told, but I trudge through it here because as it is lived and experienced by thousands of people, day in and day out, it remains an outlier. Academic circles may have theorized its redundancy thirty years ago, but coming out has yet to go *out of style*. In fact, coming out has gone virtual as many youth use YouTube as a platform for the confessional act. In a study of thirty-five different coming out videos within four Anglophone countries (the United States, Ireland, Britain, and Australia), cultural theorist Michael Lovelock writes that coming out on YouTube serves as a community-building strategy to share experiences of "being queer in a straight world."[51] Paying heed to the same queer scholarship that has grown tired of the coming out trope, Lovelock's research findings tell a more nuanced story as he describes the current era of coming out on YouTube as less about a revelation of self than it is a process of self-validation.[52] Likewise, the *coming in* event represents steps of self-determination for Two Spirit people, much as the term Two Spirit operates as a culturally specific term that is applied to both gender and sexuality.

Any coming out story/story about coming out then demonstrates that the coming out event is not easily placed. On the one hand, coming out is the paramount act of "giving an account of oneself," while on another it still references a progress narrative of bringing a hidden "truth" to the fore. In all of its expressions, coming out is entangled with the thick tale of pasts, presents, and futures, which anchors it to not only its teller, but also every single listener for years to come. No subject is free from the sinews, tendons, families (chosen or not), traumatic experiences, or ridiculous celebrations that have layered and unfolded upon one another in the time-body we each call "me."

So how do we live complicated, messy, embodied, desiring, sexed, and gendered lives without *fixing* a static subjectivity? How do we express ourselves outside of the gender binary and without leaning in to progress narratives about what the future should be, could be? The easiest answer is that such transgressive enactments are already taking place. They have been taking place for centuries as humans have always exceeded our categories of analysis (*conditions of possibility*). For effectively, *there is nothing new*, there is just alternate ordering, new assemblages, various contractions of the past that open up novel futures. As this plays out in more specific terms it means that *we are already* balancing the legitimating force of identity with the creativity and self-determination of our practices of giving account of oneself. *We are already* telling stories that resist rather than restrict. *We are already* living queer lives that make more than history, but rather make novel futures and it is through the apparatus of the living present that these lines of flight are brought into view. In particular, the uptake involves a collapse between the dualism of nature-culture and a move toward a Deleuzian subjectivity, which is much less about a subject than it is about assemblages, rivers, and *time-bodies*.

Time-Bodies: The Deleuzian (Non)Subject

Two decades into the twenty-first century, and more than fifty years after the word "post-structuralism" made its debut on the theoretical stage, it is not a stretch to say that we *live* in a post-structural world.[53] That is, we are immersed in a world where plurality, diversity, and change are the norms, we participate daily in the collapse of the divisions between local/global, virtual/real, and singular/multiple via cyberspace and an increasingly global media, and we are constantly faced with a plethora of options about who we want to be and how to shape ourselves as subjects. Queer theory has been at the forefront of these activities, arguing particularly that sexuality and gender are cultural and historical constructs and thereby function more as regulatory fictions than coherent narratives. The benefits of this thread include troubling any attempts to define, naturalize, and biologize both sexuality and gender and the tradition of queer theory has thus given us the tools to understand sexuality and gender as both have been policed, expressed, enjoyed, and lived throughout the centuries. Really, where would we be without Butler's "*In imitating gender, drag implicitly reveals the imitative structure of gender itself—as well as its contingency*" or Derrida's "there is nothing outside of the text"?[54]

Butler's *Giving an Account of Oneself* veers away from her early focus in the 1990s on gendered subject formation to look at the problematic gap that surfaces when we address the subject as the product of our social and cultural makings, and yet still needs a ground for responsibility and accountability.[55] If all we are is performative beings, the product of an external world, what impetus do we have to act ethically? Butler addresses this by arguing that we are ultimately relational beings, and this position makes us vulnerable to one another. As well, even though it is through the act of giving an account of oneself that we position ourselves within the world, we can only ever give partial accounts; we are only ever opaque, both to ourselves and to others. Butler writes that "there is no making of oneself (poiesis) outside of a mode of subjectivation (assujettisement) and hence, no self-making outside of the norms that orchestrate the possible forms that a subject may take."[56] As this connects to our subjectivity, it means not only that our relationships with one another are mediated through an existing social world, but also that our knowledge of ourselves is also mitigated by such a terrain.

Let's think about this in relation to coming in/coming out. As itself an act of poiesis, coming out is entirely contingent upon its contexts. The fact that the act exists at all is a product of the queer cultural imaginary that tells us it is so. At the same time, in many ways we have—at least in a linguistic and theoretical sense— entirely over-conscribed the self, and thus dismissed the body. Butler herself queries, "Have we perhaps unwittingly destroyed the possibility for agency with all this talk about being given over, being structured, being addressed?"[57] Speaking to the gap between our over-conscription to a social constructivism and our wish for agency, Butler draws on our absolute relationality, noting that "none of us is fully bounded, utterly separate, but, rather, we are in our skins, given over, in each other's hands, at each other's mercy."[58] What an affective sentence this is in the context of coming out to an unpredictable audience, as is often the case. When it comes to ethical or moral responsibility, it is precisely this intimacy, this closeness to that which we did not choose, that forms the conditions under which we are to assume responsibility. Although this intimate responsibility has a great deal of uptake (and I return to this in Chapter 6), the affective power of the Butler-Foucauldian subject-performance has a great deal of force within queer contexts, and this performance has its drawbacks.

The theory of gender performativity renders "gender" the consequence of institutions, practices, and discourses acting on the body, and the body, concomitantly, the product of *acting* out the scripts that it has been given. Put another way, performativity is the process of making material what is given discursively (or socially) and, in so doing, revealing gender's contingency. The subversive potential, then, lies in the active construction of meaning that occurs in each and every act, actions that walk a fine line between their adherence to the norm and the fact that there is no original to which they refer.[59] Performativity contracts Foucault's technologies of production, which also illustrate the ways in which gender is regulated, reiterated, and reinforced by hegemonic discourses, and yet is always a process of subjectivation—of subject creation.[60] For both Butler and Foucault, freedom is possible in those rare moments of subversion (the drag performance, homosexual pleasures) and yet more often than not we are trapped within Foucault's panoptic stronghold. As both Butler's concept of performativity and Foucault's concept of freedom demonstrate, we have long been invested in the subversive, the transgressive, the abject, or alterior acts, rather than in unhindered actions of transformation and social change.

That said, rather than assuming that the cracks in the concrete are tied to tiny slivers of freedom, I am delighted by true lines of flight; the powerful actions of chance, intention, life, and transformation that are happening everywhere and all around us, in all pasts, presents, and futures. Coming out is not only transgressive, it is also powerful; asking for trans-specific healthcare in the Yukon is not only subversive, it is also transformative. As feminist and queer scholars, we are often so focused on the practice of critique that we fail to see that we are always already exceeding every technology of power, every restriction of the gender binary, every refusal of bodies and pleasures. Taking up this affirmative stance with zeal, many feminist scholars have worked to reveal the dangers of arguments that the self is wholly given over to systems of control and subjectivation, and thus have shepherded affirmative and hopeful narratives about the body's agency within a seemingly prescribed sphere.[61] As Chapter 3 demonstrated at length, the material turn indicates a shift in our understandings of *matter*—a shift that views matter and more significantly *life* as an assemblage of autonomy, choice, freedom, anticipation, memory, triggers, thrills, and various unfoldings of experience and *affect*.

As a criticism of feminist post-structuralism and its seeming failure to account for the bodies, matter, materiality, and "life itself" that make up our lived experiences, feminist new materialists draw in a durational living present as a reminder that all subjects are subtended by the stories that they tell, and those stories that are told around them. What this demonstrates is that origin stories and quests to live as one's "authentic self" are effective, not only because they are mechanisms of controlling the narrative, but also because they resonate with us as positive experiences, glimmers of hope, and warm memories. They make us feel safe, connected to a larger community, and as though we have purpose and sensibility. This does not mean that we are wholly given over to such narratives, but rather that it is never so easy as to assume that we can break out of the stories within which we are already being told. And also, that there is no clean moral line to be drawn between what a story should and should not include.

The material turn also demonstrates that we cannot fully understand our own environments and experiences without also understanding the effects we have on those things (whether people, plants, highways, or animals) around us, and, concurrently, the effects that such "things" have on us. For an all-too-real example of this co-creative process, let's take up Harry Benjamin's *The Transsexual Phenomenon*, originally published in the 1960s as a clinical guide for the medical community. Benjamin's text relies heavily on the "being born in the wrong body" narrative, which reproduces static understandings of sex and gender as existing entirely apart from medical encounters.[62] Analyzing the impacts of this, J. R. Latham outlines the modes through which Benjamin's text has become self-referential as its step-by-step guide for assessing and classifying trans patients was precisely the text that trans clients were reading in order to access surgery.[63] Latham writes that the "medical phenomenon of 'transsexuality' is self-referentially constituted" on account of the feedback loop between outmoded clinical guidelines and the strategic alignment with said guidelines in order to access desired procedures.[64] This trans identity is locked in to medical categories that require an adherence to binary classifications. The coming out event operates within a similar feedback loop. It exists because it is the story that we tell; it is required because we ask for its relay.

I discussed the inputs of the material turn in Chapter 3 and they are invoked here as they open a door within queer theory to change the ways that we talk about gender, sexuality, expression, confession, declaration, and disclosure in the first place. *How do we make an arrow out of our queerly becoming selves?* My case is that if we move away from *who* and *what* and *how*, and instead look at the *events*, and *becomings*, through which singularities emerge, we are less beholden to the subject, and instead more interested in its *intensities*. We are more attuned to the multiplication of *affect* as each event has the power to create new ways of understanding sexuality, gender, and one's relationship with others.

To speak of *intensity* and *affect* is to shift the conversation from one of difference to one of *differenciation*.[65] Rather than thinking about identity differences as differences *in kind*, as we are accustomed to doing, even—especially?—in our multicultural, gender-diverse, and sexually diverse fields, we turn toward differenciations; that is, variations without end, multiplications without cause. Differenciations refer to the infinite expressions of *being* that are spatio-temporal; that is, expressions of being that are thick, durational contractions of corporeal experience (i.e., memories of what it is like to have homo-sex desire at the high school prom, that pinnacle of adolescent heterosexual development? Or embodied experiences of having a skin color different from 99 percent of the residents of a small settler-populated town?). These timelines also anticipate futures as they impact our movements (maybe a terrible prom experience becomes the narrative that keeps me from coming out for another twenty years) and the movements of others (an Indigenous woman is watched every time she walks into the local grocery store; the town residents construct a story about her without her consent and when a theft occurs, she has no hope in denying a tale that's already been written).

The key here, however, is that although being expresses itself, subtends itself, in varying intensities and durations, this affective spatio-temporal *being*—these time-bodies—exists in the same way for all things. Deleuze's famous claim that "a single voice raises the clamour of being" refers to the fact that everything *is* in the same way.[66] Being is not a genus, species, or a type, but only absolute expression, and so when we talk about identity, diversity, multiplicity, or difference, at base, there is univocity—sameness—and from there we have *differenciation*; that is, multiple unfoldings of difference within a groundless, shared *being*. For example, the table in front of me expresses its being through its flat, hard surface while I express being through my elastic skin. We both *are*, as in *exist* in the same way, but our extensions and durations are unique. Likewise, variations in skin color, divergent sexual desires, and unique socioeconomic contexts do not create different *species*, but rather multiple and unique expressions of a subject that is always already entangled. Differenciation is not numerical or quantitative difference, but qualitative, durational difference such that size, color, shape, presence have no impact on whether an entity or person has any more or less access to existence or being.[67] As this impacts my relationship with the table, it recognizes the equality of our being. The table may feel like a tool for my work, but its presence as an extension in space and time is not dissimilar from mine. It is not a tool "for" me, but exists and persists through, beyond, and before "me." As it impacts the relationships between subjects, univocity flattens all relationships into horizontal heterogeneities; being is the same for all things.

From here we see that our time-bodies are vertical, as well as horizontal. This vertical univocity is not indicative of a hierarchy, but rather a signal of a living timeslice that thickens the present of all beings at the same time that they are in horizontal (and co-creative) relationships with all others. Through this we are able to open up the space for a reworking of the neoliberal paradigm, one that hinges on precisely the most feared postmodern move: the denial of the autonomous, rational, and distinctly humanist subject. This denial does not abandon us as fragmented selves, nor does it turn us into the intersectionally raced, gendered, sexed, classed, and aged subject who reads each identity category alongside the other in an effort to produce a richer genealogy. Instead, subjectivity is multiple; the "I" is entangled, and self is just an offshoot of an otherwise rhizomatic field. This means that not only do the table and I have distinct affective capacities, despite being one and the same in being, but also that our variations or differenciations of being exist only through our entanglement with one another. My elastic skin sits on the hard face of the table—its surface having an expression different from the hardback books that lay beside my arms. Likewise, my elastic skin unfolds as sharp and hard when I poke a finger through a soap bubble, or it expresses as a layered porosity when a needle glides through it, drawing blood from the blue vein within.

For our genderqueer selves, univocity shifts the frame of identity from one of diversity to one of duration. This means that rather than taking difference as our starting point (2-S-L-G-B-T-Q), we might do well to think of gender and sexuality as durational (anticipated harmony notes in a many-part chorus). More clearly, this could be the difference between obsessing over *who* and in what *way* one desires, and using that difference as a basis for identity (i.e. I desire women so I am a lesbian), and instead taking the fact that as desiring *beings*, we are directed toward various others in expressions of longing, dislike, affection, and want, and that these affects are as much a part of our expressed gender as they are a part of our limbs, hormones, genitals, skin. As well, it is through our experiences as desiring beings that we come to know our opaque selves.

The criticism, of course, is that if we flatten the differences between gender, sexuality, sex, and other distinct "pieces" of identity, then we fail to account for the differences in experience or, much more importantly, that we are entirely disloyal to the power differences that impact and shape us. For example, a politic that collapses gender and sexuality fails to see the nuances between being gay in Toronto, Canada, and being transgender in Sokol, Russia. Unfortunately, our anxieties about doing away with identity categories entirely are bound up in the fact that we live to tell linear tales; that is, we require progress narratives that reinforce the hetero-patriarchal modes in which we subjectivize, name, colonize, and identify one another. Thinking being as univocal, and gender and sexuality as durational, means that desire, expression, gender, affection, and even anatomy, are just various unfoldings of a spatio-temporal becoming. This is contrary to the politics of identity that focuses on a variety of unique differences as they comingle; this is contrary to a performative subjectivity, made only in the *doing* that has been the north star of queer theory for the last thirty years. And this even diverges from intersectionality, which, like Jasbir Puar, I argue, relies on a stable fixing of identity across space and time through its need for a logic of equivalence and analogy.[68] Making a case for queerness as assemblage, Puar determines that intersectionality relies too heavily on its component parts (race, class, sexuality, nation, gender), whereas the assemblage is made up of "mutually implicated and messy networks" that operate through organic and nonorganic forces.[69] This move to thinking race and sex (along with other identities) as *events*, rather than static categories, means that such entities are no longer tied to a particular subject *position*, but instead to expressions of a world that is primarily one of process after all. In this way, Puar's terrorist assemblages are a "cacophony of informational flows, energetic intensities, bodies, and practices that undermine coherent identity … and by-pass entirely the Foucauldian 'act-to-identity' continuum that informs much global LGBTIQ organizing," not unlike the multiplicity of times over and above precise moments and countings that quantum physics entertains.[70]

Returning to the acronym example, if we were to approach the situation through a durational univocity, first of all, it wouldn't be helpful to just throw out the entire acronym on account of its solidification of particular identities, because this thoroughly shuts down the potentialities of the project.[71] Instead we might want to look at the situation according to those outcomes that multiply intensity and those that limit intensity. For example, does the ever-expanding acronym open up possibilities for expressions of sexuality? Yes, in some ways it does: it provides a space for people to find a sense of belonging and support. Does it limit such expressions? Yes, the very delineations of "straight," "lesbian," or "gay" have acted as the structural determinations of how one understands oneself and consequently how one expresses oneself at the expense of other possibilities. The mere addition of other "types" to the list, then, remains caught within this territorializing paradigm. Puar might describe this as a tool of "diversity management" such that when identities are so easily cleaved we remain fixated on positioning ourselves within specific locales and fixed timelines.[72] This ensures that we do not see subjectivity as durational (as an unfolding process) and that we continue with processes of "excavation, restoration, and visibility" rather than upheavals of the unquestioned ground.[73] Instead we might want to look at things like the following: What possibilities does a practice of *coming in* engender? What possibilities of expression are enabled when a family works diligently, bravely, fiercely to raise a child without pronouns? Or how do the hauntings of our queer archives give us both cement-soled shoes and wings for flight?

This means that what I am calling my own queerness is not some inherent essence of sexuality or desire, nor am I the mere product of technologies of power as they enclose upon me. I am instead an interplay between social, technological, biological, and cultural factors and the key is not to gloss over each contributing factor, as this is not just an act of hand-waving at multiplicity, but an acknowledgment of differenciation. The social makes sexuality through inclusions and exclusions, through memories of a friend leaning in with curiosity when I come out and anticipations of another going cold and stiff. Each of these experiences (even those yet to come) acts on the present as I gauge my audience, position my body, or select a location for the "event." The technological makes sexuality through various reproductive technologies as they serve and do not serve queer couples looking to reproduce. Queer families are made and understood through adoption, acquiring sperm from friends and sperm banks, or tens of thousands of dollars' worth of debt for those that venture into surrogacy and in vitro. The biological makes sexuality through the gendered coding of genitalia, it also does so through discoveries of the complex sexes, biologies, sexualities, and expressions that show up in animals, plants, and nature.[74] Finally, just as each of these is an unfolding differenciation and not a unique *affect*, culture is influenced by nature, sociality, and technology as it ebbs and flows throughout all aspects of production.

To think of selfhood and this ephemeral and fierce thing called identity in this way is to embrace an onto-epistemological shift in understanding.[75] The shift is ontological in the sense that *being* must be rethought according to an embodied and contingent framework, and epistemological because the meanings and knowledges we associate with bodies are also the product of these relations. Consequently, Jason Collins's performative speech act as the first openly gay athlete operates within an embedded apparatus, one that includes, among other things, the sporting environment he is a part of (from advertising to uniforms), the material anxieties that surround the queer sporting body, and the marking of the male as the universal human subject, a marking that overwrites a history of female athletes. All of these factors contribute to the intelligibility of Collins's newly queer *life*, and his anticipated path toward self-actualization.

While we tend to trace the telltale signs of queerness to a known "identity," or read the lack of signs as indication of an even deeper closet, even greater artifice, the durational, univocal subject works to destabilize a structural understanding of signs and symbols as referents to an elusive ideal. For, in fact, there is no "real," no queer, no lesbian, no gay man to which one's behaviors do or do not refer; there is only an entangled bodily comportment, not unlike that confluence of forces that makes up the event. Put more philosophically, life is always a radical immanence so that "there is no inside/outside, no origin and end."[76] There is no gap between the sign and its referent, between culture and nature that allows us to read a biological body apart from its entanglement within various systems of language, feelings, and politics. And although I draw on Deleuze for this argument, it is not his argument to make, for the absolute entanglement of matter and meaning, self and other, the "you" and the "I" is as old as it gets. Deleuze attributes univocity to Duns Scotus, Spinoza, and Nietzsche[77]—but we can also find echoes of durational univocity (a living present) in Indigenous worldviews and philosophy, in Buddhist and Taoist teachings.[78] Each of these exemplifies the case that "the self does not stop with just you, with your body. The self penetrates other things and they penetrate you."[79]

This is the living present. By collapsing a structural understanding of the subject, so reconfiguring not only the teleological "coming out" narrative, but also the monomythic and retroactive temporality that makes a coherent queer subject, we can understand the event as one among many, as an opening onto the multiple ruptures that occurred in my childhood, adulthood, adolescence. These ruptures, as spatially situated (my thrilling and terrifying first visit to Diva's Gay Bar) and temporally affective (the contraction that takes place every time I see—or think of—the back-alley entrance), serve as memorials to past fears, and open upon a present queer self that moves joyfully ahead. I am not denying that there is a retroactive telling that will inevitably happen, nor that there is not value in remembering those moments when I did not adhere to heteronormativity, or when I was afraid, but those moments are not mine alone. To adhere to an origin story that retells my life according to a closeted queer identity is to stagnate and solidify the many events that were already rupturing a normative timeline, the events that are stagnated just as much by a queer identity as they are by a heterosexual identity. The myth that one can actually "come out" only once erases the hundreds of times that one must continue to negotiate awkward phone calls, heteronormative assumptions, and, hence, must come out again and again and again.

This "uneasy and erratic becoming" *queer* is relational movement. It is a future that remembers and a thick time that remakes the past in the present. This becoming-queer pays no heed to realizing and actualizing the self; it "does not flourish into presence, but bears a capacity to annihilate itself, to refuse its *ownness*," as Colebrook writes in "Queer Aesthetics."[80] For becoming-queer is to never arrive. It is an opening up to Deleuze and Guattari's thousand tiny sexes, but a refusal to name a single one. Although the coming out narrative will continue to have temporal weight in a rights-based moral economy, a Deleuzian (non)subject demonstrates that, indeed, to "come out" is not to open the door on a life that has been closeted, but rather it is an encounter between a life and a set of material forces that always have the potential to overcome the self-as-subject-of-desire. To queer time, then, is to refuse to make a life, any life, structurally coherent, for the potential for becoming-otherwise only works when a queer life is an event out-of-time.

5

Thick Time: Echoes of the Anthropocene

Every text is a time capsule and a time machine, containing the present, but sending the present into a future that the present cannot control.
—Claire Colebrook, "The Anthropocene and the Archive"

The most important thing to know about prehistoric humans is that they were insignificant animals with no more impact on their environment than gorillas, fireflies, or jellyfish.
—Yuval Noah Harari, *Sapiens*

Imagine you are back in your high school biology classroom.[1] The walls are lined with charts, maps, and pictures of flora and fauna. There's a pet turtle at the back of the room in an old aquarium and a row of dusty glass jars holding insects, reptiles, and eyeballs suspended in clear jelly. There may be a poster of Darwin's species of finches from *On the Origin of Species* on the wall, or maybe even the iconic image that shows human evolution from apes (see Figure 5.1). A blue-and-green globe sits idly on your teacher's desk, used more to play the game of "where will I live when I grow up" than for geographic education.

Though it is far from a tidy tale, "man's" evolution is often presented according to the linear pathway in Figure 5.1, whereby an ape reaches progressively upward until he is standing upright, his arms have shortened, his legs lengthened, and his civility has been sufficiently archived. In this map, evolution is a series of stages. Pre-"man" is Australopithecus, who overlaps slightly with homo habilis, all the way to "modern man": homo sapiens. The progression is cumulative as "man" evolves, acquires skills, and creates tools. This arborescent model is familiar to us; it satisfies our longings for progress and our addictions to the hero's journey. The more interesting thing, however, is that rather than representing a single species, or a lone hero, as recently as 100,000 years ago there were possibly six different species of the genus *homo* that lived in different parts of the Earth *at the same*

Figure 5.1 Human evolution
Source: Tkgd2007 © CC BY-SA 3.0 (https://creativecommons.org/licenses/by-sa/3.0>, via Wikimedia Commons).

time (see Figure 5.2). In a popular nonfiction book called *Sapiens*, Yuval Noah Harari disrupts the fable of the mono-species by tracing the timelines of many species of what we now call *human* and, in so doing, Harari weaves rhizomatic webs instead of arborescent trees. Deleuze and Guattari contrast arborescence with the rhizome, where the former refers to theories and ideas that are built like a tree, from the ground up, while the latter forms webs and random growths, like the roots of strawberries or grass. The difference is the creation of vertical and hierarchical ideas in the case of arborescent thought systems and horizontal and decentered systems in the case of the rhizome.[2] Harari's popular nonfiction text is far from a scientific study, but he is not wrong in his multiplication of the species *homo* nor in his claim that early clans of human beings were no different from a smack of jellyfish or a herd of giraffes in terms of environmental and intra-animal impact. It wasn't until somewhere between 12,000 and 30,000 years ago that homo sapiens began to make a name for themselves. Whether through uses of language, social patterns, the development of more sophisticated tools, or their swift rise from the middle to the top of the food chain, humans started to take steps toward industry, economic systems, infrastructure, and capitalism.

Today, "man's" pinnacle position is a given. Not only are we the masters of time, history, and language, but we also increasingly think about the world as a global landscape. In many ways this is valuable, as we can trace the impacts of

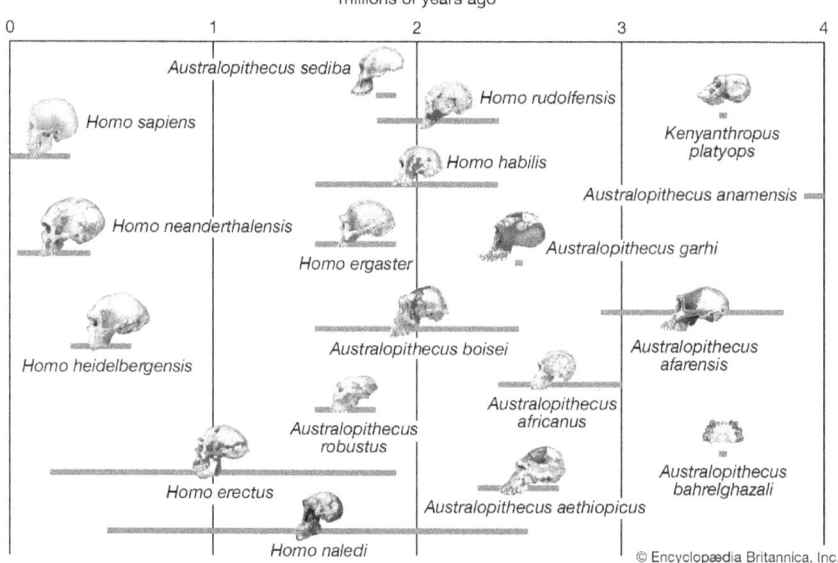

Figure 5.2 Tentative phylogenetic schemes for hominid evolution
Source: 2018 by © Encyclopaedia Brittanica, Inc. (reproduced with the permission from Encyclopaedia Brittanica).

garbage that has been dumped into the Atlantic Ocean for fifty years to the rising temperatures and increased acidity of the Mediterranean Sea. At the same time, it is dangerous as it breeds apathy in our day-to-day choices; if we are just one among millions, what can our actions really matter? Hopefully our knowledge of widespread human impact on the Earth gives us pause, but more likely it reinforces the sense that the small spinning desk globe from our high school biology classes is merely our plaything; the world is small and, in the global landscape, it is seemingly within our grasp.

I bring up these old stories about evolution because so many of the stories that we tell, the histories that we make, and the futures we create are bound up in our grand human ego. We fixate on our capacity for rational thought, opposable thumbs, the ability to walk upright, self-awareness, propensity toward cooperation, and our mastery of fire, as skills and characteristics that set us apart, but remember that we also have the "dubious distinction of being the deadliest species in the annals of biology."[3] Like Harari, many climate change philosophers have spent a great deal of time flattening the landscape and reminding us that homo sapiens are just one species among many.[4] Not only are we one human species among many nonhuman species, but throughout Earth's duration we are just one human species among many others, and many that lived much longer than homo sapiens is likely to live. Perhaps more than any other topic I have discussed in this work, the landscape of evolution, human and geological history, and the lightning fast (and terribly slow) speeds of climate change are indications of the need for both an apparatus of the living present and, relatedly, for a renewed relationship to *time*.

In most of today's contemporary "climate change imaginary" we are caught between the desire to save or sustain an abstract "environment" and a tendency toward denial or a deflection of environmental concerns.[5] The former may be enacted through alarm bells about decreasing populations of the honeybee and satisfied by our efforts to eat locally or to purchase honey that has been marked with a label of "sustainable," while the latter comes into play when the warnings reach their tipping point, when our imagined potential to *act* gives way to derealization and apathy. *I am not responsible. I cannot do anything to change this.* The parallel operations of each of these projects, however, construct "climate" as something far away, disconnected from our everyday experiences, and they indicate that rather than imagining (and creating) new possibilities for thinking about and engaging with *Earth, climate, history*, we are often bound by anticipations of a future that is already determined.

This politics of futurity is directly connected to the language of sustainability, the framing of efforts to *sustain* or *maintain* the Earth's ability to meet the needs of future generations. And although the stamp of "sustainable produce" whets the whistle of a growing population of young, upwardly mobile adults, a critical understanding of what constitutes sustainability, or rather, sustainable development remains absent. Not only does sustainable development assume the "inexhaustibility of natural resources," but alongside warnings of glacial melt, endangered animal populations, and the loss of plant species, it also endorses a view of nature as the fixed and external milieu against which human beings construct and maintain civilization.[6] The ubiquitous "environment" is perceived as outside of and beyond us, and it is clear that to *sustain* is to *hold up* a world reliant on liberal humanism's firm dichotomy between human and nonhuman, a world in which human civilization is able to prosper.

But what if nature is "neither a passive surface awaiting the mark of culture" nor "the end product of cultural performances" as Karen Barad writes?[7] What if the processes of a multispecies *materiality*—homo sapiens, homo erectus, bodies, plants, highways, discarded bottles—are creative in the makings and unmakings of this thing we call "climate change," this thing we call "world"? Donna Haraway's naturecultures have long indicated this entanglement, as they illustrate the co-constitutive relationships between the imagined categories of "nature" and "culture."[8] Building on Haraway's naturecultures, Barad has enlivened our understandings of matter by making visible the quantum enactments of materiality, that is, the way that material particles do not preexist the encounter with an objective observer, but rather come into being/meaning through the dynamism of a relational interaction.[9] Each of these developments demonstrates that our anthropocentric framings of nature always enact a violence as they position the human subject as the pole around which ecology is ordered. This model ensures that "nature" itself has no agential role in the climate change imaginary or, put another way, this ensures that earth, land, and sky have no agential roles in our dreams of a future that is otherwise.

Now, I cannot transcend this human body, assembled of flesh, bones, and thoughts that I take to be my own, so I cannot represent the thoughts of naturecultures, *or the practices of the honeybee*, any more than I can assume that my white, academic ponderings on climate are at all relevant to another's lived experience. But I can *imagine* collaborative rhizomes that try to invert, upset, or otherwise trouble a human-centered approach. I am also reminded that we have been here before and we will be here again; there is no "new," there is only an eternal *differenciating* return. In order to explore the thick time of climate change, and to see the impacts of a thick time on our living present, we must reorient the frames through which we ordinarily construct meaning about Earth. This involves talking about our environments, climates, and even our naturecultures in ways that dig deeper than causal crisis narratives, and it involves changing the ways in which we frame and differentiate between things, beings, time, and space.

I characterize this anticipatory politic as an "echo of the future." An echo, in this context, is a powerful contraction of the past that opens upon unknowable futures. One such echo is the Anthropocene, a potential new epoch that scientists are presently debating. By mapping both the scientific and philosophical engenderings of the Anthropocene as it is already at play in our naturecultures, we are able to see the ways that it demonstrates the entanglement of matter and meaning. In a very material sense, it represents the geographical time-scale that is as much a part of our time-telling (and history-making) as it is part of the futures we are creating. Following this, this chapter diffracts conversations about climate with bodies, knowledges, and environmentalisms as they serve as powerful contractions (*echoes?*) of a thick materialist temporality. An uptake of this durational echo is its demonstration of the fact that the future can never be "new," that is, the future can never be produced in a vacuum; it is deeply connected to the conditions that lead to its emergence, the material pasts that are layered within any experience (the eternal return that cycles us back to the hero's journey, again and again). Thus, both the actual events of climate change and the discourse surrounding it (as if these aren't already entirely connected) serve as clarifying examples for a methodology of the living present as a means by which to look, listen, and learn from a durational time.

Echoes of the Anthropocene

> And at once, I knew I was not magnificent.
> —Bon Iver, "Holocene"

Thinking the "new" is no stranger to philosophy. We are addicted to new technologies, new bodies, new theories, new models, a new epoch, a new *Earth*. The map of "man's" evolution satisfies this desire with its ever-forward movement, its figure that transforms from mere animal to civilized being. This *being* stands upright, is taller than the rest, and no longer carries a weapon, for his weapon is his mind. There is often a sense of longing that accompanies our want of the new: maybe the future will be more interesting, compelling, unique, we wonder. Maybe it will ease our pain, lessen our burdens. Ultimately the new is inspiring not because it is unknown, but because it is a reprieve. It tells us that there is a future that we haven't even thought of yet. There are possibilities beyond our present and past imaginations. *There is hope.*

The call for the new surfaces in most writing around climate change, such as Melissa Nelson, who reminds us that "we cannot solve our global crisis with the same thought process that created it," a phrase that contracts Einstein's famous "we cannot solve our problems with the same thinking we used when we created them," and diffracts Audre Lorde's "the master's tools will never dismantle the master's house."[10] This game of repetition and difference reminds us that the sensationalized fears of climate change, global pollution, and overpopulation are translated into a discourse of global crisis. As well, they echo philosophical and scientific scholars around the world who are increasingly calling for a paradigmatic shift in the way we view the relationship between human beings and the natural world, given that our current methods only offer the same outcomes *over and over again*. So, what if what we call "new" is instead an echo?

The eternal return of the same? Because thinking about an echo, alongside this urgency, reminds us that calls for paradigmatic shifts in thinking are not *new*. Talk of needing to renew the relationship between human beings and the natural world is not *new*. Arguments that hierarchical, neoliberal ideologies govern environmental, social, and political policies globally and will continue to perpetuate inequities between different cultures, between humans and nature, and between humans and nonhuman animals if they carry on the way that they are, *are not new*. And yet, we hope that the alternatives will be "new," "unthought," "transformative." We hinge our hopeful hearts on the possibility that the future will be unlike the present, and even less like the past, and, yet, we continue to repeat without difference.

The echo is a contraction of the past. *All pasts*. At the same time, an echo stretches forward as it reverberates an eternal return through its repetition. *An eternal return that is only the return of difference*. An echo of the future, then, is both the anticipatory politic that fixes our timeline and the novel event that Deleuze's third synthesis of time promises us. As we stretch out along timelines that are short (the life cycle of a honeybee) and long (the 22-million-year life cycle of stratigraphic rock formations), we engage with various speeds and slows, various temporal events as they change our spatial landscape. Throughout this, we also recognize that, on account of the historic linguistic gaps between "nature" and "culture," *ecological echoes may well be the hardest to hear.*

Today we are still in the epoch known as the *Holocene*. The Holocene followed the last ice age and, throughout its nearly 12,000-year life span, it has provided a relatively stable incubation for the proliferation of humans, plants, and animals. That said, as I type this sentence, the world stage is holding its breath in anticipation of a new epoch within the Geological Time Scale. This epoch is the *Anthropocene*, and, although it is the subject of hundreds of scientific articles and arguments, the term has been popularized primarily within philosophy and critical theory as it presents rich fodder for political and ethical conversations. Scientists define the Anthropocene as the age of human impact, such that geologists and stratigraphers are now able to measure anthropocentric processes as they have added to Earth's landscape.[11] The term was coined by Eugene Stoermer in the 1980s, and gained traction through its use by Paul Crutzen and Stoermer in the early 2000s.[12] Although Crutzen and Stoermer originally dated its inception to 1784—the invention of the coal-fueled steam engine—the Working Group on the Anthropocene charts its emergence within the middle of the twentieth century, the dawn of the nuclear age.[13]

When scientists say that the proposed Anthropocene marks human changes to Earth's landscape, they are not referring only to the warming of our atmosphere (and glacial melts) or to Northern wastelands where resource extraction has ravaged the land, and ecosystems are not able to re-root. They are referring to the layers of plastic, microplastics, discarded metal and bricks that have *become* part of our stratigraphic layers. There are rocks forming on the coasts of Hawaii that are called plastiglomerates and are made up of fused molten plastics, basalt clasts, and coral fragments.[14] The proliferation of dams across rivers means that riverbeds are sediment-starved and their composite layers lack stable material entirely and cannot physically support the increased water flows from glacial melts.[15] And the combinations of overfishing and warming sea temperatures have meant that jellyfish are reproducing at record-breaking rates.[16] So, riverbeds are washing away, Hawaiian beaches are *becoming-plastic*, and jellyfish are plotting world domination, all indicating that the Anthropocene is not only a record of "man's" devastation of the Earth, but also of our human-made materials becoming a part of the natural ground beneath our feet, the air that we breathe, the water that we drink. This fusing of nature-technology-culture-biology is the ultimate spatial-temporal-material entanglement, though it is much less a site of wonder and awe than it is one of horror.

Despite its widespread use within scientific, cultural, and political texts, formal adoption of the Anthropocene as a geological time period (thus indicating the end of the Holocene) requires scientific justification in the form of a clear stratigraphic sign reflected in the geological timescale. There is an anticipatory angle to the debates about instantiating a new epoch, as they evaluate the Anthropocene on whether or not geologists (thousands or millions of years in the future) will be able to look back to see a human trace. What a curious yardstick. To think that an age, which is predictively bringing about mass extinction of animals, plants, and fauna, and, most likely, all of humanity, can only exist if it can be determined that it will be recognized by mythical geologists *to come*. Also, although origin stories for various timescales are very much a part of our present, the boundary-making of a new epoch has never aligned with a calendar date that living humans have themselves crossed. And likewise, the death of an epoch has never occurred simultaneously with our written history.

In a mock obituary *Time* magazine remembers the Holocene epoch as a "warm, stable climate" that made possible the "flourishing of Homo Sapiens." Its accomplishments included a hospitable climate for plant and animal life, as well as the invention of writing, while its fallbacks include the extinction of the woolly mammoth and widespread deforestation.[17] The *Time* article's levity counteracts the intense debate that is waged around the adoption of the Anthropocene, as another argument centers on the fact that we can't move to another epoch because we haven't had enough *time* to measure it (its physical manifestation is too small). A shift to the Anthropocene would drastically shorten the Holocene's life span, which, at only 11,650 years, is much younger than its ancestors—the Pleistocene lasted 2.5 million years, while the Eocene was 22 million years long. Again we are confronted with various measures, speeds, and slows, as evaluations of the Anthropocene's validity hinge largely upon how *fast* it has impacted the Earth, thus demonstrating by default that the slow and stable movements of the earlier Holocene are preferable. Somehow human "intervention" has "sped up" the timeline, but no one is asking to whose timeline we defer.

Today, geologists, stratigraphers, and environmentalists haven't levied a final verdict on the Anthropocene, but that hasn't stopped (and has likely encouraged) philosophers from employing the term in full force. Bringing the scientific and literary longings in line, Claire Colebrook asserts that we are propelled forward through imaginings of a present-made-future whereby "we might then imagine our own present, our own self-archiving as if it were already being read by nonhumans, beyond our own existence."[18] Anticipation of a posthumanity to come (just like the geologist-to-come) impacts our archive (and our science), and philosophers recognize the ethical potential for such an anticipatory rupture as it brings us face to face with the best and the worst of ourselves. Andrew Revkin writes:

> Some will see this period as a "shame on us" moment. Others will deride this effort as a hubristic overstatement of human powers. Some will argue for the importance of living smaller and leaving no scars. Others will revel in human dominion as a normal and natural part of our journey as a species.[19]

Thus, the imagining (and therefore creating) of a new Anthropocentric epoch is both humiliating and egomaniacal. But what is more telling is that the Anthropocene forces us to face *nature* as no longer the background against which culture dances and turns—as it demonstrates whatever happens sticks with us. Nature is no longer an "outside" or an "away," as the supposedly "fixed" natural laws have clearly never been fixed and, further, the perceived autonomy of politics and culture has been nothing but a hopeful dream, given the heated political import of plastiglomerates and impending jellyfish attack.[20] What this shows us is that we are well beyond the point of "purity," the topsy-turvy world(s) of the Anthropocene actually overthrows our progress-oriented politics, despite desperate grabs at order. Our messy, devastating, and often hopeless, present provides a continual reminder that we are always "in the middle of things"; there will be no end to climate change, just as there was no beginning. What really matters is our ability to better understand our complex and multiple present accountabilities within an otherwise incomprehensible process of change.

The Anthropocene may be terrifying but, more than anything before, it demonstrates that humans, trees, air, texts, and even plastiglomerates are all time-bodies. Remember that time-bodies are the embodied recognition that we (rocks, tables, humans, woolly mammoths) are the *makers of time.* In its most prolific uptake outside of scientific circles, the Anthropocene has been the justification for the material turn explored in Chapter 3. Feminist materialisms arguably provide material evidence for the entanglements of human-nature-meaning-climate. The field has been dominated by feminist and queer scholars as contemporary feminist arguments do not simply fight for personhood (first wave) or for equal rights between two genders (second wave), nor even for intersectional inclusion of multiple forms of structural power (the Butlerian-Foucauldian third wave). These feminist materialisms are critical to conversations about time and matter as they illustrate the preeminence of the text and its failure to write *life*.

Ultimately, the material turn is not about dismissing discourse; rather it is about reconsidering the onto-epistemological boundaries that hold nature and culture, body and mind, self and other at arm's length in the first place. And so, what do we do with these naturecultures? How is the Anthropocene more than a stratigraphic layer? How are our water bodies echoes of the future? One place to start is through not thinking of the human body as a distinct, autonomous entity, and instead as "always intermeshed with the more-than-human world"; always "inseparable from 'the environment.'"[21] Our habits of viewing nature as the background to our human activities or the store of resources for human consumption all fail to comprehend a world of "fleshy beings, with [its] own needs, claims, and actions."[22] We are, therefore, pushed to comprehend not only the corporeality, that is, the *bodily natures* of plants, bodies of water, birds, and amoebas, but also the agency of these entities; they each operate in millions of seen and unseen ways. In fact, once we are attuned to it, it is easy to see, feel, and smell the ways that our seemingly distinct human lives are absolutely interconnected with all other *bodily natures*: for nature "is always as close as one's own skin—perhaps even closer."[23] This fact is no more visceral than when we endure smog warnings, or cut ourselves on a tiny sliver of tree-turned-paper.

Think back to the dusty globe on your biology teacher's desk. The fact that we have a physical entity, this spherical and contained Earth, lends itself to our understanding of a world. This is the "kick back" without causal force, for remember that this process is passive where passivity refers not to slowness or absence, but to an indiscriminating affectivity. It is demonstrated by the slow roll of our desert stone, just as much by the melting ice caps that kick back with floods that wipe out entire cities, and sea levels that creep up to cover homes and fields. This returns us to the "climate change imaginary" that I attended to in the introduction to this chapter, a narrative that is far less a story about the past's impact on future climate than it is an anticipatory creation of a future in peril. Through each of these scenarios, it is clear that agential realism is not a concept of autonomous agency (which depends upon a human consciousness or a sense of intentionality), but rather the activity of the *agential*, that is, a force that doesn't necessarily need a conscious mover. It is the very processes of creative encryption, as Kirby describes them. It is the biotechnologies that have shown us the vitality of embryonic stem cells, it is the colonial unfoldings of water, it is the slow movement of a desert stone. None of these processes attend to a teleological narrative and, yet, each clearly transforms and enacts the stuff of "life itself."

Climate *Matters*

The material turn, along with the intra-activity of agential realism, provides a method for reimagining our environmental processes as well as contemporary climate change discourses, not only because they open us up to an entangled terrain of naturecultures, but also because they reveal the agential role of the stories that we tell in making a *time* of climate—that is, in telling an origin story about climate change, solidifying its impact and its identity, and, in so doing, limiting or proliferating its possibilities for past, present, and future events. Let's walk through this temporal uptake alongside the example of the jellyfish.

As a result of warming ocean temperatures and overfishing, jellyfish have enjoyed ideal conditions for growth and reproduction. The consequence is that environmentalists and marine biologists are raising alarm bells with articles about the anticipated invasions of the "cockroaches of the sea." Stacy Alaimo takes up the discourse surrounding the jellyfish, noting that "the jelly-fish, which seems barely to exist as a creature, not only because it is a body without organs but because it is nearly indistinguishable from its watery world ... [is] nonetheless thriving, provoking fear of a clear planet in which jellies over-populate the degraded oceans, causing harm to fisheries, mining operations, ships, and desalination plants."[24] In this predictive future, jellyfish are our apocalyptic aliens, representing the roles of victim and villain. And as neoliberal platforms operate, the "kick back" of nature, or its refusal to operate according to "man-made" systems, is an important point here, for this capitalist system will undoubtedly cast the jellies as enemies, as harming not only human production, but also the ecosystem of the ocean. Such a framing legitimates forms of human intervention, control, and policing. But, what does it look like if the jellyfish is neither victim nor villain, and instead the protagonist in an altered tale? If we take a diffractive materialist reading of the situation, we can think of the jellies as agential phenomena. As Alaimo notes, by submersing into the world of the jellyfish, we may be able to create "complex mappings of agencies and interactions in which—for humans as well as for pelagic and benthic creatures—there is, ultimately, no firm divide between mind and matter, organism and environment, self and world."[25] Jellyfish, in fact, enact ethical and cultural scenarios that we would do well to take account of before wiping them out, just as Haraway's naturecultures create new worlds each time they are invoked in place of our familiar dualisms.

For example, in a short film that I often use in an intro queer theory class, the jellyfish is stretched around queer fluidity. Coral Short's "Genderless Jellyfish" (2014) shows images of pink, purple, and yellow jellyfish moving through the sea while the narrator gushes about this unique creature: "Oooo, so flexible, so fluid. That's because they are made of over 95% water."[26] Here, the jelly is the ultimate water body as its watery subjectivity is a body-without-organs-without-bones. Short whispers, "Did you know some jellyfish have male and female organs in their body? They don't give a shit about gender. They are badass." In this story-telling-world-making, jellies are the genderpunks who have never even heard of the binary. Jellyfish also disrupt any timeline as they stretch beyond the Anthropocene, beyond the Holocene, beyond the Paleocene and the Eocene. Short continues, "Floating around all happy, free-swimming marine animals. They have been around longer than dinosaurs. Five hundred million years!" Ultimately jellyfish are the eternal return par excellence as they don't die from old age; they just cycle through their lives repeatedly in an endless stream of differenciation. Short's closing, "nothing can stop that jellyfish. Nothing," is then both an echo of the future and a contraction of the past, as jellyfish occupy a much longer timeline than our short homo sapiens life span and will likely enjoy a much longer future. The jellyfish, with their absence of identity, fixed mass, clear life span, or marked gender, are clearly the greatest villain we have ever seen as they embody every vulnerability of the anthropod and so propel us toward identity-without-borders.

The material entanglements of jellyfish bring us face-to-face with the ethical implications of the material turn, as it has the potential to give us a different starting point for thinking about climate change. This doesn't mean simply learning how to recycle or buying electric cars, but to see that processes of worlding are *us* and our vulnerable, fleshy bodies are themselves *worlding*.[27] Jellyfish may be creatures of the sea, but their becoming-jellyfish is as natural as it is cultural as it is economic. Likewise, our choices between MDF (medium density fiberboard) or real wood material for kitchen cabinets has an impact on our world. MDF has a shorter production time and a much lower construction cost than wood, which has a long production time (we must actually grow the tree), and deforestation depletes a great deal of energy and resources. However, once placed in a home, MDF has a shorter "shelf" life; it cannot be repaired and reused as wood can, it loses its integrity quickly, and it cannot be recycled as it is made with heavy-duty resins, formaldehydes, and waxes that don't break down (and in fact give off toxic gases in our homes). If we diffract this simple decision alongside a living, contracting, anticipating present, we may stretch the timeline of wood cabinets to a long and slow life span. *Sustainability* in this context references the sustainability of the cabinets themselves. MDF cabinets, on the other hand, occupy a short and compacted timeline as they are fast and cheap to produce and more quickly become refuse. That said, once disposed, wood will break down and decompose, returning back to the earth, while MDF does not break down: it *sustains* its shape and material beyond any timeline that we know. Climate change writ large is nearly impossible to understand; everything we do, say, and dream, has an impact on "climate." And so, in an effort to continue to bring the conversation *home*, that is, to the social, natural, and cultural worlds that we live in, the choices that we make, and the worlding that we do, I close this chapter with a return to the impacts of our progress and sustainability narratives, particularly as they frame our novel futures and our regrettable pasts.

Remembering the End

> There is something uncanny about the very word Anthropocene. Perhaps it is in the way it seems to arrive too early and too late.
>
> —McKenzie Wark[28]

Hollywood has always been infatuated with the idea of apocalypse. Classics such as *The War of the Worlds* (1953), *The Day the Earth Caught Fire* (1961), *The Andromeda Strain* (1971), *Dawn of the Dead* (1978), *Blade Runner* (1982), *Independence Day* (1996), or *Armageddon* (1998), show decades of fascination with all varieties of postapocalyptic futures ranging from zombie takeovers to alien invasions, climate change to techno-dystopia. Today, movies about the end of the "world" as we know it are as plentiful as romantic comedies. Every third movie or television series projects a future of impending or present destruction and in each narrative we are telling a new story about old fears. Again, the "new" operates as a horizon; it reaches for that which is yet unthought. For many, the new is that magical "aha!" moment, the cut that sends us on a new path, or the scientific discovery that literally propels us into space in search of a new Earth, a new planet to colonize. The thing about the *new*, however, is that it operates in the present through anticipation, as we have seen in earlier chapters. We may anticipate the outcome of a political action, anticipate a future of environmental destruction, or even imagine the day when our feminist onto-epistemologies will transform our political structures entirely, and, in each of these cases, anticipation assumes direct causality between our present and our future. This means that we assume that if we carry on using the Earth's resources at the degree to which we are using them, the result will be continued anthropogenic degradation of the Earth; jellyfish will take over our seas, plastiglomerates will take over our shorelines, and pollutants will fill our air. At the same time, our anticipation of a climate apocalypse breeds fear, paralysis, and apathy, as we anticipate a future outside of human control. At its most extreme, we are, as Shannon Winnubst describes us, rendered "docile, most often at a wholly unconscious bodily level, through our unwitting obedience to the future."[29]

As I have discussed earlier in this book, our activities of "preparing for," "speculating about," or anticipating future events effectively bring the future into the frame of the present. This means that our present becomes defined by the future, and often behaves exactly as anticipated.[30] Such a future is not concerned with distinctions of race, gender, sexuality, or ability as they play out on the bodies of subjects, for grand swipes of disaster, extinction, barrenness, and overpopulation rely on a logic of sameness rather than any *differenciation*. This fear-laced storytelling also immobilizes us. It flattens out and solidifies any timeline as we step into concrete blocks and gaze upon the horizon with dread. Now, does this mean that we should not be alarmed about climate change? That we should deny apocalyptic threats? Of course not; the trouble is that, just as we have done in so many other timelines, we have let ourselves be lulled into a narrative of history whereby our past, present, and future are linear and, even more significantly, they are only and always read through the continuity of human experience.[31]

So how do we break our anthropocentric timelines? The short answer is that we will never be able to think outside the "human," for we are grossly limited by our own frames. But a longer answer involves a vertical and horizontal thickening of not only our human timelines, but also the entangled landscape of space-time-bodies. The final chapter of this book will take up the ethical compartments (if they are to exist at all) of this thickening in greater detail, but for our purposes here, it can include, among many other options, an embrace of Harari's discussion of the fact that homo sapiens are not *the* species, but *a* species among many, many other human species, many animal species, many species of flora and fauna. This shift to species thinking takes some of our human exceptionalism away, for we are no more significant than any other species—though just as parasitic and just as prone to extinction. "Earth," actually, even more frighteningly, "life" will go on without us, as Isabelle Stengers captures in her sublime claim:

> Of the Earth, the present subject of our scenarios, we can presuppose a single thing: it doesn't care about the questions we ask about it. What we call a catastrophe will be, for it, a contingency. Microbes will survive, as well as insects, whatever we let loose. ... From the viewpoint of the long history of the Earth itself, this will be one more "contingent event" in a long series.[32]

Rocks will not remember we were here, but they will embody human contributions by way of the Anthropocene-ic "orange rope" that snakes through stratigraphic layers the world over.[33] And of course, our anticipations of a future that lacks human narrative is only an echo of the past, as Chakrabarty and other historians remind us of the period called "deep history," or the time period before which we have any written record.[34]

Just as the anticipation of mass extinction is awe-inspiring in all of the most terrifying ways, the allure of a deep history lies in its indefinability. We can never know all of the details about what took place, what "life" was like, what stories were told. A deep history echoes arguments that "the planet does not need to be saved; it existed before organic life, and will go on to exist for some time (probably) well after humans and well after organisms," though it feels a bit irresponsible and careless to toss our heads back with "oh the planet will survive" or "life will go on without us."[35] Either way, the threat (and memory) of extinction/absence is a compelling wake-up call for many, as we anticipate homo sapiens' tumble from the top of the food chain.

Now, before we get too caught up in the end as inevitable, and the insignificance of human life, let's return to the sparkle of hope—the "promise of the new" that feminist scholars have dangled before us.[36] This *new* expresses the potentialities of the unknown as that which really does have the potential to transform our present lot. New feminist materialism, and actually much of feminist philosophy, has a stake in an open-ended future. Projects of revitalizing our present are critical parts of social and political change; as Grosz has argued, "unless we develop concepts of time and duration that welcome and privilege the future, that openly accept the rich virtualities and divergent resonances of the present, we will remain closed to understanding the complex processes of becoming that engender and constitute both life and matter."[37] Grosz's future relies on an infectious optimism that imagines not only *change* but renewed epistemologies as they engender new ways of thinking, being, and *doing*. Despite my hesitance around uncritical embraces of the "new," a living present does indeed indicate that the future is new. In this context, new does not mean better, but instead references a ladenness, a thickness. The new has a heaviness that is not a weight, but a force. The future of a living present, then, builds upon and changes the past in an infinite number of ways, knowing that every framing can lead to different outcomes. We cannot predict these outcomes in the present, for they are contingent on every story that we tell, move that we make, gum wrapper that we throw away.

If we think durationally we continue to question direct causality between past and present: the belief that anything that occurs could have been foreseen by a mind with adequate information. This assumes that the idea preexists its realization. A living, durational time instead allows us to see the perpetual activity and movement of life, movements that are not possible without the intra-active objects, voices, signs, and histories that echo around us. Is this a vibrancy of matter? Absolutely. Is it an active and determined agency? Yes, it is that as well. But is it the agency of an anthropocentric neoliberal humanism? *Not even close.* A living present denies a stable, agential, and autonomous human subject. Its proliferation of identities and movements places the emphasis not on coherence, sameness, or identity, but on *difference-in-itself*. This means that a durational temporality includes the becoming of all its participants: the becoming of the overture as it swells to a crescendo, the becoming of the jellyfish as they glide through the sea. None is more significant than the other, and all are involved in the making of a future-present-past.

Grosz's project of time as the engendering of the new—an echo of a differentiating interpretation—is not only intent on shifting the way we understand identity, difference, and temporality but, also, as a philosophy of immanence, it grounds itself in a complex materiality, therefore filling out those projects that may be too focused on the unknowable future. As such, we resist the neoliberal subject, or an ontology that grounds itself in human consciousness. It frees us from the dualism between interiority/exteriority—time as inside or outside of us—and instead reminds us of our time-bodies. Moving us to feel a history to which we are inexorably bound, and to listen as the sound waves carry on, the echo operates within Deleuze's temporality of difference and repetition whereby the *future* is never disconnected from the past. It is deeply bound to the heavy material memories of the physical and ideological pasts from which it came. But this doesn't mean that the future is causal or linear because unlike the unfettered, autonomous subject of neoliberalism, these "heavy material memories" hang in a thick fog around us.

In this vein, this chapter was inspired by a workshop held by Astrida Neimanis in Linköping, Sweden, where she encouraged transcorporeal engagements with the weather through a practice of "groundwriting." Groundwriting is an embodied project of rethinking the boundaries of one's body in relation to the surrounding climate or environment. By encouraging us to write "with" rather than "about" the ground, Neimanis engendered an entanglement of limbs and thoughts with weather and land in order to help us imagine (and thus create) alternate narratives of our relationships with weather changes, as well as a changing global climate. I was able to participate in the workshop at the *New Materialisms IV* Conference in Turku, Finland, May 2013, and I remember it being a beautiful sunny day, as our little group went outside with our pens and our paper to try this "groundwriting." Our instructions included touching the ground, feeling the street, the sidewalk, imagining where the cement stopped and earth began. We were invited to smell the air. How does exhaust frame, blend, and relay the city? Listen to the sounds: Is there a lone rustling tree in a cement pot? Is there laughter or anger in the honking horns? Is there a patch of grass that adds vibrant color to an otherwise grey landscape? Just as we began, it started to rain. Big raindrops blotted my sheet of "groundwriting," as I darted for the cover of a tree and then to the overhang of a neighboring building. Today, eight years later, I can still remember the hot, tar smell of city rain, as well as the deep belly laugh we all had about the Earth's sense of humor. It was a memorable event in an otherwise ordinary (and thus forgettable) conference experience that diffracted not only the plateaus of city and ground, weather and writing, but also the firm boundaries between theory and body, nature and culture, that as much as we resist, we cannot help but replicate.

There is both a slowing down and a speeding up that occurs during groundwriting as it flattens the "human," the "nature," the "culture" into a plane of univocity.[38] Just as univocity shows us that our identity politics are wrongheaded, univocity of climate shows us the horizontal heterogeny that pushes us beyond a difference *from*, and toward the multiple unfolding of different forces, moments, and relations in time. Within this plane, our familiar frames fall away, so that we may begin to recognize that Cohen's "climate change imaginary" is not a push-pull between human exceptionalism and absolute paralysis, and instead inclusive of the historical and material contingency of our neoliberal progress narratives as they anticipate a future that requires us to *sustain* a particular present. Of course, "sustainability" is arguably one of the most loaded terms of the twenty-first century. To *sustain* is to trap ourselves within an ethic of sameness, while the concept of *sustainability* calls for the thickening of our temporal horizons that a living present affords. The term is used both to inspire and to close down possible paths and, so, in line with the complicated and critical new materialisms, living presents, and vibrant materialities, we will end this chapter where we began—that is, with a question about sustainability.

sus·tain (sə'stān/)

verb

1. strengthen or support physically or mentally. "this thought had sustained him throughout the years"
2. *synonyms:* comfort, help, assist, encourage, succor, support, give strength to, buoy up, carry, cheer up, hearten, endure,

sus·tain·a·bil·i·ty (sə͵stānə'bilədē/)

noun

1. the ability to be maintained at a certain rate or level. "the sustainability of economic growth"

2. avoidance of the depletion of natural resources in order to maintain an ecological balance. "the pursuit of global environmental sustainability"
3. *synonyms:* continual, viable, worthwhile, unceasing, feasible, livable[39]

As I digest an ethic of sustainability, I want to think about sustainability alongside the questions of sustainable for *whom*? Whose needs? Which future? And it may encourage us not to write *about* climate change and practices of sustainability, but to write, teach, and act *sustainably, climactically.* We might want to explore questions such as

1. What does it mean for the Saskatchewan Glacier to (buoy up, endure) a changing climate?
2. How can we (give strength to) the needs of the North Saskatchewan River to flow fast and furiously from the Columbia Icefield to Lake Winnipeg?
3. How do the prairie wheat fields of Manitoba continue to (make viable) their consumption by human beings?
4. Why do the honeybees (unceasingly allow) human and nonhuman animals to share in their resources?

These queries take seriously the phrase that "the way we live in the world is bound to what we imagine the world to be,"[40]—such that our narratives of resource management, extinction, water, flows, and glacier melt hinge upon their relationship with *us*; we are forever the sun, while nature is our planetary orbit. Sustainability is our Janus-faced launchpad, giving us arguments for capitalism and its enemies. The key to a living present as a method of understanding is that it includes a Copernican revolution so that each ecological phenomenon becomes the center of the universe, even if only for a moment. We could imagine that honeybees have waged war on centuries of human theft or that glacier melt is their process of letting go and clearing away human refuse (including humans themselves) through the rise in sea level, increased floods, redistribution of the toxic chemicals that were previously trapped in ice layers.

I can never access the "mind" of a glacier, for no such thing exists, nor can I embody the winged-body of a honeybee, but I can imagine environment *otherwise*, and the above questions and diffractive reframings each play a role in the anticipatory politics of climate change and thus play a role in *making* the future. Though there are differences between the anticipatory fear of the future discussed above, and the open-ended future of feminist and new materialist scholarship, I am far more interested in their diffraction patterns (their overlaps and differenciations) than any argument about right or wrong, for each is a response to the force of neoliberal time as it has become unwieldy. Neoliberalism is easily able to co-opt terms such as agency, tolerance, the new, and the future as part of an ideological agenda that has much less to do with the transformative capacities of the subject, and much more to do with framing *agency* as the individual capacity to direct one's own successful, capitalist, and autonomous future. As such, neoliberalism's time is a time of *progress*, of individualism par excellence, of building from the ground up in anticipation of the successful future. And it is no secret that even our revolutionary politics ascribe to this timeline as they "revel in the idea of progress, development, movement" whether feminist, anti-racist, queer, environmentalist, or otherwise.[41] This is the narrative that a living present ruptures; this is the point in time that we can thicken and stretch, that we can propel forward, and catch the echoes of the past.

And so, we are required to travel along a thin line, a precariously strung rope bridge over a chasm of possibility. We turn the new into novel, we substitute an indiscriminate passive vitality for teleological self-actualization, and we look sideways at "progress" as though we don't really care, all the while knowing that *all we do is care about the future.* Are we endlessly naive? Are we doomed to fail? Respectively, yes and no. The duration of the echo shows us that there can never be a "new" future, in the abstract, disconnected sense of being void of ties and conditions. Instead, each future has a duration that contracts the past resonances and virtualities from which it came, thickening the temporalities of our texts, practices, and events as they stretch toward what can still be *transformative futures*. Also, a living present is not a denial of agency, but a dislocation of the agency of the autonomous humanist subject. This is an ontological difference ungrounded in an external measure (the measure of what counts as citizenship; what story a political movement tells). It demonstrates that to apply a humanist narrative to climate change, to weather, to jellyfish, or even evolution is to ask the wrong questions, it is to deny the nonlinear temporality that demonstrates the force of a cultural memory, the force of a past that homo sapiens are so quick to forget. As the final chapter will demonstrate, there is no better answer to these questions; there are only opportunities to live, think, act, and love as the time-bodies that we are—that is, as entangled human/nonhuman becomings which recognize that "human life is now implicated in timelines and rhythms beyond that of its own borders."[42] There is no single history to uncover, no proper future we have yet to find; instead we are accountable to the millions of time-bodies with which we are always already entangled. As the living present frames climate/environment/weather/earth, we have an opportunity. We have the opportunity to imagine a world that is not in need of *sustaining* a particular present—a particular mode of development—but rather which is itself capable of enacting dynamic possibilities. And within this terrain we may just begin to contract ways of being in that world that are part of a *world becoming-otherwise.*

6

An Ethics of Entanglement

Thinking about time is to acknowledge two contradictory certainties: that our outward lives are governed by the seasons and the clock; that our inward lives are governed by something much less regular—an imaginative impulse cutting through the dictates of daily time, and leaving us free to ignore the boundaries of here and now and pass like lightning along the coil of pure time, that is, the circle of the universe.
—Jeanette Winterson, *Sexing the Cherry*

Queers face a strange choice: is it better to move on toward a brighter future or to hang back and cling to the past? Such divided allegiances result in contradictory feelings: pride and shame, anticipation and regret, hope and despair. Contemporary queers find ourselves in the odd situation of "looking forward" while we are "feeling backward."
—Heather Love, *Feeling Backward*

There is no escaping responsibility. Whether the world is beautiful and true, or ugly and degrading, hurtful or grieving, depends on us.
—Viola Fay Cordova, *How It Is*

The first time I read Deleuze and Guattari I was a young undergrad in Women's and Gender Studies at the University of Saskatchewan and, like many burgeoning Deleuzians, it was the concept of *becoming* that most caught my breath. From there, abstract concepts such as the rhizome, imperceptibility, and lines of flight not only fascinated me but also resonated with my experiences of feminism and queer theory as I lived them. In fact, Deleuze and Guattari made the difference between my following a path of cultural studies and communications (often the next logical step in the absence of many graduate programs in women's and gender studies throughout Canada) and entering the field of philosophy for graduate work. Suddenly philosophy wasn't just a game of words and arguments, it was something I could feel in my bones, something expressed in the world around me.

The first time I read Jeanette Winterson I was nineteen years old, living between two cities and sexualities. When I read *Written on the Body* I didn't even notice that it was written from the perspective of a non-gendered protagonist. Once I discovered this fact, I hungrily reread every passage, devouring the tools of narrative and description that expressed not only androgyny, but femininity, masculinity, and all multiplications thereof. Winterson's novels inspired my obsessions with temporality by opening up terrains of desire unattached to a binary, and treating the progression of time like Alice's Wonderland.

My relationships with each of these authors are easily coming-of-age narratives as I sought to find my intellectual, physical, ideological, and sexual place in the world. Deleuze was a lightning bolt, shifting my relationship with philosophy from a bystander to a full participant. Winterson's dips through time, backward and forward, her plays with memory and embrace of the physical and the sexual, expressed the thickness of the living present that birthed me into adulthood. For the first time, after years of reading Aristotle, Mill, Wollstonecraft, Marx, Foucault, and even Butler, Deleuze's texts resonated with me on a personal level and Winterson gave me a language of desire that was otherwise hidden. As I traveled from undergraduate to graduate school, I often had texts from both writers open on my desk, diffracting philosophy and literature through, over, and under one another.

Now, this may seem overly sentimental, but we are all connected to the arguments that we make. Even if we are assigned an essay for a class that makes us seethe, it is our anger that fuels the passion (or lack thereof) with which we take up arms. More often our motivations are even closer than this: a scholar of Beauvoir can recall a moment when *The Second Sex* flipped the table on their understanding of gender; a scholar of Kant may recall standing at the edge of the Grand Canyon and finally understanding the sublime; a reader of Foucault can recall millions of moments of staring in the mirror with judgment when they studied the panopticon. As we write, teach, and speak, we are always already entangled in the narratives of our lives, and it is precisely these entangled moments that capture our imaginations, drive us to one text over another, and which reveal the inextricability of memory and experience as they inform our actions. Each of our entangled time-bodies is the rhizomatic field through which the future (present and past) is made and it is our stories that do the work of creation.

The diffractive timescapes of some of the previous chapters—a deep dive into the climate change imaginary and its anticipatory grip on the present, the two-sided coin of sameness and difference as it multiplies gender, sex, and desire—each represent different ways of narrating familiar topics within feminist, philosophical, and queer terrains and, in so doing, they open up alternative lines of flight (remembering that lines of flight are connecting points between assemblages or relational subjects). However, my intention is never merely to "show and tell," for this is a book biased toward action, recognizing that storytelling has always been an agential force. Our methods of telling, our inclusions and exclusions, the cuts that we make, the lines that we draw, each participate in processes of world-making. And so I have tried to break myself from the habit of writing "we can think differently," or even "we can open alternatives" as I have just written above. Instead I want to change the narrative to "we can *do* differently and this is how we might try." The living present as a method of understanding (and telling) is also an agential force. It changes the way that I talk and write; it has impacted my methods of planning and thinking. For example, I took a position as the executive director of a 2SLGBTQ community center in December 2013 and when I walked into my first day of work there were large portraits on the walls of the center: white men who had waged hero's journeys and who had fought their way through discrimination and horror to pave a new and liberatory path for the rest of us. Over time I moved these images from their prominent spots and downsized them to postcard sizes. My intention was never to minimize, only to shift their scale and impact so that they were some *among* many, rather than one *above* others. The images are still displayed, in homage to the past, but alongside them is art by local Two Spirit and queer artists and photographs that foreground community leaders of all backgrounds. Such material shifts also include incorporating stories of women, non-binary, and trans people into our histories in order to change the stories that we tell about our pasts, and consequently in our *making* of the future. Each case of doing and telling differently actually has material and community-based effects on our imagined futures and our expanding pasts.

In order to continue to tell stories that are rhizomes rather than trees, stories that create rather than solidify, my concluding comments take up one final question, a question that has, in fact, already guided every chapter up to this point: *What is the use of a living present for social and cultural change?* This is the "so what?" This is the question about how our learnings from this book can guide us toward imagining (and bringing about) more equitable communities, needed social programs, balanced ecosystems, and places of belonging. This is a question about how we live and live *with*, how we remember and forget, how we dream and realize, and it is also a question about *ethics*. Although my aim has not explicitly been to develop an ethics within this work, the living present offers immense ethical uptake. Particularly, as *time-bodies*, we are accountable to our temporal threads. Whether through our storytelling, our purchases, our footsteps, the memories that haunt our present choices, or the force of our own expectations and anticipations of the future on present actions, we are time-makers in every word, act, and deed. This thick temporal accountability is what I mean by *the matter of time*, and it is precisely this enactment that opens us up to the ethical. That said, I am not referring to a normative or prescriptive ethics. Instead it is an ethics that is most aptly described as the always already; we are always already in the thick of the ethical, and social and cultural change is produced through admitting to our own entanglements.

An Ungrounded Ethics

> Ten years into the Deleuzian century ... few would disagree that the world as we know it is sinking into an economic, political, social, and ethical abyss of previously unimaginable depths. Back in the halcyon days when that world was still in its infancy, Deleuze was widely heralded as a visionary who would help us demystify the web of global technological and financial networks which was, at that time, just starting to be spun. Since then, the prophecies have largely come to pass; everyone from Žižek to Badiou is fond of saying that the conceptual and methodological tools with which we make sense of this age are Deleuzian tools.[1]

Now, Deleuze and Guattari are not generally heralded for their ethical contributions. In fact, they have been said to go against any sort of ethics entirely. Of course, such a charge depends on what we call *ethics* in the first place, as ethical conversations often collapse ethics and morality. While morality is the set of rules, guidelines, or principles against which to measure one's actions (a chart of right and wrong), ethics are often more linked to the bigger questions of how to live in community or what constitutes a "good" life. To say that Deleuze and Guattari offer any sort of morality, is generally wrongheaded, but if we change the conversation to one that is about an ethic or an ethos then suddenly the path clears. In particular, we are able to shift our focus from the individual (or even collective) decisions we make and why we make those decisions (morality) to one about the relationships, connections, and encounters between *bodies* (ethics).[2] Within this framing, problems occur when we limit what a body can do and, more importantly, what it can do in the world.

But wait. If we are in support of an ethic where the body/bodies have limitless power and where connection, change, expansion, are the goal, how do we differentiate between this model and a capitalist vision for new goods, increased forms of control, new commodities?[3] Some have argued that, rather than serving as the visionary in a web of global chaos, Deleuze (and Guattari) are actually complicit within the system of capitalism that propels this web. It is precisely through processes such as "mobility, fluidity" and the movements of "nomads" that a contemporary capitalism has gained ground as it enables workplace rhetoric around the need for employees to be flexible, change-oriented, and able to navigate multiple projects at once all in service of a greater reach, the ability to adeptly respond to the desires of every consumer (and to push more product), and thus to gain more control of the market.[4] Clearly Deleuze's work can support, and has supported, capitalist, sexist, and even fascist arguments. The Deleuzian "tools" of the nomad, lines of flight, concepts, the assemblage, and the rhizome are often more relevant to analyses of social media than they are to questions of *how to live*. Importantly, however, the knitting together of these various threads occurs not necessarily in accordance with some sort of original intent (on the parts of Deleuze and Guattari) but rather because our words, thoughts, and deeds have uptake well beyond us. This is the work of the "concept" that Deleuze and Guattari use in *What Is Philosophy?* and which I describe in Chapter 2. Concepts have *affects*, that is, impacts that extend beyond the intentions or words themselves. Think about shouting the word "bomb" in a shopping center, or even the word "gender," which means so many different things to so many different people. Even *becoming* has wide uptake as it links with change, fluidity, transformation, and overcoming. The point at which Deleuze's becoming becomes complicit within capitalism is the moment when we hold too tightly to the outcome, thus participating in a monomythic grip on our stories, problems, and creations. The point at which a Deleuzian ethic becomes a joke is when we assume a clear and methodical path from point A to point B. And ultimately, it is precisely *because* Deleuze bravely engages with all types of systems that we are provided with such exacting and far-reaching tools.

Just as we faced human extinction head-on in Chapter 5, extracting it from a value- or even fear-based framework, we could do so with capitalism, neoliberalism, globalization, homophobia, or sexism. It is tempting to turn these concepts into our enemies and thus to turn away from any instance where they are given air when, in fact, it is the turning away that billows their sails in the first place and the more air we give to something like sexism, the deeper it can breathe and grow, the stronger its course becomes, the greater its winds. In this way, it is never the concept which is in and of itself *bad*—we are neck deep in a philosophy of immanence after all—it is always and only a matter of how it is used, the power both taken up and given, its lines of flight. To speak of the ethical at all, within this context, is to let everything in, to start from wide open space and to acknowledge that sexism, capitalism, transphobia, and violence are as much contributors to any so-termed "ethical response" as hope, love, compassion, and care.

The more important argument is that "they—*we*—play a role in the generation, operation, and transformation of other assemblages, other machines."[5] The ethical task, then, is not to try to understand things as they are, but rather to imagine them as they might be. So, if we take sexism as a point of departure, rather than defining it as it *is*—prejudice and/or discrimination based on a person's sex or gender—we may talk about sexism as an *absence*. We may tell a story about a future where sex-based prejudice does not exist, we might imagine a university built entirely with non-gendered bathrooms, we might picture a parliamentary session that not only has as many women as men present, but which also reflects diversity in color, sexuality, age, and ability. This point of departure is precisely the condition of possibility for thinking otherwise or doing things differently. So now, as we return to the enigmatic and ephemeral *being otherwise*, we can start to see that the "otherwise" is much more than a vague gesture or a hand-waving exercise. Instead it indicates an ethical leap that is as simple as changing our narratives from teleological to open-ended tales and as difficult as rewiring ourselves to approach systems without naming them, to see people without fixating on categories, and to read histories without affirming a causal tale. The otherwise is an opening that is not prescriptive; it is a quick sidestep without normative weight, and these movements have immense material impact as they breathe air into novel processes and possibilities. Ultimately, with its refusal to name a *something* or an *actual*, the "otherwise" resists a clear landing spot; it keeps us light on our feet and open to change.

The key is that Deleuze refuses any framework that gives us a ground to stand on or that resembles moral certainty by way of a map as to how to *live* (relying on becoming over being), and so the greatest import of the living present is its denial of any normative principles as to what we might *do* or how we might *act*. The matter at hand is an ethics without *ethics* and every attempt to describe and define participates in its erasure. Consequently, the difficulty in talking about the political and social impetus of an anti-normative apparatus is that we really are walking a tightrope (many tightropes) between accountability and absolute freedom, between deep interrelatedness and wide-open possibilities.

Levi Bryant walks this tightrope between accountability and absolute freedom by focusing on the concept of the event, not unlike I have done in Chapter 4 through my discussion of the coming out event as a moment of subject formation. Remember that I discussed the way that unlike a narrative which captures one event as "the" event or the moment of transformation, the coming out event is multiple. It is an event among others and an event that is entangled with one's audience, the time of day, the television show playing in the background, the color of one's hair. Likewise, Bryant disagrees with the "ethical fetishism" of Immanuel Kant, John Stuart Mill, or Christine Korsgaard, which situates the human at the center of morality, and instead argues that all ethical frameworks (through the event) are relational: "Given the manner in which humans always employ other objects and are employed by other objects in their actions, the idea of humans acting *alone* and without the intermediary of other objects at work in their action is itself a fiction."[6]

Bryant references the production of wine to illustrate this interrelatedness and I have expanded on his example here, *because of my love for wine*. Imagine we watch a grape seed grow in its environment. Alongside the grape growers and winemakers, a grape seed is up against neighboring plants, rain and sun levels, insects and birds, and a distinct topography made up of minerals (or lacking minerals) and other materials. If the seed develops into a grapevine it continues to be entangled in various relationships with earth and air, biological divergence (will the cells divide? Will leaves grow on the first branch or the twentieth?), and then the winemaker oversees the maceration processes, the addition of other wine varietals, the timing for skin contact, and the addition of yeast according to ratios that have been tweaked and tested for generations. After they have aged (or not), laid to rest in oak (or metal) barrels, been bottled quickly (or slowly), and set aside to rest (or shipped young), bottles are sent around the world, to different climates and pressures, and paired with different foods and smells upon opening. The result is an infinite number of outcomes. Every batch (and even bottle) is unique from those that came before or after and this uniqueness is the result of human choices, the age of the oak barrels, temperature and environment, time and delay. When the glass of wine lands on my table, its aroma and taste are the furthest thing from a causal tale, for the process is so much more than the simple determination that its mineral flavors came from soil rich in limestone, its long finish is the result of lengthy skin contact. Winemaking is intra-active and inventive; it is the convergence of particulars within a collective that is novel at the same time that it is inextricably bound to its conditions of emergence.

Whether the *event* is the growth of the grapevine, the addition of chemicals, or the shipping truck whose air conditioning breaks down en route to its destination, it is always a point of departure; the event is a singularity within millions of potentialities. And alongside Bryant, I circle back to the event because if there is to be a Deleuzian ethics at all, it is something that erupts from the event. The event is "something excessive in relation to its actualization, something that overthrows worlds, individuals, and persons, and leaves them to the depth of the ground which works and dissolves them."[7] This means that the event is the moment of diffraction, the convergence of overlapping time-bodies and generative leaps, without any predetermined path. The *ethical*, then, is also inventive, but it is not a rupture in the same way that the event is. Rather than the point of departure, the ethical is the *relationship* between and through all inputting parties; the ethical is the ultimate contraction of all pasts and all futures that occurs within each and every event. Some have called this Deleuzian ethic an ethology or an ethos and others have called it an immanent ethics but, in each case, the *ethical* is an open-ended expansion of possibilities, where more possibilities are not necessarily *better* or more *valuable*, they are simply *possible* rather than not.[8] As well, like the event, the ethical is never that which we determine after the fact, nor that which we apply to a problem, but instead it lives within the problem; an immanent ethic (ethology, ethos) calls for the transformation of its subject (or collection of subjects) instantaneously with its invocation.[9]

Now, although I agree with and echo the various projects intent upon teasing out the ethical within Deleuze and Guattari's work, there is still something missing, for how is it that we know that change happens? What ties one action to the next if cause and effect is only retroactive? How is it that an infinitely multiple subject can recognize herself in the mirror over a twenty-year span? Just as the event is inexplicably temporal, ethics too are only and ever about *time*. As time-bodies we are contractions of every past and anticipations of every future, and yet we live in a thick and entangled present. We make time, but we do not control time; we change pasts and futures but this change is never ours alone. We are not autonomous and we are not even in control of our own unique heroic journeys. We are bound to our entanglements, be they partners, cities, choices, insects, just as they are bound to us and this binding occurs in and through something much more subtle than intra-activity, diffraction, or any sort of additive concept. This binding occurs through being itself, where being is univocity and differenciation, a seamless flip between difference and sameness. That we all *are* in the same way and that such being is a thick contraction of the past (all pasts) and the anticipation of the future (all futures) is precisely the *time* and therefore the *relationality* of the ethical, and thus serves as the condition of possibility for social and cultural change.

To illustrate this, I reference one final example or "timescape." Epigenetics allows for the study of gene expression governed by the genome: the cellular material on top of DNA and the science of epigenetics is a key example of the entanglement of nature and culture. While the epigenome does not change one's genetic code, it can activate or silence genes by mobilizing molecules called methyl groups (DNA methylation), which means that the cellular material on top of DNA can be changed and impacted by environmental and social factors. Now, scientists have long demonstrated that poor environmental conditions such as toxins, contaminants, dietary changes, deficient prenatal nutrition, and exposure to stressors have an impact on the body, and even that they can activate or silence genes.[10] But it is less well known that these environmentally induced changes in gene expression can also be passed down to offspring through at least one generation through a form of epigenetic inheritance. This means an individual's experience of abuse, famine, or other significant cultural and physical traumas "might influence the phenotypes of [their] offspring," or, put another way, the diets, exposure to toxins, and even the emotional stresses that our parents and grandparents experienced, can predispose us to health risks, diseases, and changes to our life spans.[11] For example, Kuzawa and Sweet demonstrate that there is a relationship between pregnant African American women's experiences of racism, discrimination, and structural inequity and increased incidences of cardiovascular disease (among other things) in their children.[12]

The epigenetic *event* has ruptured much more than the health field, as feminist scholars use epigenetics to fortify arguments that our bodies are rich compositories of past experiences and that these experiences serve as much more than haunting memories, but rather play out through patterns of illness and social behaviors.[13] A key component of this work includes recognizing that the research process itself (including the questions, hypotheses, and measurement tools) is co-determinant as the diffraction grating has already shown us, thus demonstrating that our questions or lenses are as much a part of the answer as the object of study.[14]

Although there are still many complications within the field, epigenetic inheritance reveals the contracted pasts of disease, pasts of abundance, pasts of pain and hurt, and manifests these pasts within the sociogenetic material of the human body, expressing these entanglements in bodies, cultures, and medical institutions to come. Epigenetics is particularly salient to conversations about the social, cultural, and historical effects of residential schools and continued neocolonial/liberal policies that limit the self-determination and lives of Indigenous peoples. Through epigenetics we can dig deeper, we can thicken the story to see that such discussions fail to fully understand the interconnectedness or the intersectionality of environmental and biological matters, or the way that genetics and environments "essentially coact to lead to the development of the individual" and can be transmitted across generations.[15] When we apply epigenetic inheritance to the impact of one person's residential school experience on subsequent generations, it reveals that the operations of sustained trauma, stigma, and illness can reshape specific genetic traits within a particular community, over a relatively short period of time. Thus, epigenetics brings the inter- and transgenerational impact of residential schools into sharp focus. The children and grandchildren of those who endured residential schools are not only empathetic to the experiences of previous generations, but can feel their experiences in their bones; they retell the stories of their ancestors through their bodies, their emotional and intellectual lives. Such realizations contract previous discussions within this work, such as the absence of potable water in White Bear First Nation. How does this story change when we ask how structural racism and water shortages/absences coact to materialize in the bodies of generations of White Bear residents to come? We can also ask questions about what epigenetic inheritance might look like in relation to the AIDS crisis? To survivors of Nazi internment camps? Each of these ruptures is dripping with echoes of our future politics, mental health patterns, embedded molecules of PTSD and, as well, they compel us to ask how we can ever justify harm against another (human, animal, plant, shoreline) when the impact contracts so many future generations in, as of yet, unimaginable ways? The ethical is about all our relations, a Lakota phrase that means that we are all connected—human beings, animals, rocks, air—for generations forward and generations back.

To enlist a living present as a method of understanding is to develop a different sense of the "time" of history. Rather than relying on chronology, or the construction of a politics of the subject, formed around key dates and events that represent progressive states of self-actualization, we are able to think such events "out-of-time." Foregrounding a temporal frame of accountability, the living present entangles our pasts and presents so intensely that, just as the EPR Paradox demonstrated, we are actually able to change the past through observation of the present. Take this example: marriage equality was achieved in Canada through Bill C-38, the *Civil Marriage Act*, legislation that followed on the heels of eight of ten provinces and one of three territories having already passed civil marriage legislation between 2002 and 2005. In most cases across the country, it took a group of local individuals with the courage to bring suit against outdated definitions of marriage. As these small victories piled up in various courtrooms across the country, the federal government worked through layers of bureaucracy in order to pass the countrywide Bill. Canada became the fourth country in the world to legally recognize same-sex marriage on July 20, 2005, and although a Conservative government tried to reopen the decision in 2006, they were unsuccessful.

In this chronological time-telling, the past is actual: "the set of archived and stored events that have occurred and been completed."[16] So the passing of Bill C-38, the Civil Marriage Act, constitutes a moment, forever emblazoned in the history of queer rights—the moment of emancipation. And yet, a living present alerts us to the underlying problems with such a telling of history. Here we have a group fighting for their rights and freedoms, attaining them, and then continuing to live on in a future that has *overcome* the past. The past in this narrative is a static, actual event, and the *telling* of such a past satisfies our addiction to monomythic progress narratives. If we take a look at this event through the diffractive lens of the living present, and thus enfold the present and the future, the living present introduces a responsibility to the past in the present. This is not a causal demand of the past on the present, but rather recognition that we are never free of the past or, put another way, "the present cannot absolve itself selectively of the past."[17] What this means is that a durational engagement with Bill C-38 contracts a variety of side-narratives, which are entirely overwritten within the neoliberal progress narrative of marriage equality.

For example, in a detailed presentation of these side-narratives, Bronwyn Winter identifies the operations of homonationalism, marriage's weddedness to patriarchal systems of violence and control as they are silenced by the neoliberal success story of marriage equality, and trans erasure (though she spends much less time on this last topic).[18] She writes that "the persistent opposition by most (albeit not all) Muslim countries to the decriminalisation of homosexuality has provided a new means for Western and pro-Western nations to distinguish themselves as progressive in relation to the essentialised Islamic (terrorist) other."[19] As it operates within a global imaginary, marriage equality becomes the yardstick against which national morality is measured, and consequently serves as justification for Western interventions and boycotts of those countries that do not measure up. When we contract Bill C-38 and the institution of marriage itself, the gay rights agenda (and its successful achievements) overrides any discontent around the institution of marriage itself, whether through its enforcement of a heteronormative model of coupling, or its dark history of shrouding violence against women. Clearly, and as statistics demonstrate, marriage equality will not rid us of domestic violence, nor does it do much to challenge or transform the institution of marriage.[20]

Regarding the conflicting narrative that marriage equality movements result in trans erasure, we must remember that Canada still does not provide full health coverage for gender-affirming surgeries, and provincial services are spotty and far between. A living present reminds us that our stories have affective uptake, and so we may surmise that those stories that have a great deal of public *presence* can take up much more space than those that may not follow such a positive trajectory. As long as Bill C-38 remains the poster child for gay tolerance, it will overshadow harms against trans people in judicial and medical systems, and the absence of surgical and bodily autonomy that many trans people experience.

As these diffractive narratives demonstrate, the passing of Bill C-38 is not enough to wipe the slate clean as the government might hope for; changing a law doesn't erase the homophobia, transphobia, or misogyny of the past; *allowing* queer people to wed does not erase the patriarchal system of marriage. Sara Ahmed might call this the "stickiness of the past" such that historical harms live on, not only in the body of the individual, but also in the "skin," or the intergenerational affectivity of whole communities.[21] To forget the past—and we are no strangers to such large-scale forgettings in the face of historical injustices—would repeat the violence. Our bodies, our communities, and our ecologies, remember these pasts and continue to live through them as they are folded into our presents and our futures. Further, if we only focus on a future-yet-to-come, we fail to see that there are still an infinite number of past experiences, habits, and memories that enact our particular present. For example, a homophobic slur could be examined according to its distinct spatio-temporal location: why did *that* word come from *that* individual at *this* time? By asking questions about the wider materialities at play in any event we respond to the complexity of injustices that can not only bring about change for the better, but also reveal the assemblages of violence and negation that are *different every time*.

A living present means that the past always leaves a remainder: "Each text, word, fragment and image of the past ... acts as an always present resistance (or insistence) to a simple moving forward."[22] Just as we cannot expect to jump up and run away the minute after we twist an ankle, we cannot erase a history of exclusion with the great big stroke of legalizing same-sex marriage in Canada. The past is retained in the antigay sermons of a Catholic priest and in the patriarchy that informs the concept of marriage itself. The living present is heavy with lineages that mimic, critique, and undo our assumed histories and, rather than wiping away the past, or seeking absolution for our actions, we can embrace this remainder, recognizing its ability to deepen our accountabilities to those pasts and their possible futures. In this way such a focus becomes a necessary form of ethical engagement with the world that begins not from the point of subject/object relations (or human/inhuman, nature/culture, cause/effect, for that matter) but from the position of being always already entangled in space-time-world. Consequently, Bill C-38, July 20, 2005, does not need to stand in as the day of queer rights in Canada; instead it can be folded into the present rise in trans suicides, or the staggering rates of homelessness for queer and trans youth as, both nationally and in nearly every province, 2SLGBTQ youth make up 30–40 percent of the youth homelessness statistics.[23] This is a gross overrepresentation that is due to their being kicked out of their homes, the lack of non-gendered youth housing, and the failure of available social services to adequately serve this population.

How do we read this politics of queer identity alongside the legislation of same-sex unions and the largely sanctioned bullying and exclusion of queer youth? Just as Colebrook writes that "any feminist claim in our present is in harmony and dissonance with a choir of past voices,"[24] any instances of violence against queer persons in the present echoes a past (and a future) of violence and discrimination that continues to act on our present. This method of reading entails a more careful inclusion of the apparatuses of knowledge production that contribute to the organizing narratives of history. In fact, it may lead us to interrogate (and forget) those identities, representations, and reflections that we cling to—the way that we call marriage progress, the fact that we want sameness in our rights and freedoms, without questioning the complex systems that mitigate these rights and freedoms. The living present of a feminist politic is one where we can bring Sojourner Truth's bold query "And Ain't I a Woman?" to bear on twenty-first-century identity politics, for it creates a space where we can question the effects of this category "woman": the freedoms it affords, *as well as* the deeply drawn boundaries on which it relies.

It's About Time

Returning to our questions about social and political change, it is clear that epigenetic inheritance has ethical import as it stretches our timelines far into the future and far into the past. At the same time, I hope it is becoming clear that we have already traveled decidedly ethical terrains. Tricks of time that I experienced as a child, rather than indicating failures of memory, are precisely the Deleuzian problem, whereby a problem is not something that is in my *mind*, but something that belongs to the world.[25] These points of departure, then, thicken my understanding and experience of selfhood. I stretch my understanding forward and backward through reading books and working within the human service sector pursuing graduate studies and other paths and I know that there are millions of actualizations made possible from my childhood experiences.

The living present shows us that the *now*, the present, is always our access point, but that this *now* is also an already and a not yet. Ultimately, and as I hope I have shown, it is not just recycling that teaches us about the temporality of the material, it is bodies, racisms, transphobias, institutions, and transgenerational bodies that show us how material our experiences and lives really are. The experience of living under colonialism has long-lasting biological effects at a molecular level, which persist across generations; the expanding population of jellyfish contracts thousands of years of changing ocean temperatures, and anticipates a dangerous future. The implications of the living present are vast and engender a long temporal frame, while at the same time demonstrating how insufficient our short time frames are for any level of understanding. It also demonstrates that it is because we are relational time-bodies that we can have accountability or any degree of responsibility at all.

Throughout, I have endeavored to show that when we really take heed of the fact that we live, act, and are acted upon within a living present that is always contracting the past as it reaches toward an unknowable future, we unsettle the fierce linearity of our stories about history, about tomorrow, about today. As we "thicken" the present moment to include embedded pasts (and embodied futures), we are better poised to take accountability for our position(s) in the making of the timeline and thus the creation of our social and cultural environments. Thus, the living present calls us to tend to our temporal threads, including their impacts on our political movements, our philosophical theories, our relationships with the Earth, our partners, our children. These are the stories from the living present; these are the *doings* and *becomings* of time.

Notes

Preface: The Monomyth

1 Gilles Deleuze and Felix Guattari, *A Thousand Plateaus: Capitalism and Schizophrenia*, trans. Brian Massumi (Minneapolis: University of Minnesota Press, 1987), 225–8.
2 Jeanette Winterson, *The Stone Gods* (Boston: Mariner Books, 2009), 93, emphasis added.

Introduction

1 William James, *The Principles of Psychology* (New York: Holt, 1890).
2 See Richard A. Block et al., "Human Aging and Duration Judgments: A Meta-Analytic Review," *Psychology and Aging* 13, no. 4 (1998): 584–96; Marc Wittmann and Sandra Lehnhoff, "Age Effects in Perception of Time," *Psychological Reports* 97, no. 3 (2005): 921–35.
3 Gilles Deleuze, *Difference and Repetition*, trans. Paul Patton (New York: Columbia University Press, 1994), 70.
4 Astrida Neimanis and Rachel Loewen Walker, "Weathering: Climate Change and the 'Thick Time' of Transcorporeality," *Hypatia* 29, no. 3 (2014): 561.
5 Deleuze, *Difference and Repetition*, 78.
6 Deleuze, 79.
7 James Williams, *Gilles Deleuze's Philosophy of Time: A Critical Introduction and Guide* (Edinburgh: Edinburgh University Press, 2011), 11.
8 Shazia Akhtar et al., "Fictional First Memories," *Psychological Science* 29, no. 10 (October 1, 2018): 1612–19, https://doi.org/10.1177/0956797618778831 (accessed September 12, 2020).
9 Akhtar et al., 1617.
10 Deleuze, *Difference and Repetition*, 88.
11 Deleuze, 88.
12 Deleuze, 88.
13 Jeanette Winterson, *Sexing the Cherry* (Toronto: Vintage Canada, 1989).

14 Parts of this section were previously published in Rachel Loewen Walker, "The Living Present as a Materialist Feminist Temporality," *Woman: A Cultural Review* 25, no. 1 (2014): 46–61.
15 See Donna Haraway, *Modest—Witness@Second—Millennium. FemaleMan—Meets—OncoMouse: Feminism and Technoscience* (New York: Routledge, 1997); Karen Barad, *Meeting the Universe Halfway: Quantum Physics and the Entanglement of Matter and Meaning* (Durham, NC: Duke University Press, 2007); Iris van der Tuin, "'A Different Starting Point, a Different Metaphysics': Reading Bergson and Barad Diffractively," *Hypatia* 26, no. 1 (2011): 22–42.
16 See Diana Coole and Samantha Frost, *New Materialisms: Ontology, Agency, and Politics* (Durham, NC: Duke University Press, 2010); Elizabeth Grosz, *Time Travels: Feminism, Nature, Power* (Durham, NC: Duke University Press, 2005); Rosi Braidotti, *Metamorphoses: Towards a Materialist Theory of Becoming* (New Jersey: Wiley, 2002).
17 Mary Wollstonecraft, *A Vindication of the Rights of Women & a Vindication of the Rights of Men* (New York: Cosimo, 2008), 42.
18 Barad, *Meeting the Universe Halfway*, 67–77.
19 Emma Goldman, *Anarchism and Other Essays* (New York: Mother Earth Publishing Association, 2010).
20 Barad, *Meeting the Universe Halfway*, 30.
21 See Constance Borde and Sheila Malovany-Chevallier, "Translating the Second Sex," *Books & Ideas*, November 17, 2011, https://booksandideas.net/Translating-the-Second-Sex.html (accessed August 25, 2019).
22 For example, the discovery of DNA was accomplished through an analysis of the diffraction grating in order to understand the structure of the substance in question. See Barad, *Meeting the Universe Halfway*, 84.
23 Barad, 87.
24 Barad, 91.
25 Barad, 91.
26 Sara Ahmed, *Living a Feminist Life* (Durham, NC: Duke University Press, 2017), 18.
27 Viviane Namaste, "Undoing Theory: The 'Transgender Question' and the Epistemic Violence of Anglo-American Feminist Theory," *Hypatia* 24, no. 3 (2009): 27.
28 Stacey Alaimo, *Bodily Natures: Science, Environment, and the Material Self* (Indianapolis: Indiana University Press, 2010), 2.
29 I borrow the term "actant" from Latour, who defines it simply as "something that acts" and as such serves as a catalyzing force. The concept of *actant* is differentiated from *agent* as it is neither subject, nor object, and thus unable to be subjectivized as "agency" often is. I return to the concept of "actant" in Chapter 3 in my discussion of immaterial and inorganic time-bodies but, in this case, I use it in order to reveal a nuance between the actancy of the story itself as it moves and affects others beyond

the intentions of the *teller*. See Bruno Latour, *Pandora's Hope: Essays on the Reality of Science Studies* (Cambridge, MA: Harvard University Press, 1999).

1 Telling Time: From Deleuze to Heraclitus and from Queer Theory to Indigenous Ways of Knowing

1 Rob Nixon, *Slow Violence and the Environmentalism of the Poor* (Cambridge, MA: Harvard University Press, 2011), 2, as quoted in Claire Colebrook, "Fast Violence, Revolutionary Violence: Black Lives Matter and the 2020 Pandemic," *Journal of Bioethical Inquiry* 17 (2020): 496.
2 See Melissa Gregg, *Counterproductive: Time Management in the Knowledge Economy* (Durham, NC: Duke University Press, 2018); Paul Gibbs et al., eds., *Universities in the Flux of Time: An Exploration of Time and Temporality in University Life* (New York: Routledge, 2014); and Mark Rifkin, *Beyond Settler Time: Temporal Sovereignty and Indigenous Self-Determination* (Durham, NC: Duke University Press, 2017).
3 Mark Muldoon, *Tricks of Time: Bergson, Merleau-Ponty and Ricoeur in Search of Time, Self and Meaning* (Pittsburgh, PA: Duquesne University Press, 2006), 24.
4 Isaac Newton, *The Principia: Mathematical Principles of Natural Philosophy [1687]* (Berkeley: University of California Press, 1999), 6.
5 In actuality, it would never be anywhere close to a full second ahead at a higher elevation—it only amounts to an increase of 90 billionths of a second over a seventy-nine-year lifespan. See C. W. Chou et al., "Optical Clocks and Relativity," *Science* 329 (2010): 1630–3. In fact, Einstein's famous "twin paradox" hypothesized that if one twin was to stay on Earth and the other traveled through space in a spacecraft, the twin in the spacecraft would age slower than the one that stayed behind. Of course, this hypothesis has since been proven true through time dilation or the findings that the elapsed time measured by two observers differs based on either varied velocities of the two observers, or divergent gravitational fields.
6 Heraclitus, *Fragments*, trans. T. M. Robinson (Toronto: University of Toronto Press, 1991), Fragment 91a and b.
7 Charles M. Sherover, *The Human Experience of Time: The Development of Its Philosophic Meaning [1975]* (Evanston, IL: Northwestern University Press, 2001), 3.
8 Sherover, 4.
9 Heraclitus, *Fragments*, Fragment 1.
10 Friedrich Nietzsche, *Twilight of the Idols*, trans. Walter Kaufmann (New York: Viking, 1954), 481.
11 Aristotle, *Physics*, IV.11 219b 1–2.
12 Aristotle, 219a 2–3.

13 Aristotle, III.1.
14 Aristotle, III.1, 30–1.
15 Aristotle, VI.9.
16 Plato, *Timaeus*, trans. B. Jowett(Aeterna Press: London, 2015.), 37d4.
17 Plato, 47a4–7.
18 Adrian Bardon, *A Brief History of the Philosophy of Time* (Oxford: Oxford University Press, 2013), 25.
19 Augustine, *Confessions*, trans. R. S. Pine-Coffin (Harmondsworth: Penguin, 1970), Book XI, 20, 269.
20 Augustine, Book X, Chapter 8, 218–19.
21 Akhtar et al., "Fictional First Memories."
22 For feminist works see Elizabeth Grosz, *Space, Time, and Perversion: Essays on the Politics of Bodies* (New York: Routledge, 1995); *Becomings: Explorations in Time, Memory, and Futures* (Ithaca, NY: Cornell University Press, 1999); *Time Travels: Feminism, Nature, Power* (Durham, NC: Duke University Press, 2005); *Becoming Undone: Darwinian Reflections on Life, Politics, and Art* (Durham, NC: Duke University Press, 2011); Elizabeth Freeman, *Time Binds: Queer Temporalities, Queer Histories* (Durham, NC: Duke University Press, 2010); J. Jack Halberstam, *In a Queer Time and Place: Transgender Bodies, Subcultural Lives* (New York: New York University Press, 2005); Claire Colebrook, "Stratigraphic Time, Women's Time," *Australian Feminist Studies* 24, no. 59 (2009): 11–16. For transnational texts see Cynthia Enloe, "Feminism, Nationalism, and Militarism: Wariness without Paralysis," in *Feminism, Nationalism, and Militarism* (Arlington, VA: Association for Feminist Anthropology/American Anthropological Association in collaboration with the International Women's Anthropology Conference, 1996), 42–54; Jasbir K. Puar, *Terrorist Assemblages: Homonationalism in Queer Times* (Durham, NC: Duke University Press, 2007); Carolyn Dinshaw et al., "Theorizing Queer Temporalities: A Roundtable Discussion," *GLQ: A Journal of Lesbian and Gay Studies* 13, no. 2–3 (2007): 177–95. For intersections with critical disability studies and "crip" theory, see Rachel Loewen Walker, Danielle Peers, and Lindsay Eales, "New Constellations: Lived Diffractions of Dis/Ability and Dance," in *Feminist Philosophies of Life*, ed. Hasana Sharp and Chloe Taylor (Montreal: McGill-Queen's University Press, 2016), 129–45. For anti-teleological projects see Lee Edelman, *No Future: Queer Theory and the Death Drive* (Durham, NC: Duke University Press, 2004); José Esteban Muñoz, *Cruising Utopia: The Then and There of Queer Futurity* (New York: New York University Press, 2009); Madhavi Menon, "Spurning Teleology in Venus and Adonis," *GLQ: A Journal of Lesbian and Gay Studies* 11, no. 4 (2005): 491–519; Elizabeth Grosz, *The Nick of Time: Politics, Evolution, and the Untimely* (Durham, NC: Duke University Press, 2004). For its crossovers with philosophy see Carla Freccero, *Queer/Early/Modern* (Durham,

NC: Duke University Press, 2005); "Queer Times," *South Atlantic Quarterly* 106, no. 3 (2007): 485–94; Shannon Winnubst, *Queering Freedom* (Bloomington: Indiana University Press, 2006); "Temporality in Queer Theory and Continental Philosophy," *Philosophy Compass* 5, no. 2 (2010): 136–46; Rachel Loewen Walker, "The Living Present as a Materialist Feminist Temporality," *Woman: A Cultural Review* 25, no. 1 (2014): 46–61; Sara Ahmed, *Queer Phenomenology: Orientations, Objects, Others* (Durham, NC: Duke University Press, 2006). And for ethical projects see Neimanis and Loewen Walker, "Weathering: Climate Change and the 'Thick Time' of Transcorporeality"; Rosi Braidotti, *Transpositions: On Nomadic Ethics* (Cambridge: Polity, 2006).

23 Christopher Nealon, *Foundlings: Lesbian and Gay Historical Emotion before Stonewall* (Durham, NC: Duke University Press, 2001), 182.
24 Ahmed, *Queer Phenomenology*, 68.
25 Ahmed, 68.
26 For more political engagements see Wendy Brown, *Politics Out of History* (Princeton: Princeton University Press, 2001); *Undoing the Demos: Neoliberalism's Stealth Revolution* (New York: MIT Press, 2015); Puar, *Terrorist Assemblages: Homonationalism in Queer Times*; and Vincanne Adams, Michelle Murphy, and Adele E. Clarke, "Anticipation: Technoscience, Life, Affect, Temporality," *Subjectivity* 28, no. 1 (2009): 246–65. For others see Edelman, *No Future*; Leo Bersani, *Homos* (Cambridge, MA: Harvard University Press, 2009); Muñoz, *Cruising Utopia*; Grosz, *Time Travels*; Grosz, *The Nick of Time*; Freeman, *Time Binds*.
27 Edelman, *No Future*, 3.
28 Muñoz, *Cruising Utopia*, 95.
29 Muñoz, 185.
30 See Grosz, *Time Travels*, 14–18; *The Nick of Time*.
31 Grosz, *Time Travels*, 26.
32 Grosz, 181.
33 Grosz, 29.
34 E. L. McCallum and Mikko Tuhkanen, "Becoming Unbecoming: Untimely Mediations," in *Queer Times, Queer Becomings* (New York: State University of New York, 2011), 9.
35 Viola Faye Cordova, *How It Is: The Native American Philosophy of V.F. Cordova*, ed. Kathleen Dean Moore et al. (Tuscon: University of Arizona Press, 2007), xiii.
36 Cordova, xiii.
37 Cordova, xiv.
38 Cordova, 175.
39 Rifkin, *Beyond Settler Time: Temporal Sovereignty and Indigenous Self-Determination*, 36.

40 Juan Alejandro Chindoy Chindoy, *A Decolonial Philosophy of Indigenous Colombia: Time, Beauty, and Spirit in Kamëntšá Culture* (London: Rowman & Littlefield, 2020), 18.
41 Chindoy, 18.
42 Williams, *Gilles Deleuze's Philosophy of Time: A Critical Introduction and Guide*, 37. An earlier and shorter version of this chapter is published as Loewen Walker, "The Living Present as a Materialist Feminist Temporality."

2 The Living Present: A Co-Creative Conversation between Deleuze and Winterson

1 Winterson, *The Stone Gods*, 62.
2 Winterson, *The Stone Gods*, 92.
3 Winterson, 93.
4 Gilles Deleuze, "I Have Nothing to Admit," trans. Janis Forman, *Semiotext(e), Anti-Oedipus* 2, no. 3 (1977): 113. For example, Deleuze's work on Kant interprets him in an atypical way by pulling out his theory of the unified subject and reading it instead as one of conflict and difference. Likewise, his explorations of Nietzsche's "will to power" turn the dictum into a vitalist and affirmative philosophy of all matter (human, nonhuman, and otherwise), rather than a psychological drive to overcome resistance, as others have interpreted him. See Gilles Deleuze, *The Critical Philosophy of Kant*, trans. Hugh Tomlinson and Barbara Habberjam (Minneapolis: University of Minnesota Press, 1984); Gilles Deleuze, *Nietzsche and Philosophy*, trans. Hugh Tomlinson (Minneapolis: University of Minnesota Press, 1983).
5 Deleuze, *The Critical Philosophy of Kant*.
6 For Deleuze's texts on literature see Gilles Deleuze, *Proust and Signs: The Complete Text*, trans. Richard Howard (Minneapolis: University of Minnesota Press, 2003); Gilles Deleuze and Felix Guattari, *Kafka: For a Minor Literature*, trans; Dana Polan (Minneapolis: University of Minnesota Press, 1986). For texts on music see Gilles Deleuze, *The Fold: Leibniz and the Baroque*, trans. Tom Conley (Minneapolis: University of Minnesota Press, 1993); Gilles Deleuze, *Cinema I: The Movement-Image*, trans. Hugh Tomlinson and Barbara Habberjam (Minneapolis: University of Minnesota Press, 1986); Gilles Deleuze, *Cinema II: The Time-Image*, trans. Hugh Tomlinson and Barbara Habberjam (Minneapolis: University of Minnesota Press, 1986).
7 Winterson, *The Stone Gods*, 183, emphasis added.
8 Gilles Deleuze and Felix Guattari, *What Is Philosophy?* (New York: Columbia University Press, 1994), 5.
9 Deleuze and Guattari, 34.

10 Winterson, *The Stone Gods*, 88.
11 Winterson, 151.
12 Claire Colebrook, *Understanding Deleuze* (Crows Nest: Allen and Unwin, 2002), 17.
13 Winterson, *The Stone Gods*, 88, emphasis added.
14 Gilles Deleuze, *Negotiations, 1972–1990*, trans. Martin Joughin (New York: Columbia University Press, 1997), 136.
15 And many philosophers have made precisely this case. See Beverley Clack, *Misogyny in the Western Philosophical Tradition: A Reader* (New York: Routledge, 2016); Nancy Tuana, *Woman and the History of Philosophy* (New York: Paragon Press, 1992); Michèle Le Doeuff, *Hipparchia's Choice: An Essay Concerning Women, Philosophy, Etc.* (Cambridge, MA: Blackwell, 1991); Susan Moller Okin, *Women in Western Political Philosophy* (Princeton: Princeton University Press, 1988); Genevieve Lloyd, *The Man of Reason: Male and Female in Western Philosophy* (Minneapolis: University of Minnesota Press, 1984).
16 See Charles J. Stivale, *Gilles Deleuze: Key Concepts* (New York: Routledge, 2014); Eugene B. Young, Gary Genosko, and Janell Watson, *The Deleuze and Guattari Dictionary* (London: Bloomsbury Academic, 2013); Adrian Parr, *Deleuze Dictionary Revised Edition* (Edinburgh: Edinburgh University Press, 2010); Williams, *Gilles Deleuze's Difference and Repetition: A Critical Introduction and Guide*; Colebrook, *Understanding Deleuze*.
17 Gilles Deleuze, *The Logic of Sense*, trans. Mark Lester (New York: Columbia University Press, 1990), 3.
18 Deleuze, 3.
19 Deleuze, 3.
20 Gilles Deleuze and Claire Parnet, *Dialogues* (London: Athlone Press, 1987), 39, emphasis added.
21 Henri Bergson, *Creative Evolution*, trans. Arthur Mitchell (Mineola, NY: Dover, 1998), 14.
22 Henri Bergson, *Time and Free Will: An Essay on the Immediate Data of Consciousness* (Mineola, NY: Dover, 2001), 100–1.
23 Bergson, *Creative Evolution*, 7.
24 Henri Bergson, *The Creative Mind* (Whitefish, MT: Kessinger, 2007), 22–3.
25 Deleuze and Guattari, *A Thousand Plateaus: Capitalism and Schizophrenia*, 239.
26 Deleuze, *Difference and Repetition*, 41.
27 Angela Gosetti-Murrayjohn, "Sappho as the Tenth Muse in Hellenistic Epigram," *Arethusa* 39, no. 1 (2006): 21–45.
28 Margaret Reynolds, *The Sappho Companion* (London: Vintage, 2001).
29 Sappho 31, verses 1–15, trans. Julia Dubnoff. https://www.uh.edu/~cldue/texts/sappho.html%20https://www.uh.edu/~cldue/texts/sappho.html (accessed January 29, 2020).

30 Todd May, "When Is a Deleuzian Becoming?," *Continental Philosophy Review* 36 (2003): 147. https://link-springercom.cyber.usask.ca/article/10.1023/A:1026036516963 (accessed August 25, 2019).
31 Deleuze, *Difference and Repetition*, 72.
32 Deleuze, 72.
33 Deleuze, 74.
34 Deleuze, 75.
35 Williams, *Gilles Deleuze's Philosophy of Time: A Critical Introduction and Guide*, 60.
36 Deleuze, *Difference and Repetition*, 75.
37 Deleuze, 75.
38 Bergson, *The Creative Mind*, 200.
39 Deleuze, *Difference and Repetition*, 80.
40 Colebrook, *Understanding Deleuze*, 64.
41 Friedrich Nietzsche, *The Gay Science*, trans. Walter Kaufmann (New York: Vintage, 1974), 341.
42 Deleuze, *Nietzsche and Philosophy*, 49.
43 Williams, *Gilles Deleuze's Philosophy of Time: A Critical Introduction and Guide*, 37; Winterson, *The Stone Gods*, 86, 119, 207.
44 Williams, *Gilles Deleuze's Philosophy of Time: A Critical Introduction and Guide*.
45 Williams, 37.
46 Adams, Murphy, and Clarke, "Anticipation," 247.
47 Adams, Murphy, and Clarke, 248, emphasis in original.
48 Jana Sawicki, "Disciplining Mothers: Feminism and the New Reproductive Technologies," ed. Janet Price and Margrit Shildrik (New York: Routledge, 1999), 194.
49 Adams, Murphy, and Clarke, "Anticipation," 251.
50 Winterson, *The Stone Gods*, 22.
51 Brown, *Politics Out of History*, 5.
52 Brown, 6.
53 Sawicki, "Disciplining Mothers," 194.
54 Winnubst, "Temporality in Queer Theory and Continental Philosophy," 138.
55 See Halberstam, *In a Queer Time and Place: Transgender Bodies, Subcultural Lives*; Ahmed, *Queer Phenomenology*; Edelman, *No Future*; Winnubst, *Queering Freedom*.
56 Edelman, *No Future*.
57 Halberstam, *In a Queer Time and Place: Transgender Bodies, Subcultural Lives*, 152.
58 "It Gets Better," emphasis added. https://itgetsbetter.org/ (accessed February 19, 2019).
59 Jason Tseng, "Does It Really Get Better?: A Conscientious Critique," *The Bilerico Project* (blog), October 3, 2010, http://bilerico.lgbtqnation.com/2010/10/does_it_really_get_better.php (accessed February 18, 2019).

60 Though it does exert real and dangerous force on people's lives, the "heteronormative trajectory" that queer theorists address here exerts force on *all* lives, not only 2SLGBTQ people. I reference this point of clarity again in Chapter 4.
61 See Rebecca Coleman and Debra Ferreday, eds., "Hope and Feminist Theory," *Journal for Cultural Research* 14, no. 4 (2010): 313–21; Erin McKenna, *The Task of Utopia: A Pragmatist and Feminist Perspective* (Lanham, MD: Rowman & Littlefield, 2001); Christine De Pizan, *The Book of the City of Ladies* (University of Michigan: Persea Books, 1982).
62 Rebecca Coleman and Debra Ferreday, "Introduction: Hope and Feminist Theory," *Journal for Cultural Research* 14, no. 4 (2010): 313–21.
63 Sara Ahmed, *The Cultural Politics of Emotion* (New York: Routledge, 2004), 187, emphasis added.
64 Ahmed, 187.
65 The famous five included Nellie McClung, Henrietta Muir Edwards, Louise McKinney, Emily Murphy, and Irene Parlby. The Persons Case was argued in 1927 because, despite most women having attained the right to vote in Canada, they were still not recognized as "persons" due to the British North America Act of 1867, and therefore not allowed to be appointed to the Canadian Senate.
66 Rebecca Coleman, "Past and Future Perfect? Beauty, Affect and Hope," *Journal for Cultural Research* 14, no. 4 (2010): 357–73.
67 Winterson, *The Stone Gods*, 119.
68 In fact, one of Winterson's editors *did* leave a copy of the unfinished manuscript at an Underground station in south London, where a fan found it and then returned it to the publisher.
69 Winterson, *The Stone Gods*, 202.
70 Winterson, 86, 119, 207.
71 Winterson, 80, emphasis in original.

3 Quantum Materialism: Bringing Time and Matter Together in a Feminist Future

1 Philip Ball, *Beyond Weird: Why Everything You Thought You Knew about Quantum Physics Is Different* (Chicago: University of Chicago Press, 2018), 11.
2 Melissa K. Nelson, *Original Instructions: Indigenous Teachings for a Sustainable Future* (Rochester, NY: Simon and Schuster, 2008), 11; Audre Lorde, "The Master's Tools Will Never Dismantle the Master's House," in *Sister Outsider* (Berkeley: Crossing Press, 1984).
3 Ball, *Beyond Weird*, 19.
4 Barad, *Meeting the Universe Halfway*, 198.

5 Karen Barad, "Posthumanist Performativity: Toward an Understanding of How Matter Comes to Matter," *Signs: Journal of Women in Culture and Society* 28, no. 3 (2003): 801.
6 Barad, 821, fn. 26.
7 Claire Colebrook, "On Not Becoming Man: The Materialist Politics of Unactualized Potential," in *Material Feminisms*, ed. Stacey Alaimo and Susan Hekman (Bloomington, IN: Indiana University Press, 2008), 68.
8 Vicki Kirby, *Quantum Anthropologies: Life at Large* (Durham, NC: Duke University Press, 2011), 73.
9 Kirby, 73.
10 Kirby, 73.
11 Kirby, 72.
12 Jacques Derrida, "Structure, Sign and Play in the Discourse of the Human Sciences," in *Margins of Philosophy* (Chicago: University of Chicago Press, 1982), 158.
13 Kirby, *Quantum Anthropologies: Life at Large*, 83.
14 Nikolas S. Rose, *The Politics of Life Itself: Biomedicine, Power, and Subjectivity in the Twenty-First Century* (Princeton: Princeton University Press, 2007); see also Rosi Braidotti, "The Politics of 'Life Itself' and New Ways of Dying," in *New Materialisms: Ontology, Agency, and Politics*, ed. Diana Coole and Susan Frost (Durham, NC: Duke University Press, 2010), 201–19.
15 Michel Foucault, *History of Sexuality: An Introduction* (New York: Vintage, 1990), 140.
16 Rose, *The Politics of Life Itself*, 14.
17 Landecker, as quoted in Rose, 17.
18 Rose, 17.
19 Ackerman, Jennifer, "White Bear First Nation to Receive $9.2 Million for New Water Treatment System," *Regina Leader-Post*, July 25, 2017, http://https://leaderpost.com/news/local-news/white-bear-first-nation-to-receive-9-2-million-for-new-water-treatment-system (accessed August 18, 2020).
20 Astrida Neimanis, *Bodies of Water: Posthuman Feminist Phenomenology* (London: Bloomsbury, 2017), 1, emphasis added.
21 Jane Bennett, *Vibrant Matter: A Political Ecology of Things* (Durham, NC: Duke University Press, 2009), 63.
22 See Hans Driesch, *The Science and Philosophy of the Organism: The Gifford Lectures Delivered before the University of Aberdeen in the Year 1907* (London: Adam and Charles Black, 1908); Bergson, *Creative Evolution*.
23 Gilles Deleuze, *Negotiations, 1972–1990*, European Perspectives (New York: Columbia University Press, 1995), 143.
24 Deleuze, 143.
25 Deleuze and Guattari, *What Is Philosophy?*
26 Bennett, *Vibrant Matter*, 3.
27 U.S. Department of Health and Health Services, as quoted in Bennett, 91.

28 Spinoza, as quoted in Bennett, 2.
29 Spinoza, as quoted in Bennett, 2.
30 Latour, as quoted in Bennett, 9.
31 Bennett, 9.
32 Claire Colebrook, "Queer Aesthetics," in *Queer Times, Queer Becomings*, ed. E. L. McCallum and Mikko Tuhkanen (New York: SUNY Press, 2011), 25.
33 Colebrook, 32–3.
34 Colebrook, 31.
35 Colebrook, 31.
36 Claire Colebrook, *Deleuze and the Meaning of Life* (London: Continuum Books, 2010), 137.
37 Patrice Haynes, "Creative Becoming and the Patiency of Matter: Feminism, New Materialism, and Theology," *Angelaki* 19, no. 1 (2014): 137.
38 Braidotti, "The Politics of 'Life Itself' and New Ways of Dying," 202.
39 Paul-Antoine Moreau et al., "Imaging Bell-Type Nonlocal Behavior," *Science Advances* 5, no. 7 (July 1, 2019): 1–8, https://doi.org/10.1126/sciadv.aaw2563 (accessed February 26, 2021).
40 Karen Barad, "Agential Realism: Feminist Interventions in Understanding Scientific Practices," in *The Science Studies Reader*, ed. Mario Biagioli (New York: Routledge, 1999), 3.
41 Barad, "Posthumanist Performativity: Toward an Understanding of How Matter Comes to Matter," 823, emphasis in original.
42 Idle No More is a protest movement begun by four Indigenous and non-Indigenous women in Saskatoon, SK, Canada, in November 2012. It has since sparked a wide variety of political action in Canada and around the globe, particularly aimed at protesting governmental legislation intent upon reducing environmental protections. Acts of solidarity and activism such as public round dances, teach-ins, and flash mobs argue for Indigenous sovereignty and protest against the continued discrimination against Indigenous peoples.
43 Rebecca Adamson, "First Nations Survival and the Future of the Earth," in *Original Instructions: Indigenous Teachings for a Sustainable Future*, ed. Melissa K. Nelson (Rochester, VT: Bear, 2008), 34.
44 Adamson, 33.
45 Gregory Cajete, *Native Science: Natural Laws of Interdependence* (Sante Fe, NM: Clearlight, 2000).
46 Cajete, 5.
47 Cajete, *Native Science: Natural Laws of Interdependence*; Nelson, *Original Instructions*.
48 I borrow this phrase from Cajete's *Native Science: Natural Laws of Interdependence*; Lila, "The Pace of Queer Time," *Autostraddle*, March 16, 2016, https://www.autostraddle.com/the-pace-of-queer-time-329459/ (accessed February 26, 2019).

4 "An Erratic and Uneasy Becoming": Queering Time, Reworking the Past

1 Deleuze, *Negotiations, 1972–1990*, 141.
2 Deleuze and Guattari, *A Thousand Plateaus: Capitalism and Schizophrenia*; Elizabeth Grosz, "A Thousand Tiny Sexes: Feminism and Rhizomatics," *Topoi* 12, no. 2 (1993): 167–79.
3 Chelle Matthews, Rachel Loewen Walker, and Miki Mappin, "Policy Recommendation: Toward the Inclusion of Gender Identity and Expression as Protected Grounds in the Saskatchewan Human Rights Code" (Saskatoon, SK: The Avenue Community Centre for Gender and Sexual Diversity, 2014).
4 Adrienne Rich, "Compulsory Heterosexuality and Lesbian Existence," *Women: Sex and Sexuality* 5, no. 4 (1980): 631–60.
5 Michael Lovelock, "'My Coming Out Story': Lesbian, Gay and Bisexual Youth Identities on YouTube," *International Journal of Cultural Studies* 22, no. 1 (2019): 70–85; Julia Golda Harris, "Without Closets: A Queer and Feminist Re-Imagining of Narratives of Queer Experience," Honors Thesis, https://digitalcommons.oberlin.edu/cgi/viewcontent.cgi?article=1288&context=honors (accessed January 29, 2019); (Oberlin College, 2014); Lal Zimman, "'The Other Kind of Coming Out': Transgender People and the Coming Out Narrative Genre," *Gender & Language* 3, no. 1 (May 2009): 53–80; Alex Wilson, "N'tacimowin Inna Nah'" *Canadian Woman Studies* 26, no. 3/4 (2008): 193–9.
6 As I indicated in the preface, I have found Viviane Namaste's article "Undoing Theory: The 'Transgender Question' and the Epistemic Violence of Anglo-American Feminist Theory," 11–31, particularly inspiring on a number of fronts, not the least of which includes its overarching argument that feminist research and theory has often failed to involve the lived experiences of those it purports to address.
7 Puar, *Terrorist Assemblages: Homonationalism in Queer Times*, 91; Gloria Anzaldua, "To(o) Queer the Writer—Loca, Escritora y Chicana," in *The Gloria Anzaldúa Reader*, by Gloria Anzaldua, ed. AnaLouise Louise Keating et al. (Durham, NC: Duke University Press, 2009), 166.
8 Dinshaw et al., "Theorizing Queer Temporalities," 181.
9 Lila, "The Pace of Queer Time."
10 Rachel Loewen Walker, "Toward a FIERCE Nomadology: Contesting Queer Geographies on the Christopher Street Pier," *PhaenEx* 6, no. 1 (2011): 90–120.
11 See Elizabeth Grosz, *Architecture from the Outside: Essays on Virtual and Real Space* (London: MIT Press, 2001); Gordon Brent Ingram, Anne-Marie Bouthillette, and Yolanda Retter, *Queers in Space: Communities, Public Places, Sites of Resistance* (Seattle, WA: Bay Press, 1997); bell hooks, "Choosing the Margin as a Space of Radical Openness," *Framework* 36 (1989): 15–23; Dereka Rushbrook, "Cities, Queer

Space, and the Cosmopolitan Tourist," *GLQ: A Journal of Lesbian and Gay Studies* 8, no. 1/2 (2002): 183–206; Nancy Duncan, "Renegotiating Gender and Sexuality in Public and Private Spaces," in *Bodyspace: Destabilizing Geographies of Gender and Sexuality*, ed. Nancy Duncan (London: Routledge, 1996); David Bell et al., *Pleasure Zones: Bodies, Cities, Spaces* (New York: Syracuse University Press, 2001); Wayne Myslik, "Renegotiating the Social/Sexual Identities of Places: Gay Communities as Safe Havens or Sites of Resistance?," in *Bodyspace: Destabilizing Geographies of Gender and Sexuality*, ed. Nancy Duncan.

12 Michel Foucault, "Of Other Spaces: Utopias and Heterotopias," trans. Jay Miskowiec, *Architecture/Mouvement/Continuité*, 1984, 1–9, http://web.mit.edu/allanmc/www/foucault1.pdf (accessed August 28, 2019).

13 Michel Foucault, *The Order of Things: An Archaeology of the Human Sciences* (New York: Vintage Books, 1994).

14 Foucault, xviii.

15 Foucault, xviii.

16 Foucault, "Of Other Spaces: Utopias and Heterotopias," 93.

17 Foucault, 93.

18 See Angela Jones, "Queer Heterotopias: Homonormativity and the Future of Queerness," *Interalia* 14, no. 4 (2009): 1–20; Duncan, "Renegotiating Gender and Sexuality in Public and Private Spaces"; Myslik, "Renegotiating the Social/Sexual Identities of Places: Gay Communities as Safe Havens or Sites of Resistance?"; Edward W. Soja, *Thirdspace: Journeys to Los Angeles and Other Real-and-Imagined Places* (Oxford: Blackwell, 1996); Homi Bhabha, *The Location of Culture* (New York: Routledge, 1994); hooks, "Choosing the Margin as a Space of Radical Openness"; Gloria Anzaldua, *Borderlands/La Frontera: The New Mestiza* (San Francisco: Spinsters/Aunt Lute, 1987); Victor Turner, "Liminality and Communicatas," in *The Ritual Process: Structure and Anti-Structure* (Chicago:, 1969), 94–130.

19 Gayle Salamon, "Last Look at the Lex," *Studies in Gender and Sexuality* 16, no. 2 (2015): 147.

20 Salamon, 146.

21 Foucault, "Of Other Spaces: Utopias and Heterotopias," 6.

22 Foucault, 7.

23 Wilson, "N'tacimowin Inna Nah," 197.

24 Wilson, 196.

25 See Halberstam, *In a Queer Time and Place: Transgender Bodies, Subcultural Lives*; Edelman, *No Future*; Muñoz, *Cruising Utopia*.

26 Kathryn Bond Stockton, *The Queer Child, or Growing Sideways in the Twentieth Century* (Durham, NC: Duke University Press, 2009), 6.

27 McCallum and Tuhkanen, "Becoming Unbecoming: Untimely Mediations," 1.

28 Lila, "The Pace of Queer Time."
29 J. Jack Halberstam, *The Queer Art of Failure* (Durham, NC: Duke University Press, 2011), 27.
30 Halberstam, 29.
31 Halberstam, 80.
32 Halberstam, 81.
33 Orson Welles, *Citizen Kane*, Drama, Mystery, 1941; Stanton and Unkrich, *Finding Nemo*. Note that my reference to *Citizen Kane* is tongue-in-cheek as Deleuze spent a great deal of time discussing the film in *Cinema II: The Time-Image*, trans. Hugh Tomlinson and Barbara Habberjam (Minneapolis: University of Minnesota Press, 1986).
34 Eve Kosofsky Sedgwick, *Epistemology of the Closet* (Berkeley: University of California Press, 1990), 4.
35 Kosofsky Sedgwick, *Epistemology of the Closet*; Judith Butler, "Imitation and Gender Insubordination," in *Inside/Out*, ed. Diana Fuss (New York: Routledge, 1991), 13–29.
36 Kosofsky Sedgwick, *Epistemology of the Closet*, 71.
37 Philip Bockman, "A Fine Day," *New York Native* 175 (1986): 13.
38 See William A. Henry III, "Ethics: Forcing Gays Out of the Closet," *Time*, January 29, 1990, http://content.time.com/time/subscriber/article/0,33009,969264-2,00.html (accessed April 25, 2019).
39 See Ian Lucas, *OutRage!: An Oral History* (London: Cassell, 1998); Andrew Brown, "How Outing Came in with a Vengeance," *The Independent Online*, March 21, 1995, http://www.independent.co.uk/news/uk/how-outing-came-in-with-a-vengeance-1612094.html (accessed April 25, 2019); Randy Shilts, *The Mayor of Castro Street: The Life and Times of Harvey Milk* (New York: St. Martin's Press, 1982). There is a scholarly and journalistic debate surrounding the practice of outing largely from the mid-1990s. OutRage! And Queer Nation outed public figures in order to expose their hypocrisy (in the case of gay Republicans, for example) and/or to create public role models (in the case of famous figures). The counterarguments include the case that outing removes the matter of choice from its targets, can easily put people in danger, and does not result in effective role models. See Simon Watney, "Queer Epistemology: Activism, 'Outing', and the Politics of Sexual Identities," *Critical Quarterly* 36, no. 1 (1994): 13–27, for a comprehensive overview.
40 Butler, "Imitation and Gender Insubordination," 309.
41 "NBA's Jason Collins Comes Out as the First Openly Gay Athlete in Major U.S. Team Sport," NOLA.com, April 29, 2013, http://www.nola.com/sports/index.ssf/2013/04/nbas_jason_collins_comes_out_a.html (accessed August 28, 2019).

42 To be fair, the article includes a final paragraph that states that "female athletes have found more acceptance in coming out," and then cites both Brittney Griner (a basketball player) and tennis player Martina Navratilova who has been out since 1981. Seemingly, the use of "gay" refers only to *men*, in this context; however, the author's small attempt at accuracy fails to justify its broad strokes.
43 Zimman, "'The Other Kind of Coming Out,'" 60.
44 E. van der Wal, "Crossing Over, Coming Out, Blending In: A Trans Interrogation of the Closet," *South African Review of Sociology* 47, no. 3 (2016): 44-64.
45 Wilson, "N'tacimowin Inna Nah," 197.
46 Rifkin, *Beyond Settler Time: Temporal Sovereignty and Indigenous Self-Determination*, 12.
47 Rifkin, 16.
48 Deleuze, *Negotiations, 1972-1990*, 1997, 170.
49 Deleuze, *Negotiations, 1972-1990*, 1995, 170-1.
50 Wilson, "N'tacimowin Inna Nah," 197.
51 Lovelock, "'My Coming Out Story,'" 83.
52 Lovelock, 83.
53 Though there is clearly no official "date" to indicate the beginning of post-structuralism I am referencing, the symposium on "The Languages of Criticism and the Sciences of Man" that took place at Johns Hopkins University in 1966 is sometimes cited as the point at which post-structuralism began to ripple through the field. This is also the symposium where Derrida gave the paper "Structure, Sign, and Play in the Discourse of the Human Sciences," in *Margins of Philosophy*, 201-331, which offers a critique of structuralism. For further discussion of this origin story see Graham Allen, *Roland Barthes* (New York: Routledge, 2003), 67.
54 Butler, 175, emphasis in original; Jacques Derrida, *Of Grammatology*, trans. Gayatri Chakravorty Spivak (Baltimore: JHU Press, 1998), 158.
55 Judith Butler, *Giving an Account of Oneself* (New York: Fordham University Press, 2005).
56 Butler, 17.
57 Butler, 99.
58 Butler, 101.
59 Butler, *Gender Trouble: Feminism and the Subversion of Identity*.
60 Foucault never himself addressed gender, but instead developed the technologies of production in relation to the construction of male identity and sexuality Foucault, *History of Sexuality: An Introduction*.
61 Braidotti, "The Politics of 'Life Itself' and New Ways of Dying"; *The Posthuman* (Cambridge, MA: Polity Press, 2013); Iris van der Tuin, "The New Materialist 'Always Already': On an A-Human Humanities," *NORA – Nordic Journal of*

Feminist and Gender Research 19, no. 4 (2011): 285–90; Van Der Tuin, "A Different Starting Point, a Different Metaphysics"; Barad, *Meeting the Universe Halfway*; Manuel DeLanda, *Philosophy & Simulation: The Emergence of Synthetic Reason* (London: Continuum, 2010).

62 J. R. Latham, "Axiomatic: Constituting 'Transexuality' and Trans Sexualities in Medicine," *Sexualities* 22, no. 1–2 (2019): 14; Harry Benjamin, *The Transsexual Phenomenon*, 1996, https://journals.sagepub.com/doi/full/10.1177/1363460717740258. As a positive improvement on this, in many cities in Canada, at the urging of local activists and community groups, healthcare providers are increasingly encouraged to use the Standards of Care as developed by the World Professional Association for Transgender Health (WPATH). In Canada, the Canadian Professional Association of Transgender Health (CPATH) endorses these standards of care and offers an annual conference and training summit (http://cpath.ca/en/). See "Standards of Care for the Health of Transsexual, Transgender, and Gender Nonconforming People, 7th Version" (WPATH), https://www.wpath.org/publications/soc (accessed September 29, 2019).

63 Latham, "Axiomatic: Constituting 'Transexuality' and Trans Sexualities in Medicine," 17. Latham relies on Sandy Stone's analysis of this feedback loop in "The Empire Strikes Back: A Posttranssexual Manifesto," in *The Transgender Studies Reader*, ed. Susan Stryker and Steven Whittle (New York: Routledge, 2006), 221–35.

64 Latham, "Axiomatic: Constituting 'Transexuality' and Trans Sexualities in Medicine," 26.

65 Deleuze discusses "differenciation" in *Bergsonism*, trans. Hugh Tomlinson and Barbara Habberjam (Brooklyn, NY: Zone Books, 1988), and in *Difference and Repetition*, 208–11. While differentiation refers to mathematical division, for Deleuze, differenciation is a process of becoming different; it is the process of variation and variability.

66 Deleuze, *Difference and Repetition*, 35.

67 Deleuze, 37.

68 Puar, *Terrorist Assemblages: Homonationalism in Queer Times*, 212.

69 Puar, 211.

70 Puar, 222.

71 This is tantamount to using a sledgehammer rather than a fine file, as Deleuze and Guattari indicate in *A Thousand Plateaus: Capitalism and Schizophrenia*, 177. By this they are referring to the difficulty inherent in any attempts at desubjectification.

72 Puar, *Terrorist Assemblages: Homonationalism in Queer Times*, 212.

73 Puar, 212.

74 Joan Roughgarden, *Evolution's Rainbow: Diversity, Gender, and Sexuality in Nature and People* (Berkeley: University of California Press, 2004).

75 Karen Barad uses the phrase "onto-epistem-ology" to indicate that being and knowledge are inseparable (see *Meeting the Universe Halfway*, 185).
76 Tuin, "The New Materialist 'Always Already,'" 288.
77 Deleuze, *Difference and Repetition*, 35–41.
78 See Rifkin, *Beyond Settler Time: Temporal Sovereignty and Indigenous Self-Determination*; Nelson, *Original Instructions*; Tony See, "Deleuze and Buddhism: Two Concepts of Subjectivity?," *Deleuze and Guattari Studies* 13, no. 1 (2019): 104–22.
79 Gloria Anzaldua, as quoted in Mikko Tuhkanen, "Mestiza Metaphysics," in *Queer Times, Queer Becomings* (New York: State University of New York, 2011), 162.
80 Colebrook, "Queer Aesthetics," 31.

5 Thick Time: Echoes of the Anthropocene

1 Sections of this chapter are taken from and inspired by my short article titled, "Environment Imagining Otherwise," *Journal of Curriculum and Pedagogy* 10, no. 1 (June 1, 2013): 34–7.
2 Deleuze and Guattari, *A Thousand Plateaus: Capitalism and Schizophrenia*.
3 Yuval Noah Harari, *Sapiens: A Brief History of Humankind* (Toronto: McClelland & Stewart, 2014), 74.
4 Tom Cohen, Claire Colebrook, and J. Hillis Miller, *Twilight of the Anthropocene Idols* (London: Open Humanities Press, 2016); Claire Colebrook, "The Anthropocene and the Archive," *The Memory Network*, 2014, http://thememorynetwork.com/blog/2014/01/27/the-anthropocene-and-the-archive/ (accessed August 13, 2020;)Dipesh Chakrabarty, "The Climate of History: Four Theses," *Critical Inquiry*, no. 35 (2009): 197–222; Alaimo, *Bodily Natures: Science, Environment, and the Material Self*.
5 Tom Cohen, "Anecographics," in *Impasses of the Post-Global: Theory in the Era of Climate Change*, ed. Henry Sussman (University of Michigan: Open Humanities Press, 2012), 50.
6 Robert Markley, "Time," in *Telemorphosis: Theory in the Era of Climate Change*, Vol. 1, ed. Tom Cohen= (University of Michigan: Open Humanities Press, 2012), 85.
7 Barad, *Meeting the Universe Halfway*, 183.
8 Donna Haraway, *When Species Meet* (Minneapolis: University of Minnesota Press, 2008).
9 Barad, *Meeting the Universe Halfway*.
10 Nelson, *Original Instructions*, 11; Lorde, "The Master's Tools Will Never Dismantle the Master's House."

11 Jan Zalasiewicz et al., "Making the Case for a Formal Anthropocene Epoch: An Analysis of Ongoing Critiques," *Newsletters on Stratigraphy* 5, no. 2 (2017): 208.
12 Paul Crutzen and Eugene Stoermer, "The Anthropocene," *Global Change Newsletters* 41 (2000): 17–18; Paul Crutzen, "Geology of Mankind," *Nature* 415 (2002): 23.
13 Zalasiewicz et al., "Making the Case for a Formal Anthropocene Epoch."
14 See Zalasiewicz et al., 212.
15 Colin N. Waters et al., "The Anthropocene Is Functionally and Stratigraphically Distinct from the Holocene," *Science* 351, no. 6269 (January 8, 2016), http://science.sciencemag.org/content/351/6269/aad2622 (accessed August 13, 2020).
16 Celia, "Jellyfish Overpopulation—a Threat to the Oceans?," *Marine Science Today* (blog), 2009, http://marinesciencetoday.com/2009/06/11/jellyfish-overpopulation-a-threat-to-the-oceans/ (accessed August 13, 2020); Richard Stone, "Massive Outbreak of Jellyfish Could Spell Trouble for Fisheries," *Yale Environment 360* (blog), January 13, 2011, https://e360.yale.edu/features/massive_outbreak_of_jellyfish_could_spell_trouble_for_fisheries (accessed August 13, 2020).
17 Chris Wilson, "Obituary: Remembering the Holocene Epoch," *Time*, August 9, 2016, http://time.com/4471327/holocene-epoch-end-anthropocene/ (accessed August 15, 2020).
18 Colebrook, "The Anthropocene and the Archive," para. 7
19 Andrew C. Revkin, "Confronting the 'Anthropocene,'" *Dot Earth Blog* (blog), May 11, 2011, https://dotearth.blogs.nytimes.com/2011/05/11/confronting-the-anthropocene/ (accessed August 20, 2020).
20 David Chandler, *Ontopolotics in the Anthropocene: An Introduction to Mapping, Sensing and Hacking* (London: Routledge, 2018).
21 Alaimo, *Bodily Natures: Science, Environment, and the Material Self*, 2.
22 Alaimo, 2.
23 Alaimo, 2.
24 Alaimo, 283.
25 Alaimo, 283.
26 Coral Short, *Genderless Jellyfish* (Group Intervention Video, 2013).
27 I draw on Heideger's concept of "worlding" here, as a process of world-making, or becoming-world. For Heidegger, worlding is always bound to Dasein, or the primal nature of "being" that is always bound to an entity. Therefore, it is restricted to man's being and excludes animals, minerals, plants, and materials from any worlding activities. Martin Heidegger, *Being and Time*, trans. John Macquarrie and Edward Robinson (Oxford: Basil Blackwell, 1927).
28 Wark, as quoted on the back cover of Cohen, Colebrook, and Miller, *Twilight of the Anthropocene Idols*.
29 Winnubst, *Queering Freedom*, 128.
30 Adams, Murphy, and Clarke, "Anticipation," 248.

31 Chakrabarty, "The Climate of History: Four Theses."
32 Isabelle Stengers, *The Invention of Modern Science* (Minneapolis: University of Minnesota Press, 2000), 144.
33 Zalasiewicz et al., "Making the Case for a Formal Anthropocene Epoch."
34 Chakrabarty, "The Climate of History: Four Theses."
35 Cohen, Colebrook, and Miller, *Twilight of the Anthropocene Idols*, 7.
36 Grosz, *Becomings*; *Time Travels*; Braidotti, "The Politics of 'Life Itself' and New Ways of Dying"; Braidotti, "The Ethics of Becoming-Imperceptible," in *Deleuze and Philosophy*, ed. Constantin V. Boundas (Edinburgh: Edinburgh University Press, 2006), 133–59; Coole and Frost, "Introducing the New Materialisms," in *New Materialisms: Ontology, Agency, and Politics*, 1–46; Alaimo, *Bodily Natures: Science, Environment, and the Material Self*.
37 Grosz, *Becomings*, 15–16.
38 Deleuze, *Difference and Repetition*, 35.
39 "Sustain; Sustainability," in *Oxford Dictionary Online*, https://en.oxforddictionaries.com/definition/sustainability (accessed October 2, 2018).
40 Jenna Tiitsman, "Planetary Subjects after the Death of Geography," in *Planetary Loves: Spivak, Postcoloniality, and Theology*, ed. Stephen D. Moore and Mayra Rivera (New York: Fordham University Press, 2011), 150.
41 Grosz, *Becomings*, 17.
42 Claire Colebrook, *Death of the PostHuman: Essays on Extinction, Vol. 1* (Ann Arbor, MI: Open Humanities Press, 2014), 59–60.

6 An Ethics of Entanglement

1 Nathan Jun, "Introduction," in *Deleuze and Ethics*, ed. Nathan Jun and Daniel W. Smith (Edinburgh: Edinburgh University Press, 2011), 1.
2 Gilles Deleuze, *Spinoza: Practical Philosophy*, trans. Robert Hurley (San Francisco: City Lights Books, 1988), 18.
3 Luc Boltanski and Eve Chiapello, *The New Spirit of Capitalism* (New York: Verso, 2007), 467.
4 Boltanski and Chiapello, 147.
5 Jun, "Introduction," 3.
6 Levi R. Bryant, "The Ethics of the Event: Deleuze and Ethics without Αρχή," in *Deleuze and Ethics*, ed. Daniel W. Smith and Nathan Jun (Edinburgh: Edinburgh University Press, 2011), 28.
7 Deleuze, *The Logic of Sense*, 167–8.
8 Anthony Uhlmann, "Deleuze, Ethics, Ethology, and Art," in *Deleuze and Ethics*, ed. Daniel W. Smith and Nathan Jun (Edinburgh: Edinburgh University Press,

2011), 154–70; Erinn Cunniff Gilson, "Responsive Becoming: Ethics between Deleuze and Feminism," in *Deleuze and Ethics*, ed. Daniel W. Smith and Nathan Jun (Edinburgh: Edinburgh University Press, 2011), 89–107; John Lundy, "The Stroll: Reflections on Deleuzian Ethics," *Rhizomes: Cultural Studies in Emerging Knowledge* 26, no. 1 (2014), http://www.rhizomes.net/issue26/lundy.html (accessed February 19, 2019); Daniel W. Smith, "Deleuze and the Question of Desire: Towards and Immanent Theory of Ethics," in *Deleuze and Ethics*, ed. Daniel W. Smith and Nathan Jun (Edinburgh: Edinburgh University Press, 2011), 123–41; Kathrin Thiele, "Of Immanence and Becoming: Deleuze and Guattari's Philosophy and/as Relational Ontology," *Deleuze Studies* 10, no. 1 (2016): 117–34.

9 Bryant, "The Ethics of the Event: Deleuze and Ethics without Αρχή," 36.
10 Lawrence V. Harper, "Epigenetic Inheritance and the Intergenerational Transfer of Experience," *Psychological Bulletin* 131, no. 3 (2005): 340–60; Christopher W. Kuzawa and Elizabeth Sweet, "Epigenetics and the Embodiment of Race: Developmental Origins of US Racial Disparities in Cardiovascular Health," *American Journal of Human Biology: The Official Journal of the Human Biology Council* 21, no. 1 (2009): 2–15; Sarah C. P. Williams, "Epigenetics," *Proceedings of the National Academy of Sciences* 110, no. 9 (2013): 3209.
11 Harper, "Epigenetic Inheritance and the Intergenerational Transfer of Experience," 341.
12 Kuzawa and Sweet, "Epigenetics and the Embodiment of Race."
13 Noela Davis, "The Sociality of Biology: Epigenetics and the Molecularisation of the Social" (paper presented at Mattering: Feminism, Science, and Materialism, City University of New York, 2013). Note as well that epigenetics is not always used to support arguments that we would call transformative or open-ended; in fact, the knowledge that our social environments can have impacts on biology for generations to come has been used to bolster narratives that put the blame on individuals (especially pregnant women); see Mark A. Rothstein, Yu Cai, and Gary E. Marchant, "The Ghost in Our Genes: Legal and Ethical Implications of Epigenetics," *Health Matrix Clevel* 19, no. 1 (2009): 1–62.
14 Megan Warin and Anne Hammarström, "Material Feminism and Epigenetics: A 'Critical Window' for Engagement?," *Australian Feminist Studies* 33, no. 97(2018): 11.
15 Lawrence Harper, "Epigenetic Inheritance and the Intergenerational Transfer of Experience," 340–1.
16 Colebrook, "Stratigraphic Time, Women's Time," 12.
17 Williams, *Gilles Deleuze's Philosophy of Time: A Critical Introduction and Guide*, 18.
18 Bronwyn Winter, "'The Ties That Bind Us': The Hidden Knots of Gay Marriage," *PORTAL Journal of Multidisciplinary International Studies* 11, no. 1 (2014): 3296.
19 Winter, n.p.; See also Puar, *Terrorist Assemblages: Homonationalism in Queer Times.*

20 Winter, n.p.
21 Ahmed, *The Cultural Politics of Emotion*, 33–4.
22 Colebrook, "Stratigraphic Time, Women's Time," 13.
23 See James Bar, "'Hey Faggot': Understanding That the Current Homeless System, Planning Policy, and Land Use Planning Tools Is Not Designed to Address the Socialized and Insitutionalized Disregard for the LGBTQ Homeless Youth Population" (Toronto: Ryerson University, 2013); Saskatoon Housing Initiatives Partnership and OUTSaskatoon, "Need and Demand Assessment of Affordable Rental Housing for LGBTQ Youth in Saskatoon," Need and Demand (Saskatoon, 2016).
24 Colebrook, "Stratigraphic Time, Women's Time," 13–14.
25 Deleuze, *Difference and Repetition*, 280.

References

Adams, Vincanne, Michelle Murphy, and Adele E. Clarke. "Anticipation: Technoscience, Life, Affect, Temporality." *Subjectivity* 28, no. 1 (2009): 246–65.

Adamson, Rebecca. "First Nations Survival and the Future of the Earth." In *Original Instructions: Indigenous Teachings for a Sustainable Future*, edited by Melissa K. Nelson, 27–35. Rochester: Bear, 2008.

Ahmed, Sara. *The Cultural Politics of Emotion*. New York: Routledge, 2004.

Ahmed, Sara. *Living a Feminist Life*. Durham, NC: Duke University Press, 2017.

Ahmed, Sara. *Queer Phenomenology: Orientations, Objects, Others*. Durham, NC: Duke University Press, 2006.

Akhtar, Shazia, Lucy V. Justice, Catriona M. Morrison, and Martin A. Conway. "Fictional First Memories." *Psychological Science* 29, no. 10 (October 1, 2018): 1612–19.

Alaimo, Stacey. *Bodily Natures: Science, Environment, and the Material Self*. Indianapolis: Indiana University Press, 2010.

Allen, Graham. *Roland Barthes*. New York: Routledge, 2003.

Anzaldua, Gloria. *Borderlands/La Frontera: The New Mestiza*. San Francisco: Spinsters/Aunt Lute, 1987.

Anzaldua, Gloria. "To(o) Queer the Writer—Loca, Escritora y Chicana." In *The Gloria Anzaldúa Reader*, edited by Ana Louise Keating, Walter D. Mignolo, Irene Silverblatt, and Sonia Saldívar-Hull, 163–75. Durham, NC: Duke University Press, 2009.

Aristotle. *Physics*, n.d.

Augustine. *Confessions*. Translated by R. S. Pine-Coffin. Harmondsworth: Penguin, 1970.

Ball, Philip. *Beyond Weird: Why Everything You Thought You Knew about Quantum Physics Is Different*. Chicago: University of Chicago Press, 2018.

Bar, James. "'Hey Faggot': Understanding That the Current Homeless System, Planning Policy, and Land Use Planning Tools Is Not Designed to Address the Socialized and Institutionalized Disregard for the LGBTQ Homeless Youth Population." Toronto: Ryerson University, 2013. Major Research Paper. https://digital.library.ryerson.ca/islandora/object/RULA%3A2410/datastream/OBJ/view (accessed April 30, 2020).

Barad, Karen. "Agential Realism: Feminist Interventions in Understanding Scientific Practices." In *The Science Studies Reader*, edited by Mario Biagioli, 1–11. New York: Routledge, 1999.

Barad, Karen. *Meeting the Universe Halfway: Quantum Physics and the Entanglement of Matter and Meaning*. Durham, NC: Duke University Press, 2007.

Barad, Karen. "Posthumanist Performativity: Toward an Understanding of How Matter Comes to Matter." *Signs: Journal of Women in Culture and Society* 28, no. 3 (2003): 801–31.

Bardon, Adrian. *A Brief History of the Philosophy of Time*. Oxford: Oxford University Press, 2013.

Bell, David, Jon Binnie, Ruth Holliday, Robyn Longhurst, and Robin Peace. *Pleasure Zones: Bodies, Cities, Spaces*. Syracuse: Syracuse University Press, 2001.

Benjamin, Harry. *The Transsexual Phenomenon*. Michigan: Human Outreach & Achievement Institute, 1966.

Bennett, Jane. *Vibrant Matter: A Political Ecology of Things*. Durham, NC: Duke University Press, 2009.

Bergson, Henri. *Creative Evolution*. Translated by Arthur Mitchell. Mineola, NY: Dover, 1998.

Bergson, Henri. *The Creative Mind*. Whitefish, MT: Kessinger, 2007.

Bergson, Henri. *Time and Free Will: An Essay on the Immediate Data of Consciousness*. Mineola, NY: Dover, 2001.

Bersani, Leo. *Homos*. Cambridge, MA: Harvard University Press, 2009.

Bhabha, Homi. *The Location of Culture*. New York: Routledge, 1994.

Block, Richard A., Dan Zakay, Peter A. Hancock, and Richard A. Block. "Human Aging and Duration Judgments: A Meta-Analytic Review." *Psychology and Aging* 13, no. 4 (1998): 584–96.

Bockman, Philip. "A Fine Day." *New York Native*, 25 August 1986, 12-–13.

Boltanski, Luc, and Eve Chiapello. *The New Spirit of Capitalism*. New York: Verso, 2007.

Borde, Constance, and Sheila Malovany-Chevallier. "Translating the Second Sex." *Books & Ideas*, November 17, 2011. https://booksandideas.net/Translating-the-Second-Sex.html (accessed August 25, 2019).

Braidotti, Rosi. "The Ethics of Becoming-Imperceptible." In *Deleuze and Philosophy*, edited by Constantin V. Boundas, 133–59. Edinburgh: Edinburgh University Press, 2006.

Braidotti, Rosi. *Metamorphoses: Towards a Materialist Theory of Becoming*. New Jersey: Wiley, 2002.

Braidotti, Rosi. "The Politics of 'Life Itself' and New Ways of Dying." In *New Materialisms: Ontology, Agency, and Politics*, edited by Diana Coole and Susan Frost, 201–19. Durham, NC: Duke University Press, 2010.

Braidotti, Rosi. *The Posthuman*. Cambridge, MA: Polity Press, 2013.

Braidotti, Rosi. *Transpositions: On Nomadic Ethics*. Cambridge, UK: Polity, 2006.

Brown, Andrew. "How Outing Came in with a Vengeance." *The Independent Online*, March 21, 1995. http://www.independent.co.uk/news/uk/how-outing-came-in-with-a-vengeance-1612094.html (accessed April 25, 2019).

Brown, Wendy. *Politics Out of History*. Princeton: Princeton University Press, 2001.
Brown, Wendy. *Undoing the Demos: Neoliberalism's Stealth Revolution*. New York: MIT Press, 2015.
Bryant, Levi R. "The Ethics of the Event: Deleuze and Ethics without Αρχή." In *Deleuze and Ethics*, edited by Daniel W. Smith and Nathan Jun, 21–43. Edinburgh: Edinburgh University Press, 2011.
Butler, Judith. *Gender Trouble: Feminism and the Subversion of Identity*. New York: Routledge, 1990.
Butler, Judith. *Giving an Account of Oneself*. New York: Fordham University Press, 2005.
Butler, Judith. "Imitation and Gender Insubordination." In *Inside/Out*, edited by Diana Fuss, 13–29. New York: Routledge, 1991.
Cajete, Gregory. *Native Science: Natural Laws of Interdependence*. Sante Fe, NM: Clearlight, 2000.
Celia. "Jellyfish Overpopulation—a Threat to the Oceans?" *Marine Science Today* (blog), 2009. http://marinesciencetoday.com/2009/06/11/jellyfish-overpopulation-a-threat-to-the-oceans/ (accessed August 13, 2020).
Chakrabarty, Dipesh. "The Climate of History: Four Theses." *Critical Inquiry* 35, no. 2 (2009): 197–222.
Chandler, David. *Ontopolotics in the Anthropocene: An Introduction to Mapping, Sensing and Hacking*. London: Routledge, 2018.
Chindoy, Juan Alejandro Chindoy. *A Decolonial Philosophy of Indigenous Colombia: Time, Beauty, and Spirit in Kamëntšá Culture*. London: Rowman & Littlefield, 2020.
Chou, C. W., D. B. Hume, T. Rosenband, and D. J. Wineland. "Optical Clocks and Relativity." *Science* 329, no. 5999 (2010): 1630–3.
Clack, Beverley. *Misogyny in the Western Philosophical Tradition: A Reader*. New York: Routledge, 2016.
Cohen, Tom. "Anecographics." In *Impasses of the Post-Global: Theory in the Era of Climate Change*, edited by Henry Sussman, 32–57. University of Michigan: Open Humanities Press, 2012.
Cohen, Tom, Claire Colebrook, and J. Hillis Miller. *Twilight of the Anthropocene Idols*. London: Open Humanities Press, 2016.
Colebrook, Claire. "The Anthropocene and the Archive." *The Memory Network*, 2014. http://thememorynetwork.com/blog/2014/01/27/the-anthropocene-and-the-archive/ (accessed August 13, 2020).
Colebrook, Claire. *Death of the PostHuman: Essays on Extinction, Vol. 1*. Ann Arbor, MI: Open Humanities Press, 2014.
Colebrook, Claire. *Deleuze and the Meaning of Life*. London: Continuum Books, 2010.
Colebrook, Claire. "Fast Violence, Revolutionary Violence: Black Lives Matter and the 2020 Pandemic." *Journal of Bioethical Inquiry*, 17 (2020): 495–9,.

Colebrook, Claire. "On Not Becoming Man: The Materialist Politics of Unactualized Potential." In *Material Feminisms*, edited by Stacey Alaimo and Susan Hekman, 52–84. Bloomington: Indiana University Press, 2008.

Colebrook, Claire. "Queer Aesthetics." In *Queer Times, Queer Becomings*, edited by E. L. McCallum and Mikko Tuhkanen, 25–46. New York: SUNY Press, 2011.

Colebrook, Claire. "Stratigraphic Time, Women's Time." *Australian Feminist Studies* 24, no. 59 (2009): 11–16.

Colebrook, Claire. *Understanding Deleuze*. Crows Nest, Sydney: Allen and Unwin, 2002.

Coleman, Rebecca. "Past and Future Perfect? Beauty, Affect and Hope." *Journal for Cultural Research* 14, no. 4 (2010): 357–73.

Coleman, Rebecca, and Debra Ferreday. "Introduction: Hope and Feminist Theory." *Journal for Cultural Research* 14, no. 4 (2010): 313–21.

Coleman, Rebecca, and Debra Ferreday. "Introduction: Hope and Feminist Theory." *Journal for Cultural Research* 14, no. 4 (2010): 313–21.

Coole, Diana, and Samantha Frost. "Introducing the New Materialisms." In *New Materialisms: Ontology, Agency, and Politics*, 1–46. Durham, NC: Duke University Press, 2010.

Coole, Diana, and Samantha Frost. *New Materialisms: Ontology, Agency, and Politics*. Durham, NC: Duke University Press, 2010.

Cordova, Viola Faye. *How It Is: The Native American Philosophy of V.F. Cordova*. Edited by Kathleen Dean Moore, Kurt Peters, Ted Jojola, and Amber Lacy. Tuscon: University of Arizona Press, 2007.

Crutzen, Paul. "Geology of Mankind." *Nature* 415 (2002): 23.

Crutzen, Paul, and Eugene Stoermer. "The Anthropocene." *Global Change Newsletter* 41 (May 2000): 17–18.

Cunniff Gilson, Erinn. "Responsive Becoming: Ethics between Deleuze and Feminism." In *Deleuze and Ethics*, edited by Daniel W. Smith and Nathan Jun, 89–107. Edinburgh: Edinburgh University Press, 2011.

Davis, Noela. "The Sociality of Biology: Epigenetics and the Molecularisation of the Social." Paper presented at Mattering: Feminism, Science, and Materialism, City University of New York. New York, 2013.

DeLanda, Manuel. *Philosophy & Simulation: The Emergence of Synthetic Reason*. London: Continuum, 2010.

Deleuze, Gilles. *Bergsonism*. Translated by Hugh Tomlinson and Barbara Habberjam. Brooklyn, NY: Zone Books, 1988.

Deleuze, Gilles. *Cinema I: The Movement-Image*. Translated by Hugh Tomlinson and Barbara Habberjam. Minneapolis: University of Minnesota Press, 1986.

Deleuze, Gilles. *Cinema II: The Time-Image*. Translated by Hugh Tomlinson and Barbara Habberjam. Minneapolis: University of Minnesota Press, 1986.

Deleuze, Gilles. *The Critical Philosophy of Kant*. Translated by Hugh Tomlinson and Barbara Habberjam. Minneapolis: University of Minnesota Press, 1984.

Deleuze, Gilles. *Difference and Repetition*. Translated by Paul Patton. New York: Columbia University Press, 1994.

Deleuze, Gilles. *The Fold: Leibniz and the Baroque*. Translated by Tom Conley. Minneapolis: University of Minnesota Press, 1993.

Deleuze, Gilles. "I Have Nothing to Admit." Translated by Janis Forman. *Semiotext(e), Anti-Oedipus* 2, no. 3 (1977): 111–16.

Deleuze, Gilles. *Kafka: For a Minor Literature*. Translated by Dana Polan. Minneapolis: University of Minnesota Press, 1986.

Deleuze, Gilles. *The Logic of Sense*. Translated by Mark Lester. New York: Columbia University Press, 1990.

Deleuze, Gilles. *Negotiations, 1972–1990*. European Perspectives: A Series in Social Thought and Cultural Criticism. New York: Columbia University Press, 1995.

Deleuze, Gilles. *Negotiations, 1972–1990*. Translated by Martin Joughin. New York: Columbia University Press, 1997.

Deleuze, Gilles. *Nietzsche and Philosophy*. Translated by Hugh Tomlinson. Minneapolis: University of Minnesota Press, 1983.

Deleuze, Gilles. *Proust and Signs: The Complete Text*. Translated by Richard Howard. Minneapolis: University of Minnesota Press, 2003.

Deleuze, Gilles. *Spinoza: Practical Philosophy*. Translated by Robert Hurley. San Francisco: City Lights Books, 1988.

Deleuze, Gilles, and Felix Guattari. *What Is Philosophy?* New York: Columbia University Press, 1994.

Deleuze, Gilles, and Claire Parnet. *Dialogues*. London: Athlone Press, 1987.

Deleuze, Gilles, and Felix Guattari. *A Thousand Plateaus: Capitalism and Schizophrenia*. Translated by Brian Massumi. Minneapolis: University of Minnesota Press, 1987.

Derrida, Jacques. *Of Grammatology*. Translated by Gayatri Chakravorty Spivak. Baltimore: JHU Press, 1998.

Derrida, Jacques. "Structure, Sign and Play in the Discourse of the Human Sciences." In *Margins of Philosophy*, 201–331. Chicago: University of Chicago Press, 1982.

Dinshaw, Carolyn, Lee Edelman, Roderick A. Ferguson, Carla Freccero, E. Freeman, Jack Halberstam, Annamarie Jagose, Christopher Nealon, and Nguyen Tan Hoang, "Theorizing Queer Temporalities: A Roundtable Discussion." *GLQ: A Journal of Lesbian and Gay Studies* 13, nos. 2–3 (2007): 177–95.

Driesch, Hans. *The Science and Philosophy of the Organism: The Gifford Lectures Delivered before the University of Aberdeen in the Year 1907*. London: Adam and Charles Black, 1908.

Duncan, Nancy. "Renegotiating Gender and Sexuality in Public and Private Spaces." In *Bodyspace: Destabilizing Geographies of Gender and Sexuality*, edited by Nancy Duncan. London: Routledge, 1996.

Edelman, Lee. *No Future: Queer Theory and the Death Drive*. Durham, NC: Duke University Press, 2004.

Enloe, Cynthia. "Feminism, Nationalism, and Militarism: Wariness without Paralysis." In *Feminism, Nationalism, and Militarism*, 42–54. Arlington, VA: Association for Feminist Anthropology/American Anthropological Association in collaboration with the International Women's Anthropology Conference, 1996.

Foucault, Michel. *History of Sexuality: An Introduction*. New York: Vintage, 1990.

Foucault, Michel. *The Order of Things: An Archaeology of the Human Sciences*. New York: Vintage Books, 1994.

Foucault, Michel. "Of Other Spaces: Utopias and Heterotopias." Translated by Jay Miskowiec. *Architecture/Mouvement/Continuité*, 1984, 1–9. http://web.mit.edu/allanmc/www/foucault1.pdf (accessed August 28, 2019).

Freccero, Carla. "Queer Times." *South Atlantic Quarterly* 106, no. 3 (2007): 485–94.

Freccero, Carla. *Queer/Early/Modern*. Durham, NC: Duke University Press, 2005.

Freeman, Elizabeth. *Time Binds: Queer Temporalities, Queer Histories*. Durham, NC: Duke University Press, 2010.

Gibbs, Paul, Oili-Helena Ylijoki, Carolina Guzmán-Valenzuela, and Ronald Barnett, eds. *Universities in the Flux of Time: An Exploration of Time and Temporality in University Life*. New York: Routledge, 2014.

Goldman, Emma. *Anarchism and Other Essays*. New York: Mother Earth Publishing Association, 2010.

Gosetti-Murrayjohn, Angela. "Sappho as the Tenth Muse in Hellenistic Epigram." *Arethusa* 39, no. 1 (2006): 21–45.

Gregg, Melissa. *Counterproductive: Time Management in the Knowledge Economy*. Durham, NC: Duke University Press, 2018.

Grosz, Elizabeth. *Architecture from the Outside: Essays on Virtual and Real Space*. London: MIT Press, 2001.

Grosz, Elizabeth. *Becoming Undone: Darwinian Reflections on Life, Politics, and Art*. Durham, NC: Duke University Press, 2011.

Grosz, Elizabeth. *Becomings: Explorations in Time, Memory, and Futures*. Ithaca, NY: Cornell University Press, 1999.

Grosz, Elizabeth. *The Nick of Time: Politics, Evolution, and the Untimely*. Durham, NC: Duke University Press, 2004.

Grosz, Elizabeth. *Space, Time, and Perversion: Essays on the Politics of Bodies*. New York: Routledge, 1995.

Grosz, Elizabeth. "A Thousand Tiny Sexes: Feminism and Rhizomatics." *Topoi* 12, no. 2 (1993): 167–79.

Grosz, Elizabeth. *Time Travels: Feminism, Nature, Power*. Durham, NC: Duke University Press, 2005.

Halberstam, J. Jack. *In a Queer Time and Place: Transgender Bodies, Subcultural Lives*. New York: New York University Press, 2005.

Halberstam, J. Jack. *The Queer Art of Failure*. Durham, NC: Duke University Press, 2011.

Harari, Yuval Noah. *Sapiens: A Brief History of Humankind*. London: McClelland & Stewart, 2014.

Haraway, Donna. *Modest—Witness@Second—Millennium.FemaleMan—Meets—OncoMouse: Feminism and Technoscience*. New York: Routledge, 1997.

Haraway, Donna. *When Species Meet*. Minneapolis: University of Minnesota Press, 2008.

Harper, Lawrence V. "Epigenetic Inheritance and the Intergenerational Transfer of Experience." *Psychological Bulletin* 131, no. 3 (2005): 340–60.

Harris, Julia Golda. "Without Closets: A Queer and Feminist Re-Imagining of Narratives of Queer Experience." Oberlin College, 2014. Honors Thesis, https://digitalcommons.oberlin.edu/cgi/viewcontent.cgi?article=1288&context=honors (accessed January 29, 2019).

Haynes, Patrice. "Creative Becoming and the Patiency of Matter: Feminism, New Materialism, and Theology." *Angelaki* 19, no. 1 (2014): 129–50.

Heidegger, Martin. *Being and Time*. Translated by John Macquarrie and Edward Robinson. Oxford: Basil Blackwell, 1927.

Henry III, William A.. "Ethics: Forcing Gays Out of the Closet." *Time*, January 29, 1990. http://content.time.com/time/subscriber/article/0,33009,969264-2,00.html (accessed April 25, 2019).

Heraclitus. *Fragments*. Translated by T. M. Robinson. Toronto: University of Toronto Press, 1991.

hooks, bell. "Choosing the Margin as a Space of Radical Openness." *Framework* no. 36 (1989): 15–23.

Ingram, Gordon Brent, Anne-Marie Bouthillette, and Yolanda Retter. *Queers in Space: Communities, Public Places, Sites of Resistance*. Seattle, WA: Bay Press, 1997.

It Gets Better. "It Gets Better." https://itgetsbetter.org/ (accessed February 19, 2018).

James, William. *The Principles of Psychology*. New York: Holt, 1890.

Jones, Angela. "Queer Heterotopias: Homonormativity and the Future of Queerness." *Interalia* 14, no. 4 (2009): 1–20.

Jun, Nathan. "Introduction." In *Deleuze and Ethics*, edited by Nathan Jun and Daniel W. Smith, 1–4. Edinburgh: Edinburgh University Press, 2011.

Kirby, Vicki. *Quantum Anthropologies: Life at Large*. Durham, NC: Duke University Press, 2011.

Kosofsky Sedgwick, Eve. *Epistemology of the Closet*. Berkeley: University of California Press, 1990.

Kuzawa, Christopher W., and Elizabeth Sweet. "Epigenetics and the Embodiment of Race: Developmental Origins of US Racial Disparities in Cardiovascular Health." *American Journal of Human Biology: The Official Journal of the Human Biology Council* 21, no. 1 (2009): 2–15.

Latham, J. R. "Axiomatic: Constituting 'Transexuality' and Trans Sexualities in Medicine." *Sexualities* 22, no. 1–2 (2019): 13–30.

Latour, Bruno. *Pandora's Hope: Essays on the Reality of Science Studies*. Cambridge, MA: Harvard University Press, 1999.

Le Doeuff, Michèle. *Hipparchia's Choice: An Essay Concerning Women, Philosophy, Etc.* Cambridge, MA: Blackwell, 1991.

Lila. "The Pace of Queer Time." *Autostraddle*, March 16, 2016. https://www.autostraddle.com/the-pace-of-queer-time-329459/ (accessed February 26, 2019).

Lloyd, Genevieve. *The Man of Reason: Male and Female in Western Philosophy*. Minneapolis: University of Minnesota Press, 1984.

Loewen Walker, Rachel. "Environment Imagining Otherwise." *Journal of Curriculum and Pedagogy* 10, no. 1 (2013): 34–7.

Loewen Walker, Rachel. "The Living Present as a Materialist Feminist Temporality." *Woman: A Cultural Review* 25, no. 1 (2014): 46–61.

Loewen Walker, Rachel. "Toward a FIERCE Nomadology: Contesting Queer Geographies on the Christopher Street Pier." *PhaenEx* 6, no. 1 (2011): 90–120.

Loewen Walker, Rachel, Danielle Peers, and Lindsay Eales. "New Constellations: Lived Diffractions of Dis/Ability and Dance." In *Feminist Philosophies of Life*, edited by Hasana Sharp and Chloe Taylor, 129–45. Montreal: McGill-Queen's University Press, 2016.

Lorde, Audre. "The Master's Tools Will Never Dismantle the Master's House." In *Sister Outsider*. Berkeley: Crossing Press, 1984.

Lovelock, Michael. "'My Coming Out Story': Lesbian, Gay and Bisexual Youth Identities on YouTube." *International Journal of Cultural Studies* 22, no. 1 (2019): 70–85.

Lucas, Ian. *OutRage!: An Oral History*. London: Cassell, 1998.

Lundy, John. "The Stroll: Reflections on Deleuzian Ethics." *Rhizomes: Cultural Studies in Emerging Knowledge* 26, no. 1 (2014). http://www.rhizomes.net/issue26/lundy.html (accessed February 19, 2019).

Markley, Robert. "Time." In *Telemorphosis: Theory in the Era of Climate Change, Vol. 1*, edited by Tom Cohen. University of Michigan: Open Humanities Press, 2012.

Matthews, Chelle, Rachel Loewen Walker, and Miki Mappin. "Policy Recommendation: Toward the Inclusion of Gender Identity and Expression as Protected Grounds in the Saskatchewan Human Rights Code." Saskatoon, SK: The Avenue Community Centre for Gender and Sexual Diversity, 2014.

May, Todd. "When Is a Deleuzian Becoming?" *Continental Philosophy Review* 36 (2003): 139–53. https://link-springercom.cyber.usask.ca/article/10.1023/A:1026036516963 (accessed August 25, 2019).

McCallum, E. L., and Mikko Tuhkanen. "Becoming Unbecoming: Untimely Mediations." In *Queer Times, Queer Becomings*, 1–24. New York: State University of New York, 2011.

McKenna, Erin. *The Task of Utopia: A Pragmatist and Feminist Perspective*. Lanham, MD: Rowman & Littlefield, 2001.

Menon, Madhavi. "Spurning Teleology in Venus and Adonis." *GLQ: A Journal of Lesbian and Gay Studies* 11, no. 4 (2005): 491–519.

Moller Okin, Susan. *Women in Western Political Philosophy*. Princeton: Princeton University Press, 1988.

Moreau, Paul-Antoine, Ermes Toninelli, Thomas Gregory, Reuben S. Aspden, Peter A. Morris, and Miles J. Padgett. "Imaging Bell-Type Nonlocal Behavior." *Science Advances* 5, no. 7 (July 1, 2019): 1–8. https://doi.org/10.1126/sciadv.aaw2563 (accessed February 26, 2021).

Muldoon, Mark. *Tricks of Time: Bergson, Merleau-Ponty and Ricoeur in Search of Time, Self and Meaning*. Pittsburgh, PA: Duquesne University Press, 2006.

Muñoz, José Esteban. *Cruising Utopia: The Then and There of Queer Futurity*. New York: New York University Press, 2009.

Myslik, Wayne. "Renegotiating the Social/Sexual Identities of Places: Gay Communities as Safe Havens or Sites of Resistance?" In *Bodyspace: Destabilizing Geographies of Gender and Sexuality*, edited by Nancy Duncan. London: Routledge, 1996.

Namaste, Viviane. "Undoing Theory: The 'Transgender Question' and the Epistemic Violence of Anglo-American Feminist Theory." *Hypatia* 24, no. 3 (2009): 11–31.

"NBA's Jason Collins Comes Out as the First Openly Gay Athlete in Major U.S. Team Sport." NOLA.com, April 29, 2013. http://www.nola.com/sports/index.ssf/2013/04/nbas_jason_collins_comes_out_a.html (accessed April 29, 2013).

Nealon, Christopher. *Foundlings: Lesbian and Gay Historical Emotion before Stonewall*. Durham, NC: Duke University Press, 2001.

Neimanis, Astrida. *Bodies of Water: Posthuman Feminist Phenomenology*. London: Bloomsbury, 2017.

Neimanis, Astrida, and Rachel Loewen Walker. "Weathering: Climate Change and the 'Thick Time' of Transcorporeality." *Hypatia* 29, no. 3 (2014): 558–75.

Nelson, Melissa K. *Original Instructions: Indigenous Teachings for a Sustainable Future*. Rochester, NY: Simon and Schuster, 2008.

Newton, Isaac. *The Principia: Mathematical Principles of Natural Philosophy [1687]*. Berkeley: University of California Press, 1999.

Nietzsche, Friedrich. *The Gay Science*. Translated by Walter Kaufmann. New York: Vintage, 1974.

Nietzsche, Friedrich. *Twilight of the Idols*. Translated by Walter Kaufmann. New York: Viking, 1954.

Nixon, Rob. *Slow Violence and the Environmentalism of the Poor*. Cambridge, MA: Harvard University Press, 2011.

Parr, Adrian. *Deleuze Dictionary Revised Edition*. Edinburgh: Edinburgh University Press, 2010.

Pizan, Christine De. *The Book of the City of Ladies*. University of Michigan: Persea Books, 1982.

Plato. *Timaeus*. Translated by B. Jowett. London: Aeterna Press, 2015.

Puar, Jasbir K. *Terrorist Assemblages: Homonationalism in Queer Times*. Durham, NC: Duke University Press, 2007.

Revkin, Andrew C. "Confronting the 'Anthropocene.'" *Dot Earth Blog* (blog), May 11, 2011. https://dotearth.blogs.nytimes.com/2011/05/11/confronting-the-anthropocene/ (accessed August 20, 2020).

Reynolds, Margaret. *The Sappho Companion*. London: Vintage, 2001.

Rich, Adrienne. "Compulsory Heterosexuality and Lesbian Existence." *Women: Sex and Sexuality* 5, no. 4 (1980): 631–60.

Rifkin, Mark. *Beyond Settler Time: Temporal Sovereignty and Indigenous Self-Determination*. Durham, NC: Duke University Press, 2017.

Rose, Nikolas S. *The Politics of Life Itself: Biomedicine, Power, and Subjectivity in the Twenty-First Century*. Princeton: Princeton University Press, 2007.

Rothstein, Mark A., Yu Cai, and Gary E. Marchant. "The Ghost in Our Genes: Legal and Ethical Implications of Epigenetics." *Health Matrix Clevel* 19, no. 1 (2009): 1–62.

Roughgarden, Joan. *Evolution's Rainbow: Diversity, Gender, and Sexuality in Nature and People*. Berkeley: University of California Press, 2004.

Rushbrook, Dereka. "Cities, Queer Space, and the Cosmopolitan Tourist." *GLQ: A Journal of Lesbian and Gay Studies* 8, no. 1/2 (2002): 183–206.

Salamon, Gayle. "Last Look at the Lex." *Studies in Gender and Sexuality* 16, no. 2 (2015): 147–8.

Sappho 31, verses 1–15. Translated by Julia Dubnoff. https://www.uh.edu/~cldue/texts/sappho.html%20https://www.uh.edu/~cldue/texts/sappho.html (accessed January 29, 2020).

Saskatoon Housing Initiatives Partnership, and OUTSaskatoon. "Need and Demand Assessment of Affordable Rental Housing for LGBTQ Youth in Saskatoon." Need and Demand. Saskatoon, 2016.

Sawicki, Jana. "Disciplining Mothers: Feminism and the New Reproductive Technologies." In *Feminist Theory and the Body*, edited by Janet Price and Margrit Shildrik, 190–202. New York: Routledge, 1999.

See, Tony. "Deleuze and Buddhism: Two Concepts of Subjectivity?" *Deleuze and Guattari Studies* 13, no. 1 (2019): 104–22.

Sherover, Charles M. *The Human Experience of Time: The Development of Its Philosophic Meaning [1975]*. Evanston, IL: Northwestern University Press, 2001.

Shilts, Randy. *The Mayor of Castro Street: The Life and Times of Harvey Milk*. New York: St. Martin's Press, 1982.

Short, Coral. *Genderless Jellyfish*. Group Intervention Video, 2013.

Smith, Daniel W. "Deleuze and the Question of Desire: Towards and Immanent Theory of Ethics." In *Deleuze and Ethics*, edited by Daniel W. Smith and Nathan Jun, 123–41. Edinburgh: Edinburgh University Press, 2011.

Soja, Edward W. *Thirdspace: Journeys to Los Angeles and Other Real-and-Imagined Places*. Oxford: Blackwell, 1996.

Stanton, Andrew. *Finding Nemo*. Buena Vista Pictures, 2003.

Stengers, Isabelle. *The Invention of Modern Science*. Minneapolis: University of Minnesota Press, 2000.

Stivale, Charles J. *Gilles Deleuze: Key Concepts*. New York: Routledge, 2014.
Stockton, Kathryn Bond. *The Queer Child, or Growing Sideways in the Twentieth Century*. Durham, NC: Duke University Press, 2009.
Stone, Richard. "Massive Outbreak of Jellyfish Could Spell Trouble for Fisheries." *Yale Environment 360* (blog), January 13, 2011. https://e360.yale.edu/features/massive_outbreak_of_jellyfish_could_spell_trouble_for_fisheries (accessed August 13, 2020).
Stone, Sandy. "The Empire Strikes Back: A Posttranssexual Manifesto." In *The Transgender Studies Reader*, edited by Susan Stryker and Steven Whittle, 221–35. New York: Routledge, 2006.
"Sustain; Sustainability." *Oxford Dictionary Online*. https://en.oxforddictionaries.com/definition/sustainability (accessed October 2, 2018).
Thiele, Kathrin. "Of Immanence and Becoming: Deleuze and Guattari's Philosophy and/as Relational Ontology." *Deleuze Studies* 10, no. 1 (2016): 117–34.
Tiitsman, Jenna. "Planetary Subjects after the Death of Geography." In *Planetary Loves: Spivak, Postcoloniality, and Theology*, edited by Stephen D. Moore and Mayra Rivera, 149–67. New York: Fordham University Press, 2011.
Tseng, Jason. "Does It Really Get Better?: A Conscientious Critique." *The Bilerico Project* (blog), October 3, 2010. http://bilerico.lgbtqnation.com/2010/10/does_it_really_get_better.php (accessed February 18, 2019).
Tuana, Nancy. *Woman and the History of Philosophy*. New York: Paragon Press, 1992.
Tuhkanen, Mikko. "Mestiza Metaphysics." In *Queer Times, Queer Becomings*, edited by E. L. McCallum and Mikko Tuhkanen. 259–94. New York: State University of New York, 2011.
Tuin, Iris van der. "'A Different Starting Point, a Different Metaphysics': Reading Bergson and Barad Diffractively." *Hypatia* 26, no. 1 (2011): 22–42.
Tuin, Iris van der. "The New Materialist 'Always Already': On an A-Human Humanities." *NORA—Nordic Journal of Feminist and Gender Research* 19, no. 4 (2011): 285–90.
Turner, Victor. *The Ritual Process: Structure and Anti-Structure*. Chicago: Aldine, 1969.
Uhlmann, Anthony. "Deleuze, Ethics, Ethology, and Art." In *Deleuze and Ethics*, edited by Daniel W. Smith and Nathan Jun, 154–70. Edinburgh: Edinburgh University Press, 2011.
Wal, E. van der. "Crossing Over, Coming Out, Blending In: A Trans Interrogation of the Closet." *South African Review of Sociology* 47, no. 3 (2016): 44–64.
Warin, Megan, and Anne Hammarström. "Material Feminism and Epigenetics: A 'Critical Window' for Engagement?" *Australian Feminist Studies* 33, no. 97 (2018): 1–17.
Waters, Colin N., Jan Zalasiewicz, Colin Summerhayes, Anthony D. Barnosky, Clément Poirier, Agnieszka Gałuszka, Alejandro Cearreta, Matt Edgeworth, Erle C. Ellis, Michael Ellis, Catherine Jeandel, Reinhold Leinfelder, J. R. McNeill, Daniel deB. Richter, Will Steffen, James Syvitski, Davor Vidas, Michael Wagreich,

Mark Williams, An Zhisheng, Jacques Grinevald, Eric Odada, Naomi Oreskes, and Alexander P. Wolfe. "The Anthropocene Is Functionally and Stratigraphically Distinct from the Holocene." *Science* 351, no. 6269 (January 8, 2016). http://science.sciencemag.org/content/351/6269/aad2622 (accessed August 13, 2020).

Watney, Simon. "Queer Epistemology: Activism, 'Outing,' and the Politics of Sexual Identities." *Critical Quarterly* 36, no. 1 (1994): 13–27.

Welles, Orson. *Citizen Kane*. RKO Radio Pictures, 1941.

Williams, James. *Gilles Deleuze's Difference and Repetition: A Critical Introduction and Guide*. Edinburgh: Edinburgh University Press, 2003.

Williams, James. *Gilles Deleuze's Philosophy of Time: A Critical Introduction and Guide*. Edinburgh: Edinburgh University Press, 2011.

Williams, Sarah C. P. "Epigenetics." *Proceedings of the National Academy of Sciences* 110, no. 9 (2013): 3209.

Wilson, Alex. "N'tacimowin Inna Nah." *Canadian Woman Studies* 26, no. 3/4 (2008): 193–9.

Wilson, Chris. "Obituary: Remembering the Holocene Epoch." *Time*, August 9, 2016. http://time.com/4471327/holocene-epoch-end-anthropocene/ (accessed August 15, 2020).

Winnubst, Shannon. *Queering Freedom*. Bloomington: Indiana University Press, 2006.

Winnubst, Shannon. "Temporality in Queer Theory and Continental Philosophy." *Philosophy Compass* 5, no. 2 (2010): 136–46.

Winter, Bronwyn. "'The Ties That Bind Us': The Hidden Knots of Gay Marriage." *PORTAL Journal of Multidisciplinary International Studies* 11, no. 1 (2014). http://epress.lib.uts.edu.au/journals/index.php/portal/article/view/3296 (accessed September 22, 2020).

Winterson, Jeanette. *Sexing the Cherry*. Toronto: Vintage Canada, 1989.

Winterson, Jeanette. *The Stone Gods*. Boston: Mariner Books, 2009.

Wittmann, Marc, and Sandra Lehnhoff. "Age Effects in Perception of Time." *Psychological Reports* 97, no. 3 (2005): 921–35.

Wollstonecraft, Mary. *A Vindication of the Rights of Women & A Vindication of the Rights of Men*. New York: Cosimo, 2008.

The World Professional Association for Transgender Health. "Standards of Care for the Health of Transsexual, Transgender, and Gender Nonconforming People, 7th Version." WPATH, n.d. https://www.wpath.org/publications/soc (accessed September 29, 2019).

Young, Eugene B., Gary Genosko, and Janell Watson. *The Deleuze and Guattari Dictionary*. London: Bloomsbury Academic, 2013.

Zalasiewicz, Jan, Colin N. Waters, Alexander P. Wolfe, Anthony D. Barnosky, Alejandro Cearreta, Matt Edgeworth, Erle C. Ellis, Ian J. Fairchild, Felix M. Gradstein, Jacques Grinevald, Peter Haff, Martin J. Head, Juliana A. Ivar do Sul, Catherine Jeandel, Reinhold Leinfelder, John R. McNeill, Naomi

Oreskes, Clément Poirier, Andrew Revkin, Daniel deB. Richter, Will Steffen, Colin Summerhayes, James P. M. Syvitski, Davor Vidas, Michael Wagreich, Scott Wing, and Mark Williams. "Making the Case for a Formal Anthropocene Epoch: An Analysis of Ongoing Critiques." *Newsletters on Stratigraphy* 5, no. 2 (2017): 205–26.

Zimman, Lal. "'The Other Kind of Coming Out': Transgender People and the Coming Out Narrative Genre." *Gender & Language* 3, no. 1 (May 2009): 53–80.

Index

ACT UP 101
Actant, actancy 13, 78 (*see also* Latour)
Adamson, Rebecca 84
affect, affect theory 29, 61, 81, 108–9, 111–12, 114–15, 143, 156 n.29
  the affective capacity of matter 72, 74–9, 127–9
agent, agency 40–1, 79–80, 85, 108–9, 126–7, 132, 136, 156 n.29
agential realism 75, 80, 82–5, 87, 127 (*see also under* Barad, Deleuze)
Ahmed, Sarah
  feminist killjoy 11–12
  orientation toward 30, 32
  stickiness of the past 150
Alaimo, Stacy 128 (*see also* jellyfish, transcorporeality)
Anthropocene 15, 117, 121–6, 128, 130–1 (*see also* Crutzen, Stoermer, Working Group on the Anthropocene)
"The Anthropocene and the Archive" (Colebrook) 117, 125
anticipation 4, 52, 58–60, 84, 98 146–7
Anzaldúa, Gloria 91
Aphrodite. *See* Sappho
Aristotle 23–5, 28, 34
aromantic 47, 89
artefacts 29–30, 105
asexuality/ace 47, 89
authenticity 10, 92, 101, 105, 110

Baggins, Frodo 6–7
Ball, Philip 65, 67–8, 81–2
Barad, Karen
  agential realism 82–4
  Diffraction 34, 156 n.22
  intra-action 75–6, 82–3
  quantum materialism 68–70, 75, 81–4
becoming 11, 13–14, 27–8, 43–4, 46–53, 63, 75–80, 89, 91, 97–8, 139, 143–4, 153 (*see also under* Deleuze, coming out)

and Aristotle 24
becoming-jellyfish 129, 132–3
becoming-otherwise 43, 56, 106, 137
becoming-world (Heidegger) 172 n.27
becoming time-bodies 13
becoming queer 89, 116
and Heraclitus 23–4
and ontology 31–2
and Winterson 38–9, 41
Benjamin, Harry 110
Bennett, Jane 76–8 (*see also* vitalism)
Bennett, The Honorable Carolyn, Member of Parliament, Canada 74
Bergson, Henri
  and Deleuze 46–7, 69, 77
  difference 46
  duration 27, 45–6, 77
  élan vital 76–8
  intuition 46, 54
  memory 27–8
  time 27–8, 45
Bill C-16, An Act to amend the Canadian Human Rights Act and the Criminal Code 90
Bill C-38, the *Civil Marriage Act* 149–51
biopower 73, 76–7, 79 (*see also* Foucault)
bisexuality 102
Black Lives Matter 18, 36
Bodies that Matter (Butler) 71–2
Bodies of Water (Neimanis) 74
Bryant, Levi 145–6
Butler, Judith
  performativity 70–1, 101, 109
  poiesis 108
  and queer theory 72, 107–8

Cajete, Gregory 86
causality (cause and effect) 13, 28, 37, 46, 58, 61, 146, 151
  in anticipations of the future 130, 132
  in storytelling 6
Chindoy Chindoy, Juan Alejandro 35

chronos 32, 58
chronology 3, 8–9, 44, 49, 58, 60, 62, 98, 104, 148–9
cisnormativity 102
climate change 13, 15, 119–22, 126–7, 129–31, 134–6, 141
climate change imaginary 120–1, 127, 134, 141
clock 4, 7, 18, 21–4, 51–3, 98, 139
Colebrook, Claire
  becoming-queer 117
  and concepts 42
  critique of becoming 78–9
  and feminist time 151
  passive vitalism 78–80
  posthumanity 125
  slow violence, fast violence 17–18, 29
Coleman, Rebecca 60
Collins, Jason comes out 101–2, 114–15
colonialism 80, 84, 103, 152
coming in 14, 96–7, 103–4, 106, 108, 114 (*see also* Wilson)
coming out
  and becoming 70, 89, 110
  differentiated from coming in 103–4, 106, 108
  and memory 89
  narrative 14, 31–2, 90, 101–2, 115–16
  as a progress narrative 14, 29, 59, 91, 101–2, 106–7
  repetition of 14, 110, 145
  and storytelling 89, 91, 104
  temporality and 14, 29, 92, 97, 103, 116
  as transgender 102–3 (*see also* Zimman, Lal)
contraction of time. *See under* Deleuze
Cordova, Viola Fay 33–5, 82
Cosmodolphins: Feminist Cultural Studies of Technology, Animals, and the Sacred (Bryld and Lykke) 65
COVID-19 17–18, 36
Creative Evolution (Bergson) 45
Critique of Pure Reason (Kant) 39
Crutzen, Paul 123–4
Curie, Marie 65, 80

Darwin, Charles 31, 117
de Beauvoir, Simone 8, 9–10, 140
de Pizan, Christine 8, 76

Deleuze, Gilles 6, 139–40
  and agential realism 75
  Alice in Wonderland 40, 44
  becoming 14, 24, 28, 39–41, 43–4, 46–7, 51, 63, 75–7, 89, 116, 139, 143–4
  contraction of time 2–4, 54, 56–7
  ethics 142–3, 146
  difference-in-itself 46, 48, 133
  differenciation 63, 170 n.65
  eternal return 14, 52, 55–7
  living present 2, 4–7, 19, 34, 38, 51, 52–8, 107
  passivity of time 4, 19, 51–4, 56, 63–4, 78–9
  pure past 14, 19, 52, 54, 56–7
  the event 65, 89, 104–7, 114–15, 145–6
  three syntheses of time 19, 52, 56
  univocity 77, 111, 115
  vitalism 77, 79
Deleuze, Gilles and Guattari, Felix
  affects 76–7
  becoming 43, 46–7, 139
  concepts 31, 41, 143
  rhizomes 118
demi-gender 89
demisexual 89
"Des Espaces Autres" (Foucault) 94
Derrida, Jacques 70, 72, 108
difference (*see also under* Deleuze, difference-in-itself)
  and becoming 40–1, 44, 46–8, 50, 52, 63, 111
  and identity 15, 52, 133
  and repetition 50–1, 55–6, 62, 123
Difference and Repetition (Deleuze) 4, 14, 19, 50–1, 56, 63, 133, 170 n.65
differenciation 111–12, 114, 129, 131, 147, 170 n.65 (*see under* Deleuze)
diffraction 8–9, 11–12, 34, 40, 54, 87, 96, 135 146–7, 156 n.22
diffraction grating 8, 11, 69, 147, 156 n. 22
Diva's Lounge, Saskatoon, Saskatchewan 93–5, 115
Driesch, Hans 76, 77
duration (*see also under* Bergson)
  and intuition 41, 51–2
  and memory 27, 50–1

and the living present 136, 149
and univocity 112–13, 115

echoes of the future 121, 123, 129
Edelman, Lee 31, 59–60
Einstein, Albert 20–1, 23
entanglement 74, 76 (*see also* Barad, *see also under* ethics)
    of meaning and matter 7, 52, 54, 80, 112
    of nature and culture 72, 126–7, 147
    quantum 81–2
environmental racism 74
epigenetics 147–8, 152, 174
Epistemology of the Closet (Kosofsky Sedgwick) 101
EPR Paradox 81–2, 149
eternal return. *See under* Deleuze
ethics (*see also under* Deleuze)
    of accountability 15–16, 144–5, 149, 151
    of entanglement 15, 139–154
    and temporality 146
    an ungrounded ethic 142–52
evolution. *See* Darwin
existentialism 10
extinction 79, 124–5, 130–2, 135, 143

Feeling Backward (Love) 29, 139
feminist futures 14, 36, 61, 64–5, 67–8
feminist new materialism/new feminist materialisms 14, 32–3, 69–70, 72, 75–7, 80–4, 98, 126
feminist post-structuralism 70, 75, 107, 109–10, 169 n. 53
Feminist Theory (waves and traditions of) 8–9, 126
fertility 58–9
fictional first memories 5–6
Finding Nemo 91, 98–100
Foucault, Michel
    and biopower 73 (*see also* biopower)
    freedom 109
    heterotopia 93–5
    technologies of power 109, 114
    panopticon 140
framing (narratives and categorizations) 10, 42, 69, 72, 77, 92–3, 120–1, 128, 132, 135–6, 142–3

Freeman, Elizabeth. *See* temporal drag
future (*see also* eternal return, temporality, echoes of the future)
    anticipations of 16, 99, 142
    third synthesis of time 55–6, 123
    novel futures 19, 33, 36, 57, 84, 107, 129

Galilei, Galileo 20–1, 23
gender
    expression 90
    fluidity 89–90
    genderqueer 89, 112
    identity 90, 103
    performativity 70–1, 90, 101–2, 109
Gender Trouble (Butler) 71–2
Genderless Jellyfish (Short) 128
genealogy 41, 112
Geological Time Scale 123
giving an account of oneself (practice) 92, 102–3, 106–7
Giving an Account of Oneself (Butler) 108
Goldman, Emma 8, 10
Grosz, Elizabeth 65
    becoming 31–2, 89, 132–3
    and evolution 31
    a thousand tiny sexes 32, 91
groundwriting 133–4
Growing sideways (Stockton) 97

Halberstam, Jack 31, 92, 97–100
Harari, Yuval Noah 117–19, 131
Haraway, Donna 8, 72, 120–1, 128 (*see also* naturecultures)
Harry Potter 6
Heraclitus 22–4, 27, 34 (*see also* river)
hero's journey. *See monomyth*
heteronormativity 28, 31, 48–9, 59, 93, 97, 99, 101, 115–16, 150, 163 n.60
heteropatriarchy 102
heterosexuality 8, 32, 47, 63, 95, 97–8, 105, 123, 115
    compulsory heterosexuality 90, 103
Holocene 123–5, 128
homonationalism 149 (*see also* Puar)
homosexuality 29–30, 47, 63, 109, 149
hope (hopefulness) 14, 30–1, 43, 60–1, 122, 132, 150
How it is (Cordova) 34, 139,

Idle No More (Canadian Indigenous movement) 84–5, 165 n.41
Imitation and Gender Insubordination (Butler) 101
Indigenous ceremony 85 (*see also* Idle No more, Pow-Wow)
Indigenous sovereignty 18, 165 n.41
Indigenous knowledge/philosophy 14, 15, 84–7
  and new feminist materialisms 15, 68–9
  and temporality 33–6, 96, 103–4, 115
2017 International Women's marches 18
intersectionality 68, 112–13
intergenerational trauma (and epigenetics) 15, 148
Isle of Lesbos. *See* Sappho
It Gets Better (IGB) campaign 60
Iver, Bon *Holocene* 122

James, William 1
jellyfish 117–18, 124–30, 133, 136, 152

Kant, Emmanuel on the Sublime 140
Katniss Everdeen 6–7
kinship 32, 60, 97, 99
Kirby, Vicki 72, 127
  interview with Judith Butler 71

Last Look at the Lex (Salamon) 94
Latour, Bruno 78, 156 n.29 (*see also* actant)
learning to ride a bike 4, 26–7, 50–2
Lexington Bar in San Francisco (The Lex) 94–5
life itself 71–3, 77, 80, 109–10, 127
Lila 89, 100
linear time 5–10, 29, 31–2, 44, 86, 103–4 (*see also* nonlinear time)
linguistic turn 69–70, 75
Living a Feminist Life (Ahmed) 11–12
the living present. *See also under* duration
  definition of 3–4, 52–8
  the first synthesis of time (the living present) 52–4, 57
  the second synthesis of time (the pure past) 14, 19, 52, 54–7, 78
  and thick time 3, 28–9, 32, 46, 52, 63–4, 106–7, 112, 116, 121

  the third synthesis of time (eternal return) 55–6, 123
The Logic of Sense (Deleuze) 4
Lorde, Audre 67, 122
Love, Heather 29, 139
Lovelock, Michael 106

material turn 69–70, 72–3, 109–10, 126–7, 129
matter (*see also* agential realism, feminist materialisms)
  and climate 121
  entanglement of 36, 79, 85
  materialism 3, 52, 69, 72, 77, 80, 121, 126
  and meaning 7, 54, 56, 121
  and particle theory 67–8, 81–2
  inorganic 56, 77, 79
  of time 32, 57, 142
Meeting the Universe Halfway (Barad) 14, 68
"Medical phenomenon of transsexuality" (Latham) 110
Medium Density Fiberboard (MDF) 129
memory
  and Bergson 27, 45–6
  and Dory's forgetfulness (*Finding Nemo*) 98–100
  and habit 2, 4, 52–4, 63–4, 150
  inextricable from narrative 5–6, 19–20, 26–7, 140
  nostalgia 3, 26, 32, 99
  as passive contraction 63–4, 78
  and the stickiness of time 13–14, 27, 91, 105, 150
  and temporality 27, 39, 56, 99
#metoo movement 18
Milk, Harvey 101
misogyny 18, 74, 76, 93, 102, 150
monomyth 6–9, 14, 59–60, 79, 92, 102, 115, 117, 122, 141, 143, 149

"N'tacimowin inna nah': Our Coming in Stories" (Wilson) 96
Namaste, Viviane 12, 166 n.6
narrative (*see also* monomyth, *see also under* coming out)
  autobiography 5, 12
  causal narratives 19

and fiction 5–6, 27, 107
linear narratives 6–7, 28, 38, 99, 104, 113, 131
progress narratives 6, 14, 29, 34, 53, 59, 61, 69, 91, 97, 107, 113, 137, 134, 149
and time-telling 14, 16, 21, 36, 121, 149
National Institutes of Health's 2001 report 77
nationalism 59, 80 (*see also* homonationalism)
Native American 33–4, 86
Native science 86
natural laws of interdependence 86
Natural Resources 120, 135
nature/culture binary 71
naturecultures 72, 83, 120–1, 126–8
Nealon, Christopher 29–30, 105
Neils Bohr Institute 81
Neimanis, Astrida 133–4
New Materialisms IV Conference 2013 133
Newton, Isaac 13, 19, 20–1, 28, 56
Nietzsche, Friedrich 41, 55
nonlinear time 22, 32, 136
non-subject 92, 107, 116 (*see also under* Deleuze)
now (the present) 25–6, 38, 52, 57, 139, 152

obedience to the future 130
objective observer 11, 13, 18, 20, 26, 36, 67–8, 121, 157 n.5
On the Origin of Species (Darwin) 117
outing (practices of) 101, 103, 168 n.39
OutRage! 101, 168 n.39

"The Pace of Queer Time" (Lila) 89, 100
pansexuality 89, 102, 105
Parmenides 24–6, 28
passive synthesis 51–2, 63–4
past. *See* pure past
pure past 14, 19, 52, 54, 56–7 (*see also under* the living present)
patriarchy 102–3, 150–1
Philosophiæ Naturalis Principia Mathematica (Newton) 20
Pixarvolt 98–100
Plato 25–6

Play Nightclub, Edmonton, Alberta 95
Pleistocene 125
The Politics of Life Itself (Rose) 73
polysexual 89
postfeminism 8, 87
postmodernism 8, 70, 80, 85, 94, 112
post-structuralism 70–2, 75, 107, 109, 169, n.53
Pow-Wow 84, 96, 105
the present 41, 44, 52, 146 (*see also* the living present)
and thick time 3, 28–9, 32, 46, 52, 63–4, 106–7, 112, 116, 121
Prime Minister Justin Trudeau 74
Puar, Jasbir 91, 113–14

QTBIPOC (queer, trans, black, Indigenous, people of color) 36
quantum entanglement 14, 81–3
quantum materialism 14, 65–87 (*see also under* Barad)
quantum mechanics 65–8, 82, 84–5
quantum physics 19, 66–9, 81, 84, 113
quantum time 68, 63
"Queer Aesthetics" (Colebrook) 116
A Queer Art of Failure (Halberstam) 98
queer theory 32, 59, 63, 72, 78, 90–1, 94, 100–1, 107–13, 139 (*see also under* Butler)
queer/queering time 14, 28–33, 89–91, 92–100, 116
in Halberstam 92–3, 97, 99
and the elongated adolescence 60, 97

relativism 19–21, 23, 36, 68
relativity, special and general theories of. *See* Einstein
reproductive technologies 58–9
Re-membering the Future: Material Entanglements and Temporal Diffractions (Barad) 81
"Resisting Medicine, Re/Modeling Gender" (Spade) 100
Rifkin, Mark 33, 35, 103–4
storying 33, 35, 104
the river (as ever-changing) 22–4, 34, 91, 124
Rose, Nikolas 73
Rovelli, Carlo 17

"Safe Space" campaigns 95–7
Salamon, Gayle 94
Sapiens (Harari) 117–19, 131
Sappho 48–50, 57, 76
Saskatchewan Human Rights Code, 2014 change 90
Saskatchewan Human Rights Commission 90
Sawicki, Jana 58–9
The Second Sex (de Beauvoir) 9–10, 140
Sedgwick, Eve Kosofsky 101
self-determination 12, 84–6, 91–2, 106–7, 148
settler time 35, 103–4
Sexing the Cherry (Winterson) 139
sexism 17, 76, 80, 96, 143–4
Short, Coral 128 (*see also* jellyfish)
Solvay Gathering in 1924 75
Sonata in G 47–8
space
   physical space 82, 93, 95
   queer space 30, 92–3, 95–8 (*see also* safe spaces)
   relationship to time 20–1, 25, 28, 36, 113, 151, 157 n.5
   theories of space 20–1, 94 (*see also* Foucault, Michel)
space-time 20–1, 51
Spade, Dean 100
Spinoza 78, 113, 115, 134
St. Augustine 25–6, 28
Stengers, Isabelle 131
stickiness of memory 13–14, 27, 91, 105, 150
Stockton, Kathryn 97
Stoermer, Eugene 123
The Stone Gods (Winterson) 37–9, 42, 61–4
storying 33, 35, 104
storytelling 13–16, 91, 104, 131, 141–2
   monomyth/hero's journey 6–8, 99
   oral 86
   time as 19, 29, 35
subjectivity 21, 44, 53, 59, 63, 101, 128
   as a contraction 4
   Deleuzian 107–8
   relational/entangled 50, 71–2, 112–14
   as a river 91
substantivalism 21–2, 25–6, 36
sustainability 120, 129, 134–5

Tatchell, Peter 101
temporal drag 90–1, 99
temporal turn 18, 69
temporality
   ancient philosophy 22–8
   and climate change 121–2, 124, 127, 134
   and coming out 14, 29, 92, 97, 103, 116
   Einstein 20–1
   feminist temporalities 36, 61, 69, 93 (*see also* feminist futures)
   and materiality 14, 41, 52, 69, 72, 91, 105, 121–2, 124
   Newton's "container" model of time 13, 19, 20–1, 28, 56
   present 41, 44, 52, 146 (*see under* present)
   and progress narratives 59–61, 91, 97, 134 (*see also* narrative)
   queer time 28, 30–2, 60, 76, 92–3
   and storytelling 35, 142
   Winterson 38–9, 41–2, 62, 95
"Theorizing Queer Temporalities" (Halberstam quoted in) 92
Theory of Everything (TOE) 68–9
thick time 3–5, 35–6, 45–6, 52, 79, 87, 92–3, 131, 136
   and coming out 105–6, 116
   of climate change 121
   and the history of philosophy 26–8
   and the living present 63–4
third synthesis of time. *See under* the living present
time. *See* temporality
Time Binds (Freeman) 90
Time magazine's article on the Holocene 124–5
time makers 1, 4, 7, 13, 15–16, 30, 32, 36, 56, 63–4
time-bodies 13, 15, 91, 111–12, 133, 136–7, 140, 142, 146, 152, 156 n.29
   and climate 126
   and Deleuzian subjectivity 107–116
timescape 13–14, 30, 103, 141, 147
trans erasure 149–50
transcorporeality 3, 51–2, 74, 133
   Alaimo, Stacey 12–13
The Transexual Phenomenon (Benjamin) 110

transformative futures 136
transgender 29, 39–40, 90–1, 141, 144
   coming out as 102, 105, 109–10, 112–13
   excluded from feminism 12
   suicidality 151
   trans erasure 149–51
   youth 151
transphobia 150–2
Trump's inauguration 18
Tipton, Billy 29
Truth, Sojourner 151–2
Tuhkanen, Mikko 32, 98
Twinkle, Twinkle, Little Star 45, 47–8, 50, 56
Two Spirit 14, 91, 96, 104, 106, 141

United Nations Resolution 64/292 74
univocity 77, 80, 111–15, 134, 137
The Untimeliness of Feminist Theory (Grosz) 65

Vibrant Matter: A Political Ecology of Things (Bennett) 76
A Vindication of the Rights of Woman (Wollstonecraft) 9
vitalism 76–80, 87, 160 n.4

Wark, McKenzie 130
water shortages (White Bear First Nation) 12, 148

waves and particles 66–7
Western capitalism 85
What is Philosophy? (Deleuze and Guattari) 143
White Bear First Nation, Saskatchewan 73–5, 148
The Will to Power (Nietzsche) 41
Williams, James 1, 35–6, 56
Wilson, Alex 97, 103, 105
winemaking, as an example of agential realism 145–6
Winnubst, Shannon 130
Winter, Bronwyn 149
Winterson, Jeanette 37–9, 40, 62–3, 139 (*see also under* becoming, temporality)
   futurity 59, 63
   homo sapiens 37
   love 37, 41–2, 62
   robo sapiens 37–8, 42, 62
   time 7, 14, 38, 40–1, 56, 61–2, 95
Wollstonecraft, Mary 8–11, 76
Working Group on the Anthropocene 123–4
Written on the Body (Winterson) 140

YouTube 12, 84, 106

Zeno 24–6, 43
Zimman, Lal 102

www.ingramcontent.com/pod-product-compliance
Lightning Source LLC
Chambersburg PA
CBHW061829300426
44115CB00013B/2301